AMP
Real Estate Exam Prep
2015-2016

The Definitive Guide to Preparing for the National AMP Real Estate Exam

by

Jim Bainbridge, J.D.

© 2015

City Breeze Publishing
P.O. Box 12650
Marina del Rey, California 90295

ISBN: 978-1-939526-17-5

PRINTED IN THE UNITED STATES OF AMERICA

About the Author

Jim Bainbridge is a graduate of Harvard Law School and has been an active member of the California Bar for more than 30 years. He is a licensed California real estate broker, and a past recipient of a National Science Foundation Fellowship for graduate studies in mathematics at UC Berkeley. He is the author of *AMP Real Estate Practice Exams for 2015-2016, California Real Estate Principles and License Preparation* and numerous works that have been published in more than 50 journals in the USA, UK, Canada, Australia, Japan, and the Netherlands.

Mr. Bainbridge is also a member of the Real Estate Educators Association (REEA) and has been recognized as a Certified Distance Education Instructor by IDECC, which is a function of the Association of Real Estate License Law Officials.

DISCLAIMER and LIMIT of LIABILITY

Preface

In recent years many consumer protection statutes at the federal, state, and local levels have dramatically expanded the number and complexity of laws that impact real estate practice. The need for educating anyone interested in becoming a real estate professional has thereby also grown dramatically.

Contemporary real estate agents must acquire an adequate working knowledge in a wide variety of subjects: contract law, agency relationships, real estate financing, real estate appraisal, land use control, fair housing, and truth-in-lending laws, to name a few. Accordingly, many states contract with companies to develop license exams that prospective real estate salespersons and brokers must pass as a prerequisite to obtaining their desired real estate license. One of these companies is Applied Measurement Professionals, Inc (AMP), located in Olathe, Kansas.

This book is intended to provide prospective licensees with a thorough summary of the knowledge necessary to pass the national AMP real estate exam. The text is presented precisely according to AMP's published 2014 "detailed content outline" of 126 real estate topics that may appear on the AMP exam.

No Endorsement

Though this text follows AMP's published 2014 "detailed content outline" of topics that may appear on the AMP exam, neither this text nor the opinions expressed in it are endorsed by AMP.

Table of Contents

CHAPTER 1: AGENCY RELATIONSHIPS AND CONTRACTS

Section A: Agency relationships

1. Creating Agency

Creation of an Agency Relationship.

- *Express Agreement.* Usually, an agency relationship is created by express agreement between the principal and the agent, such as by a written **listing agreement** if the principal is a seller of property or by a written **property management agreement** if the principal is an owner of (usually rental) properties and is hiring the agent to manage the properties rather than to sell them. Unless the statute of frauds requires that the agreement be in writing, an express agency agreement can be oral. However, under a principle of agency law known as the **equal dignities rule**, the authorization of an agent requires the same formality as is required for the act(s) the agent is hired to perform.

- *Ratification.* By accepting or retaining the benefit of an act made by an unauthorized agent or by an agent who has exceeded his or her authority, a principal can create an agency by ratification. Ratification cannot be for merely part of a transaction conducted by an agent; ratification of a part of a transaction is ratification of the whole. In other words, a principal who has ratified a transaction cannot split the transaction into separate parts, taking the beneficial parts and disavowing the rest.

- *Implication.* Agency by implication may be created if someone reasonably believes that someone else is acting as his or her agent, and the supposed agent fails to correct the impression. In such a case, the supposed agent may in fact owe the other person the duties of an agent.

- *Estoppel.* There is a rule of equity known as **estoppel** that holds that one who causes another to rely on his or her words or actions shall be estopped (prohibited) from later taking a contrary position detrimental to the person who so relied. An agency relationship is created by estoppel in a situation where (1) an unauthorized person performs actions as if he or she were the agent of a principal, (2) the principal is aware of this conduct, and (3) the agent's actions and the principal's actions (or inactions) cause a third party to rely on the supposed agent's actions, believing that the actions are authorized by the principal.

2. Types of Agency (including implied agency)

Special Agent versus General Agent. An agent for a particular act or transaction is a **special agent**. All other agents are **general agents**.

Most general agents are an integral part of an ongoing business enterprise, such as a branch manager who is authorized to conduct business on an ongoing basis for the branch on behalf of a company. A special agent, on the other hand, is employed by a principal for a specific transaction or limited number of specific transactions. A real estate broker nearly always is a special agent because he or she is employed by a **principal** (also referred to as a **client**) only to negotiate the sale or purchase of a property or properties — not to conduct other business affairs of the principal.

Designated Agent. A *designated agent* is an agent authorized by a real estate broker to represent a specific principal to the exclusion of all other agents in the brokerage. This designated agent owes fiduciary responsibilities to the specified principal, but other agents in the brokerage may represent other parties to the same transaction that the specified principal is a party to without creating a dual agency situation. States that permit designated agency differ as to the role of the broker — in some states the broker is not seen as a dual agent if the broker remains totally uninvolved in the transaction; in other states the broker is seen as a dual agent even though the broker's salespersons are not seen as dual agents. In all states where designated agency is allowed, disclosure of the designated agency relationship is required.

Subagent. A *subagent* is an agent of an agent. Therefore, because a salesperson is an agent of a broker, and a broker is an agent of a principal, the salesperson is a subagent of the principal.

Dual Agent. A *dual agent* is a real estate broker who represents both the seller and the buyer in a real estate transaction.

Single Agent. A *single agent* is an agent who represents only one party in a given transaction.

Universal agent. A *universal agent* is an agent given *power of attorney* to act on behalf of a principal for an unlimited range of legal matters.

Ostensible Agent. *Ostensible agency* is created when a principal intentionally, or by want of ordinary care, causes a third person to believe another to be his agent who is not actually employed by the principal.

Implied Agent. An *implied agent* is an agent created by implication (see creation of agency by implication in part 1 above).

3. Rights, Duties and Obligations of the Parties

Duties to Client/Principal (buyer, seller, tenant or landlord): Regardless whether an agent's principal is a buyer, seller, tenant, or landlord, the agent owes the principal fiduciary duties — duties to treat the principal with utmost care, honesty, trust, and loyalty. Properly fulfilling these fiduciary duties includes:

- *Utmost Care*: An agent must perform his or her agency duties diligently and with utmost care, utilizing the skills the agent has acquired through education and experience.

- *Faithful Performance* (also referred to as *Obedience*): An agent has a duty to faithfully perform agency duties in accordance with the principal's instructions as long as such instructions are in compliance with law and ethics.

- *Loyalty*: An agent must always put the interests of the principal above the interests of others, including the agent's own self-interest.

- *Disclosure*: An agent must always disclose to the principal all facts known to the agent that may affect the transaction.

- *Confidentiality*: An agent must always keep the principal's financial condition and personal life confidential.

- *Accounting*: An agent is responsible for keeping careful records of all funds received from, or for, a principal or customer. In nearly all states, an agent must treat funds received on behalf of clients or customers as trust funds. Placing funds belonging to clients or customers into accounts also holding the agent's funds, or vice versa, is considered **commingling**, and is grounds for revocation or suspension of the agent's license. **Conversion** is the unauthorized use of another's funds for one's own use, and is a criminal offense. There is a slippery slope from commingling to conversion, because if client or customer funds are first co-mingled and then subsequently used, what started out as commingling ends up as conversion.

Traditional Common-Law Agency Duties: Agency law is governed by two sets of laws: **common law** and **statutory law**. Common law is law developed over time by tradition and law courts, and is often referred to as case law. Statutory law, which is often based on and informed by common law, is law enacted by legislation, for example by state legislatures, local governments, and regulatory bodies.

A broker may also be a **dual agent**, representing both the seller and the buyer, but only with the knowledge and consent of both parties. Dual agency would arise if the listing broker, who represents of the seller, also becomes the agent (actual or ostensible) of the buyer.

EXAMPLE: Except in a designated agency situation, dual agency would arise in a case where one salesperson of a broker represents the seller and another salesperson of the same broker represents the buyer.

In any dual agency, conflicts of loyalty and confidentiality can arise, such as when, for example, the buyer wants to know whether the seller is willing to take a lower price, or conversely, when the seller wants to know whether the buyer is willing to pay a higher price. In such cases, a dual agent must not disclose price concessions from either party without the consent of the other party.

Fiduciary Responsibilities: An agent occupies a special legal relationship, referred to as a **fiduciary relationship**, of loyalty to his or her principal. A real estate licensee who represents a seller (or a buyer) also owes certain legal responsibilities (such as to act fairly and to make certain disclosures) to the buyer (or to the seller, as the case may be); but to his or her principal, the real estate licensee owes this special relationship of *utmost care*, *honesty*, *trust*, and *loyalty* known as a fiduciary relationship.

Nonagents (transactional/facilitational): Some states permit a broker to act *not* as an agent who represents one or more parties to a real estate transaction, but to act as a mere middleman who brings the parties together and lets the parties do all of the negotiating among themselves. Such a nonagent broker (also referred to as a *transactional broker*, *facilitator*, *intermediary*, *coordinator*, or *contract broker*) does not owe fiduciary duties to either party and is therefore not held to the same legal standards of conduct as is a broker acting as an agent. However, the states that permit this kind of nonagent status impose an obligation on the nonagent to act fairly, honestly, and competently to find qualified buyers or suitable properties.

Deliberate Misrepresentation. **Deliberate misrepresentation** (also referred to as **intentional misrepresentation** or **fraud**) is the suggestion, as a fact, to a party that which is not true committed by another party who does not believe it to be true and who makes the suggestion with the intent to deceive the first party, who was deceived to his or her detriment, such as by being induced to enter into a contract.

If the seller committed the intentional misrepresentation, the defrauded party may rescind the contract or sue for damages. If a licensee commits intentional misrepresentation, the licensee may be sued for damages (and in many states for punitive damages) and likely would have his or her license revoked.

Errors and Omissions (E&O) Insurance. To protect against mistakes that can result in enormous liability, many real estate licensees purchase errors and omissions (E&O) insurance, which covers most of the errors and negligence that can occur in listing, advertising, and selling real estate. *It is important to note that (E&O) insurance does not cover fraudulent or criminal acts.*

Uninformed Misrepresentation. *Uninformed misrepresentation* (also referred to as *negligent misrepresentation*) is an assertion not warranted by the information of the party making the assertion that an important fact was true, which was not true, relied on by another party to that party's detriment. Negligent misrepresentation involves many of the same elements as does intentional misrepresentation, the primary difference being that whereas in intentional misrepresentation the defendant knew the representation to be false when making it, *in negligent misrepresentation the party who made the misrepresentation had no reasonable grounds for believing that the representation was true when making it.*

A licensee who makes uninformed misrepresentation may be liable for damages in an amount equal to the difference between the purchase price and the actual value of the property. Such an act may also subject the licensee to suspension or revocation of his or her license.

Commissions:

Procuring Cause. Of the many disputes that real estate professionals have with each other, probably the most common is over *procuring cause*. Procuring cause is a common law legal concept developed by the courts to determine the proportioning of commissions among agents involved in a real estate transaction. In general, an agent who is a procuring cause of a sale originated a chain of events that resulted in the sale and is thereby entitled to at least some part of the total commission generated by the sale. Problems occur if there appears to be a break in the chain of events leading up to a sale, such as a failure to contact a prospective buyer for several months, a failure to help secure financing, or a failure to diligently and responsibly fulfill other duties that licensees owe to clients and customers.

Protection Clause. A *protection clause* (also referred to as a *safety clause*) provides that the broker will earn the full commission under certain circumstances for a sale made after the termination of the agency. Typically, a protection clause provides that the broker will earn the full commission if the property is sold within a specified number of days after the termination of the listing to a buyer with whom the broker has negotiated on the property.

Referrals and Other Finder Fees:

A *finder's fee* (also referred to as a *referral fee*) is a payment made by a person or company to another person simply for referring a customer to the first person or company. The Real Estate Settlement Procedures Act (RESPA) prohibits referral fees be paid to a real estate agent for settlement services not actually performed by the agent. Therefore, an agent who receives compensation for referring a client to a title company would likely be in violation of RESPA because very few agents actually perform the services performed by title companies.

RESPA applies only to first-lien mortgages on residential properties consisting of one to four dwelling units, but many states have anti-kickback regulations that apply more broadly. Violations of RESPA's anti-kickback rules include criminal penalties of imprisonment of up to one year and civil penalties of up to $10,000.

State laws differ as to under what circumstances a finder's fee can be paid. For example, it may be permissible under state law for a licensee to accept a finder's fee for an *introduction only*, such as a fee from a builder for the introduction of a prospective purchaser, because such activity does not require a real estate license. Before accepting any finder's fee, licensees should carefully check their state law and, in any case, it is always good practice to inform clients of any such fee and to receive the clients' permission to accept the fee.

Practicing within Area of Competence: The word "ethics" comes from the Greek word *ethos*, meaning "moral character." A study of ethics can help us to pinpoint, and hopefully therefore to avoid, behavior that is likely to be harmful or unfair to others in the wide variety of human actions. Real estate law concerns itself with conduct that real estate licensees *must* observe; codes of ethical conduct attempt to go beyond the law by defining what kinds of conduct agents *should* observe. Put another way, real estate law sets minimum standards of acceptable behavior, while trade association codes of ethical conduct, courses on ethics, and religious and other cultural leaders attempt to teach and inspire us to do more than the law requires — to cultivate trustworthiness, fairness, kindness and accountability for our actions.

Trade Associations. The largest real estate trade association in the United States is the *National Association of Realtors®* (N.A.R.), which was established in 1908. It is a violation of real estate law to call oneself a *Realtor®* or a member of any other real estate organization without being a member of such real estate organization.

Another large trade association called the *National Association of Real Estate Brokers* (NAREB), which was established in 1947, is comprised primarily of African-American real estate agents. Members of the NAREB organization are called *Realtists®*.

The *National Association of Hispanic Real Estate Professionals (NAHREP)* was established in 1999 with the mission to assist real estate professionals to increase Hispanic homeownership and to serve Hispanic consumers.

The *Asian Real Estate Association of America (AREAA)* was established in 2001 with the mission to assist real estate professionals who serve Asian-American communities.

Area of Competence. Real estate agents owe their clients the fiduciary responsibilities of utmost care, honesty, trust, and loyalty — which implies that real estate agents must not only perform to the best of their abilities on behalf of their clients, but are also responsible for giving their clients the best advice they are able to give. This latter point means that if the client is in need of information or assistance that is outside the area of competence of the agent, the agent has the responsibility to refer the client to persons of competence in that area. For example, an agent may refer a client to real estate lawyers for legal opinions, to accountants or tax attorneys for tax advice, to licensed home inspectors, and to other appropriate professionals. Failure to make these recommendations to persons with competence outside the area of competence of the agent would likely be seen as a breach of the agent's fiduciary duty, thereby subjecting the agent to civil liability and to discipline by regulatory agencies.

Avoiding Unauthorized Practice of Law:

The only persons authorized to practice law are persons who have been licensed to practice law in the state or states in which they practice. Any person advertising or holding himself or herself out as practicing or entitled to practice law without being licensed to practice law is subject to criminal and civil penalties.

The difficulty for licensees in avoiding the risk of being accused of practicing law is that real estate agents are required to study many aspects of real estate law in order to acquire a real estate license (and to maintain their license through continuing education courses), and they are required by their fiduciary relationship with their clients to share this knowledge of real estate law with their clients whenever such sharing will benefit the interest of their clients. Nonetheless, real estate agents must be careful not to hold themselves out as practicing law (as opposed to fulfilling their obligations as real estate agents).

> **EXAMPLE:** While a licensee may fill in the blanks of real estate contract forms and, to the extent of their real estate knowledge, accurately advise their clients as to the meaning of the terms of a printed contract, licensees in nearly all states must not draft any of the specialized terms of a contract — a responsibility that must be placed in the hands of a licensed attorney.

4. Termination and Remedies for Non-Performance

Expiration: The agency relationship automatically terminates when its term ends. If the agency agreement did not include a termination date (which it must if it is an exclusive agency), then the agency would expire after a reasonable time. As a general rule, without a stated termination date, either party may terminate the agency at any time without liability, although the agent might be able to demand reimbursement for expenses incurred before the termination.

Completion/Performance: When the purpose of the agent's job is accomplished — such as by the sale of a property if the agent is a listing agent, or the purchase of a property if the agent is a buyer's agent — the agency ends.

Termination by Force of Law: Agency can be terminated by the force of law in the following circumstances:

- *Bankruptcy.* The trustee in a bankruptcy may choose either to terminate or to continue the agency. If the bankruptcy impairs the agent's performance, the principal may revoke the agency.

- *Change in Law.* If a change in law makes the performance of an agent's duties illegal, the agency is terminated.

- *Loss of License.* If either the agent or the principal loses a license that is necessary to perform the acts for which the agency was created, the agency is terminated.

Destruction of Property/Death of Principal: If the property that is the subject of the agency is destroyed, the purpose agency agreement becomes impossible to fill, and the agency is thereby terminated. Agency is a personal relationship, therefore, death or incapacity of either the principal or the agent would terminate the agency. Note, however, that since a corporation is considered a separate entity, the death of corporate officers of either the principal or the agent would not terminate the agency.

Mutual Agreement: An agency relationship can be terminated by *mutual agreement*. Also, because agency is a personal relationship based on trust and confidence, either party may *unilaterally terminate* the agency at any time (*unless, as discussed below, the agency is coupled with an interest*). However, though the principal may revoke and the agent may renounce the agency at any time, doing so may result in liability for breach of contract, such as if the principal revokes the agency prior to the termination of an exclusive right to sell listing and then sells the property him or herself.

An agency is *coupled with an interest* if the agent has a financial interest *in the subject of the agency* (as distinct from the compensation that may result for the agent from his or her performance as an agent), which has the legal effect of making the appointment of the agent irrevocable.

EXAMPLE: If an agent is a co-owner of a property and the other owners authorize the agent to represent the property for sale, then the other owners may not revoke the agency.

EXAMPLE: If a broker supplies financing to build a house with the stipulation that the broker will have the listing to sell the house, the broker's agency is coupled with an interest.

5. Disclosure (related to representation)

Disclosure of Agency Relationship. All states have enacted statutes that require brokers to inform parties to a real estate transaction as to whom the broker is representing. Even in those states that do not permit dual agency, agency relationship disclosures are required because many sellers believe that an agent who receives a commission from a seller is representing the seller, when, in fact, the agent who procures the sale and receives a portion of the commission may be the buyer's agent who does not represent, and owes no fiduciary duties to, the seller.

The timing as to when the agency relationship disclosure must be presented, and the wording of the disclosure, vary among the states; however, most states require that the disclosure be presented to, and consented by, a party before that party signs any agreement (listing agreement, leasing agreement, or purchase agreement) obligating the party to pay a commission, to pay rent, or to transfer ownership in the subject property.

The various types of agency listing agreements will be discussed later in this chapter, Section D, part 6.

Section B: General Legal Principles, Theory, and Concepts about Contracts

1. Unilateral/Bilateral

A *contract* is an agreement to do or to forbear from doing a certain thing. There probably is not a more important area of the law for real estate salespersons and brokers, and for their clients and customers, than the law of contracts. In nearly every business transaction, one or more contracts are involved.

In regard to the *manner of creation*, a contract may be *express* or *implied*. An express contract is one in which the parties declare their intention in words, whether orally or in writing. Nearly every real estate transaction must be express and, because of the statute of frauds, must be in writing. An *implied contract* is not written or spoken; it is implied by the actions of the parties.

> **Example:** When you sit down at a restaurant and place an order, there is no written or oral agreement between you and the restaurant that you will pay for the food ordered and delivered; however, there is an implied contract to that effect — a contract ever bit as valid and, in this context, as enforceable as if it had been written. An implied contract can arise even in cases where the actions of one of the parties was not intentional — for example, if you were to fall unconscious on a sidewalk and an ambulance came and took you to a hospital, an implied contract to pay the ambulance would be enforced.

In regard to the *content of an agreement*, a contract may be *bilateral* or *unilateral*. A bilateral contract is one in which one party gives a promise in exchange for a promise from the other party. In other words, a bilateral contract contains promises on two sides; a unilateral contract, on only one.

> **Example:** If I promise to pay you $20 if you mow my lawn on Tuesday, and you promise to mow my lawn on Tuesday, we have a bilateral contract right then and there. If I promise to pay you $20 if you mow my lawn on Tuesday, and you shrug your shoulders and say, "I'll see if I have time," we have a unilateral contract — you have not promised to do anything, but I have. Unless I withdraw my offer in the meanwhile, if you go ahead and mow my lawn on Tuesday, I will owe you $20. On the other hand, if you don't mow my lawn on Tuesday, there is no penalty to you, nor is there $20 owed by me to you.

As we will see, if you have a client who gives you an exclusive right to sell listing, your client promises to pay you a commission if you find a buyer and you promise to make an effort to find a buyer for your client. In this circumstance, you and your client have exchanged promises, thereby creating a bilateral contract. But in an open listing situation, your client promises to pay you a commission if you are the first to find a buyer; you promise nothing. In this circumstance, you and your client have a unilateral contract.

2. Validity

A. Requirements for Validity:

Essential elements for the existence of a valid contract are:

- parties capable of contracting;

- consent (offer and acceptance);

- lawful object or purpose; and

- adequate consideration

Parties Capable of Contracting. In nearly every state, all persons are capable of contracting except minors, persons of unsound mind, and persons deprived of certain civil rights. The term "persons" includes corporations, partnerships, and other business entities, which are fully capable of entering into contracts. Personal representatives of decedents are capable of entering into contracts on behalf of the decedents' estates. Real estate agents often deal with such estate representatives when the latter are interested in selling real property belonging to the estates they represent.

- o *Minors.* In most states a minor is a person under the age of 18 years and, in general, is not considered capable of contracting to purchase or sell real estate. Therefore, a real estate contract signed by a minor is voidable by the minor or by the minor's guardian. However, many states allow an ***emancipated minor*** to enter into any type of contract, including a contract for the purchase or sale of real property. Depending on state law, a minor may become emancipated by becoming validly married, serving in the military, or by court order.

- o *Incompetents.* A person who has been declared by court order to be of unsound mind does not have the capacity to enter into a contract. Similarly, if a person is entirely without understanding, even if such person has not been declared incompetent by a court, that person does not possess the power to contract. If an incompetent person enters into a contract, the contract is void or voidable, depending on state law. If the person is declared incompetent after a valid contract is entered into, the contract is voidable at the discretion of the incompetent person's guardian.

- o *Persons Deprived of Civil Rights.* Many states deprive certain classes of convicts of certain of their civil rights, including, (often after conviction of a serious crime resulting in life imprisonment or the death penalty) the right to purchase and sell real property.

Lawful object or purpose. The object or purpose of a contract is a thing that is agreed, on the part of the party receiving the consideration, to do or to forbear from doing. To be valid, the object or purpose of a contract must be lawful when the contract is made and possible when the contract is to be performed.

For a contract to be valid, both its consideration and its object or purpose must be lawful. If a contract has only one object or purpose and that object or purpose is unlawful, the entire contract is void. However, if the contract has several objects or purposes, some of which are valid, the contract would normally be valid and enforced as to the lawful objects or purposes only.

Examples of invalid contracts due to having an unlawful object or purpose in the field of real estate include:

- listing contracts of unlicensed brokers;

- contracts among brokers to fix commission rates; and

- contracts among brokers to sell property in their areas only to persons of a particular ethnicity.

Sufficient Consideration.

The fourth element of a valid contract is sufficient consideration. Consideration is something of value, such as money, property, or services. It might even be an act of forbearance, such as if a grandmother promises to pay her granddaughter $10 each visit if the young woman will desist from playing a certain kind of annoying "music."

Though in most states consideration must have some value, there is no requirement that consideration be of equal value to what is given in exchange for the consideration. One dollar given for an option to purchase a residence is generally considered sufficient consideration. However, gross inadequacy of consideration may be probative as to whether fraud was involved in a contract. Furthermore, in a court action for *specific performance*, the amount of consideration is important. Specific performance is an equitable remedy commonly sought by one party to a real estate contract seeking a court order requiring the other party to perform what was specifically stated in the contract (such as transferring the deed to the property), as an alternative to awarding damages. As a general rule, to obtain an equitable remedy (as opposed to a legal remedy of monetary damages), the fairness or adequacy of consideration will weigh heavily in the court's deliberations.

Statute of Frauds.

Modern law is more concerned with substance than with form. Therefore, as a general rule, whether the form of a contract is oral or written is immaterial unless there is a specific statutory exception that requires that the contract be in writing.

The statute of frauds grew out of a body of English common law, the purpose of which was to prevent perjury and dishonest conduct on the part of persons trying to prove the existence of certain kinds of contracts or the terms therein. In addition to common law, every state has a statute of frauds stating what kinds of contracts must be in writing to be valid. Typically, contracts that are covered by the statute of frauds and that fail to be in writing are not void but are unenforceable. Thus, a contract covered by a state's statute of frauds that fails to be in writing typically is effective for all purposes until its validity is challenged. Significant partial performance of a contract is generally deemed to be sufficient evidence of the contract, thereby excusing the lack of writing. If the contract has been fully performed, the statute of frauds does not apply.

An agreement covered by the statute of frauds that fails to be committed to writing may become enforceable if a note or memorandum signed by the party against whom enforcement of the contract is sought is subsequently made that confirms the terms of the agreement.

Most real estate transactions are covered by the statute of frauds, including leases having a sufficiently long term, generally of one year or longer. And in most states, agent agreements to purchase or sell interests in real estate must also satisfy the statute of frauds.

Parol evidence rule. As a general rule, the *parol evidence rule* prohibits the introduction of extrinsic evidence of preliminary negotiations, oral or written, and of contemporaneous oral evidence, to alter the terms of a written agreement that appears to be whole. However, contracts often are long, complicated documents, and the words used therein are sometimes subject to differing interpretations, leading to agreements with ambiguous terms. In such cases, extrinsic evidence may be admitted to clarify the ambiguities. Additionally, extrinsic evidence may be introduced when necessary to prove that a contract is unenforceable because of mistake, fraud, duress, illegality, insufficiency or failure of consideration, or incapacity of a party.

Statute of Limitations. Every state has a statute of limitations, which prescribes the time in which a legal action must be brought to enforce a contract. The policy behind this statute is that the law aids the vigilant, and anyone who "slumbers upon his rights" may lose the right to bring an action. The time for filing an action varies, depending upon the type of action, and because there are many different types of actions, there are many different limitation periods.

3. Void and Voidable

In regard to *legal effect*, a contract may be *valid*, *void*, *voidable*, or *unenforceable*. A *valid contract* is a contract that is binding and can be enforced by law. A *void contract* is not considered a contract at all and cannot be enforced by law, such as an agreement to commit a crime. A *voidable contract* is a contract that is enforceable at the option of one party but not at the option of the other, as when the consent of one party (the party who may elect to have the contract enforced) is obtained by fraud (not forgery, which would render the contract void), coercion, misrepresentation, or undue influence. An *unenforceable contract* has all the elements of a contract but is such that a court will not enforce it. For example, pursuant to the statute of limitations, a contract that originally was valid and fully enforceable may become unenforceable after the passage of a certain amount of time.

4. Notice of Delivery/Acceptance

Consent (offer and acceptance). The consent of the parties to a contract must be freely given, mutual, and communicated by each to the other.

- *Consent freely given.* Consent that is not freely given, such as consent obtained by *duress*, *menace*, fraud, or undue influence, is consent that may be *rescinded*. As we have seen, a contract obtained by such consent is voidable. Duress refers to unlawful confinement of a person or physical force used against a person in order to obtain consent of that person. Menace refers to a threat of duress or of injury to person or property of a person.
- *Mutuality of Consent.* Mutual consent (often referred to as a "meeting of the minds") is usually evidenced by an *offer* of one party that manifests contractual intention and by an *acceptance* by the other party.

An offer must not only manifest contractual intention; it must do so using terms that are clear and definite. A vague offer that does not clearly state what is being offered, even if accepted, is illusory, and an agreement based upon such an offer is unenforceable.

> **Example:** A contract that merely states that an unimproved parcel of land is to be improved with streets, but does not state where the streets should be located, how wide they should be, with what materials constructed, etc., would be unenforceable due to lack of definiteness of terms.

Note, however, that there are circumstances where clear and definite terms appear to be offered, but custom and law do not deem an offer to be made.

> **Example:** An advertisement that lists a description of, and an asking price for, real property is not considered to be an offer; it is deemed to be merely an invitation for a buyer to make an offer.

11

- *Communication of Consent.* In order for there to be the meeting of the minds that is required for mutuality of consent, both the offer and the acceptance must be communicated to the appropriate party. However, communication between the parties to a contract, especially to a real estate contract, is usually not a simple one-two process of an offer being made followed by an acceptance. Negotiations generally take the form of an offer being made by a potential buyer, rejection and counteroffer from the seller, rejection and counteroffer from the buyer, and so on (real estate agents must have patience) until the process ends — with or without a sale.
  - *Acceptance*: Acceptance is generally effective when it is sent; however, an offer can be revoked at any time before acceptance is actually received.
  - *Revocation*: An offeror can terminate (*revoke*) an offer at any time before its acceptance is received, even if the offer stated that it would remain open for a specified time (unless consideration was paid for the offer remaining open, in which case an option was created). Revocation of an offer is deemed effective when it is sent or communicated to the offeree in some manner.

    Example: If an offer was made to sell or purchase a property and the offeree learns that the property has in the meanwhile been purchased by someone else, revocation of the offer is deemed to have been communicated to the offeree.

  - *Rejection*: Rejection of an offer by the offeree terminates the offer. Even if the offeree subsequently wants to accept the offer, the offeree may not do so unless the offer is renewed by the offeror.
  - *Counteroffer*: A counteroffer is deemed to be both a rejection of the earlier offer and the creation of a new (counter) offer.
  - *Lapse of time*: An offer is terminated if the offer states that it must be accepted by a specified time and it is not accepted within that specified time. Furthermore, even if an offer does not state a specified time in which it must be accepted, an offer is terminated after a "reasonable" time. What is a reasonable time in a certain situation is something that would be determined by a court if a dispute arises.
  - *Death of the offeror*: An offer is terminated if the offeror dies or becomes incompetent before the offer is accepted. If the offer is accepted prior to the death, a valid contract would have been formed, and the offeror's estate would be obliged to perform according to the terms of the contract.

5. Executory/Executed

In regard to the **extent of performance**, a contract may be **executory** or **executed**. An executed contract is a contract that has been fully performed. An executory contract is one in which some performance by one or both parties remains to be done.

Example: If I offer to pay you $20 to mow my lawn on Tuesday and you agree to do so, our contract (bilateral) remains executory until both of us perform as agreed, at which time our contract becomes an executed contract.

Note: one must be careful to keep in mind the context in which "executed contract" is used. Because the word "executed" can mean signed, the phrase "executed contract" is also used to refer to a contract, any contract, that has been signed.

6. Enforceability

An ***unenforceable contract*** has all the elements of a contract but is such that a court will not enforce it. For example, pursuant to the statute of limitations, a contract that originally was valid and fully enforceable may become unenforceable after the passage of a certain amount of time.

Section C: Purchase Contracts (contracts between seller and buyer)

1. General Principles and Legal Concepts

A real estate purchase agreement is a contract, and therefore must contain the essential elements of a contract (discussed above) and must satisfy the statute of frauds. In addition to the basic contract elements, a real estate purchase agreement must also contain provisions detailing:

- a legal description of the property;
- the form of deed to be transferred;
- the items of personal property (if any) to be transferred;
- contingencies (if any);
- the buyer's earnest money deposit;
- the buyer's offer;
- the seller's acceptance; and
- the brokerage commission.

2. Purchase Contract (contract of sale, purchase and sale agreement, etc.)

A contract for the purchase of real estate must satisfy all of the elements necessary to form a valid contract and, pursuant to the statute of frauds, must be in writing. Though the use of a quality standard pre-printed form eliminates many of the legal problems that may befall a real estate sales transaction, several legal issues arise frequently enough to warrant special attention. A real estate purchase contract is often referred to as a ***deposit receipt***, in part because the agreement nearly always contains, among many other things, a receipt for the deposit (earnest money deposit) given by the purchaser.

Though the agent is permitted to fill in the blanks in a pre-printed purchase contract, an agent should be very circumspect when crossing out or adding words in the pre-printed sections, because making significant changes (1) risks liability to the seller and/or buyer if the wording turns out to be ambiguous or incorrect, and (2) risks the agent being charged with practicing law without a license to practice law. Any additions, deletions, or alterations that are made on the pre-printed form must be initialed by all parties to the contract.

3. Options (contractual right to buy)

Options: In an option contract, the *optionor* grants the *optionee* the right to purchase property for a specific sum at any time during the option term without creating an obligation by the optionee to do so. For this option right, the optionee pays the optionor a specified option fee, which is typically not refundable if the option is not exercised. Because when an option is exercised it becomes a purchase agreement, an ***option contract*** to purchase real estate must contain all of the necessary terms of such a purchase.

Right of First Refusal: Unlike an option to purchase, a *right of first refusal* does not create in the seller the obligation to sell if the holder of the right wishes to purchase — it only creates the right to purchase a property at the same price, terms, and conditions as is offered to third parties if and when the property is put up for sale. If the person holding the right of first refusal does not meet the price and terms offered, the seller is free to sell to a third party.

4. Basic Provisions/Purpose/Elements

Basic provisions of a purchase contract include:

Buyer's Identity: A statement of the buyer's identity. If there is more than one buyer, this statement should also include the relationship (such as husband/wife, or business partners) of the buyers.

Description of Property: A description of the property being purchased given in sufficient detail to uniquely identify the property, such as by giving a street address and an assessor's parcel number for the county in which the property is situated.

Purchase Price: The purchase price being offered by Buyer.

Confirmation of Agency Disclosures: An acknowledgment by both the buyer and seller that they have received an agency relationship disclosure statement, and an acknowledgment that the broker(s) involved may, as disclosed in the agency relationship disclosure statement, be representing both Seller and Buyer and perhaps other potential buyers.

Finance Terms: There should be a statement in the agreement concerning the initial deposit, the anticipated first loan amounts, any secondary financing and weather FHA or VA financing is to be obtained.

Contingencies: Purchase contracts usually contain many contingencies, which make one party's obligation to perform dependent on the occurrence of some event. These contingencies usually relate to financing, appraisals, inspections, and the delivery of other documents. Such contingencies can have very significant effects on the seller and/or buyer, so they should be prudently examined to be sure that they fit the situation that exists on both the seller's and the buyer's side.

Inspection Reports: Inspection for wood destroying pests and organisms, for properly working septic or sewage disposal systems, and for water potability and productivity are usually provided for, as are reports regarding natural hazard zone disclosure and other reports, if any, specified by the seller or buyer. Lenders often require a certificate of noninfestation of wood destroying pests before close of escrow.

Items Included and Excluded from the Purchase Price: As a matter of law, fixtures are included in the sale unless they are specifically excluded, and personal property is excluded from the sale unless specifically included. However, because disagreements can arise as to what is a fixture, if there is any doubt as to an item, that item should be specified as either a fixture included in the sale or as personal property excluded from the sale.

Buyer's Right to Investigate the Property: As a general rule, the buyer's acceptance of the property's condition is a contingency of the agreement. The buyer is given a specified time in which to conduct investigations at the buyer's expense. As a general policy, it is prudent for a buyer to request that professional investigations of the property be made, especially for older properties that may have been constructed using hazardous products such as asbestos and lead paint or pipes. Professional investigations can also be beneficial to the seller and real estate agents involved in the transaction, because if the buyer later sues based on alleged defects in the property, it will be much more difficult for the buyer to demonstrate reliance on the seller's or the agents' representations and disclosures.

Liquidated Damages: An offer to purchase generally is accompanied by a good-faith initial deposit, which, if the offer is accepted, is applied to the purchase price. But if the buyer defaults, an issue would arise as to whether the deposit should be returned to the buyer. To account for this situation, most purchase agreements provide that if the buyer fails to complete the purchase because of the buyer's default, the deposit will be treated as liquidated damages.

Time Is of the Essence: A time is of the essence clause in a contract is a provision stating that timely performance is an essential element of the contract. A time is of the essence clause in the contract means that a party who does not perform within the time specified is in breach of the contract as long as the nondefaulting party has made a valid tender of performance. A time is of the essence clause can be waived by agreement or by acceptance of tardy acts of performance, such as by accepting late payments.

5. Conditions for Termination/Breach of Contract

When Contract Is Considered Performed/Discharged:

A contract is fully performed (executed) when each party to the contract has done (or not done) what that party agreed in the contract to do (or not to do). A contract can be *discharged* (i.e., canceled) in a number of ways:

- by being fully performed;

- by mutual agreement of the parties;

- by destruction of the subject matter of the contract;

- if the object or purpose of the contract becomes illegal;

- if by the time the purpose of the contract is to be performed, it is impossible to do so; and

- death or incapacity of the party whose performance is the object of the contract if the contract calls for specific performance (such as the performance of an artist).

Assignment and Novation:

Unless a contract calls for specific performance or otherwise prohibits assignment, a party to a contract may assign its rights and obligations under the contract to another. The party who assigns its rights is called the *assignor*; the party receiving the rights is called the *assignee*. An *assignment* does not typically relieve the assignor of liability under the contract, so that if the assignee fails to perform adequately, the assignor may be sued for damages.

A *novation* is the substitution of one party for another (in which case the first party is entirely excused from performing under the contract) or the substitution of one contract for another with the intent of extinguishing the original contract.

Breach of Contract and Remedies for Breach:

A *breach* is a failure to perform in accordance with the terms of a contract. A breach can be either material (also referred to as major) or non-material (also referred to as nominal). A *material breach* is often said to "reach to the heart of the contract" and deprives the non-breaching party of a substantial benefit of the bargain. A material breach may, depending on the circumstances, permit the injured party to recover damages, terminate the contract and cease performing his or her part of the bargain, rescind the contract, or seek specific performance or injunctive relief. A *non-material breach* allows the injured party to sue for damages (though they may be nominal or even nonexistent); however, as a general rule such an injured party must still perform his or her part of the bargain.

- **Rescission.** Rescission extinguishes a contract and returns each party to the position it was in immediately prior to the formation of the contract. Rescission is often sought in cases of fraud, duress, mistake, failure of consideration, or undue influence.

- **Damages.** An injured party to a contract may sue to recover monetary damages incurred by the other party's material breach. Generally, monetary damages are limited to damages foreseeably arising from the breach, whereas damages that could not have been foreseen are not recoverable.

  ○ *Liquidated Damages.* Parties may agree, usually in a building contract or in a contract to purchase real estate, that if a breach occurs, a specified amount of damages, referred to as liquidated damages, will be paid in lieu of any other remedy for the breach. As long as the amount is not excessive, and provided that it would be extremely difficult to determine actual damage amounts, courts normally will enforce such liquidated damages provisions.

- **Specific Performance and Injunctive Relief.** When monetary damages cannot provide an adequate remedy, the injured party may seek the equitable remedy of specific performance, whereby a court orders the breaching party to perform his or her part of the bargain (such as transferring the deed to a property), or injunctive relief, whereby a court orders a party to refrain from threatening to breach the contract if the breach would result in irreparable damage.

Monetary damages are often considered inadequate when the transaction involves unique items that cannot be replaced with an exchange of money. Examples include real estate (every property is unique), artwork, and family heirlooms. Personal service, though unique, cannot be compelled by specific performance.

6. Offer and Acceptance (counter offers, multiple offers, negotiation, earnest money)

When Offer Becomes Binding (notification): An offer must be accepted as stated — any change will be construed as a rejection of the entire offer. The offer becomes binding after delivery of an acceptance; however, an offer may be withdrawn any time before it has been accepted, and an acceptance may be withdrawn any time prior to the delivery of the acceptance to the offeror.

Note: An MLS listing, or an advertisement for a listed property, is not an offer that can be accepted — it is merely a public notification that a certain property is available for which an offer is being solicited.

Counteroffer Cancels Original Offer: A counteroffer is both a rejection of the earlier offer and the creation of a new (counter) offer. Communication between the parties to a contract, especially to a real estate contract, is usually not a simple one-two process of an offer being made followed by an acceptance. Negotiations generally take the form of an offer being made by a potential buyer, rejection and counteroffer from the seller, rejection and counteroffer from the buyer, and so on until the process ends — with or without a sale.

Priority of Multiple Counteroffers: There is no priority among offers (or counteroffers), because until a legally binding purchase agreement has been executed, a seller may entertain all offers. Until a purchase transaction has closed, a listing agent is obligated to present all offers received to the seller, unless instructed by the seller to do otherwise.

7. Contingencies

A contingency is an event that may, but is not certain to, happen, the occurrence upon which the happening of another event is dependent. Until all contingencies in a purchase agreement are met, the agreement is voidable.

Contingencies may be placed in a purchase contract for the benefit of either the buyer or the seller. Typical contingencies for the benefit of the buyer include that the buyer is able to obtain adequate financing, that the property passes certain inspections, that the property be appraised at a certain value or above, or that the buyer is able to sell the buyer's current home. A typical contingency inserted on behalf of the seller is the seller's closing on another property in which the seller intends to reside.

8. Duties and Obligations of the Parties

Agent or Seller Liability:

Agent or Seller Liability. All states have laws that require sellers of residential real estate consisting of 1 to 4 dwelling units to disclose material facts related to the property. Real estate licensees are also required to perform some kind of (statutory and/or common law) due diligence to discover (as by visual inspection) and disclose material facts, including potential hazards, to prospective purchasers of such residential properties. Failure to do so exposes a licensee to civil liability for damages incurred by a purchaser and to regulatory action that may result in the suspension or revocation of the licensee's license. This issue of agent responsibility to disclose material facts will be discussed in greater detail in Chapter 5.

Types of Hazards. Real estate licensees are not expected to be experts on the detection and/or remediation of environmental hazards; however, they need to be aware of the kinds of environmental hazards that may exist; they need to to be able to make intelligent suggestions as to the possible need for inspections by experts; and they need know how to direct their clients and customers to relevant sources of information.

Lead-Based Paint. Pursuant to the federal ***Residential Lead-Based Paint Hazard Reduction Act*** rule, a seller (or lessor) of a residential dwelling unit built before 1978 must notify a buyer (or tenant) in writing about required disclosures for lead-based paint. The seller must disclose any knowledge he or she has about whether lead-based paint was used in the dwelling unit and must provide the buyer with an EPA pamphlet titled *Protect Your Family From Lead In Your Home,* which describes ways to recognize and reduce lead hazards. The seller must deliver this pamphlet to a prospective buyer before the contract is completed. The seller must also offer a prospective buyer 10 days to inspect for lead-based paint and lead-based paint hazards. The seller is not required to pay for this inspection.

Safe Drinking Water Act (SDWA). The SDWA authorizes the EPA to set national standards for drinking water protection from man-made and from natural pollutants. For example, the SDWA banned the use of lead pipes and lead solder in new drinking water systems.

Asbestos. Asbestos is a naturally occurring mineral composite that once was used extensively as insulation in residential and commercial buildings, in brake pads, and in fire-retardant products, such as furniture. As asbestos ages, it breaks down to small fibers that, if inhaled in sufficient quantity over sufficient time, can cause a variety of ailments, including a type of cancer known as *mesothelioma*. Though the use of asbestos has not been entirely banned, it is regulated by the EPA and the Occupational Safety and Health Administration (OSHA). Among the disclosures required of sellers of property, and licensees representing sellers and buyers, is any knowledge they may possess of asbestos-containing materials in the property.

Carbon Monoxide (CO). Carbon monoxide is a colorless, odorless, toxic gas that is dangerous because one cannot see or smell the toxic fumes. Indoors, the concentration of carbon monoxide created by unvented gas space heaters, gas water heaters, fireplaces, and other sources of combustion can easily rise to a lethal level. At lower levels, carbon monoxide can cause flu-like symptoms, such as headaches, nausea, and fatigue. Licensees should check their state laws and local ordinances, as increasing numbers of regulatory bodies have mandated the installation of carbon monoxide detectors in residential properties.

Radon. Radon is a radioactive, colorless, odorless, tasteless, naturally occurring gas, which is formed by the decay of the small amounts uranium and thorium that exist in most soils. Radon is considered the greatest cause of lung cancer in non-smokers. Radon can build up to unsafe levels in a house due to the gas coming up through cracks in the floor. In 2005, the U.S. Surgeon General issued a health advisory, warning Americans about the health risk due to exposure of radon in indoor air, noting that more than 20,000 Americans die of radon-related lung cancer each year. Since then, an increasing number of home buyers and renters have been asking about radon levels in the dwellings they are considering buying or renting. Therefore, sellers and licensees would be well advised to have their properties tested before beginning the selling or renting process. Reducing radon to acceptable levels is usually quite an inexpensive project, often consisting of venting the crawlspace beneath houses.

Mold. Mold is a naturally occurring, ubiquitous fungus that is usually quite smelly and appears as a woolly growth on damp or decaying organic substances. Most mold strains are harmless, but some, such as stachybotros and aspergillus, are potent allergens. Mold in homes is usually caused by leaking roofs, air conditioners, or plumbing, and by poor ventilation in moist areas such as bathrooms and laundry rooms. Due to increasing numbers of highly publicized legal cases involving mold, some resulting in millions of dollars in damage awards (lawyers have a saying "Asbestos is old, mold is gold"), real estate agents would be wise, as part of their duty to inspect, to use their noses to sniff for signs of mold, and to strongly suggest that a professional mold inspection be performed on the properties they represent.

Formaldehyde. Formaldehyde is a colorless, pungent-smelling gas that can cause a number of unpleasant symptoms, such as nausea and burning sensations in eyes and throat.

Formaldehyde may also trigger asthma attacks in some people. Formaldehyde is a known cause of cancer in animals and may be a cause of cancer in humans. It is used extensively to make building materials and numerous household products. The most significant source of formaldehyde in houses is pressed wood that uses adhesives containing urea-formaldehyde resins. The Formaldehyde Standards for Composite Wood Products Act of 2010 establishes limits for formaldehyde emissions from composite wood products. There are tests that can determine the level of formaldehyde in homes.

Section D. Service/Listing Buyer Contracts (contracts between licensee and seller or buyer)

1. General Principles and Legal Concepts

In order to be valid, *listing agreements* must satisfy the conditions for the validity of contracts in general, as discussed above, and, in most states, they must be in writing in order to satisfy the statute of frauds. Specific requirements for the special types of listing agreements are discussed below in part 6 of the Section.

A listing agreement is a contract between a real estate broker and a seller, wherein the broker (either directly or in association with salespersons or other brokers) solicits offers for the seller's property, usually in exchange for a commission, also called a *brokerage fee*. The commission is generally computed as a percentage of the price that the property is actually sold for, rather than as a percentage of the listing price. The listing itself is not an offer; it is an invitation to begin negotiations with, and for the submission of offers from, potential buyers. Therefore, a buyer cannot create a contract by accepting the terms of the listing.

Although listing agreements are often filled out and signed by salespersons, the contract is actually between the seller and the broker who employs the salesperson.

2. Basic Provisions/Purpose/Elements

Safety Clause (also referred to as a *protection clause* or an *extender clause*). A provision in a listing agreement, providing that the broker will earn the full commission if the property is sold within a specified number of days after the termination of the listing to a buyer with whom the broker has dealt in certain specified ways regarding the property.

Ironclad Merger Clause. A contract provision stating that no prior agreement or contemporaneous oral agreement will have any force or effect.

Severability Clause. A contract provision providing that if any term of the agreement is held to be ineffective or invalid, the remaining provisions will nevertheless be given full force and effect.

Liquidated Damages Clause. In a contract where it is anticipated that damages for a breach of the contract would be difficult to ascertain, a liquidated damages clause is a provision that specifies exactly the amount of damages to be paid by the breaching party for a breach.

Contingency Clause. A contract provision that makes performance of a certain act conditional on the occurrence of a specified event.

3. Duties and Obligations of the Parties

Disclosure When Acting As Principal or Other Conflict of Interest:

Conflict of Interest. A *conflict of interest* is a situation in which an individual or organization is involved in several *potentially* competing interests, creating a risk that one interest *might* unduly influence another interest. A conflict of interest can exist:

- regardless of any pecuniary gain;
- regardless of any actual undue influence; and
- regardless of any evidence of wrongdoing or impropriety.

Furthermore, not all conflicts of interest are considered unethical or illegal. For example, for real estate licensees the conflict of interest known as dual agency in which the agent owes fiduciary duties to both the buyer and seller is perfectly legal in many (but not in all) states as long as the appropriate disclosures are made and agreed upon by all parties to the transaction. However, dual agency must be handled with utmost care (some would say super-human care) to avoid stumbling into impropriety, thereby risking suspension or revocation of the licensee's license, as well as civil actions against the licensee.

Disclosure of a Special Relationship with Either the Buyer or the Seller. Real estate agents often act in real estate transactions on behalf of themselves, immediate family members, an entity in which they own an interest (such as a partnership), a close personal friend, a business associate, or someone else with whom they have a special relationship. In such situations the agent, because of his or her professional education, experience, and contacts, is more aware of the investment and profit opportunities of the subject property than are most other people. The *possibility* of exploiting those advantages for the benefit of anyone with whom the agent has a special relationship, *without full disclosure of this special relationship to all parties to a real estate transaction*, clearly presents an improper conflict of interest. Some state courts have even held that the fiduciary duty of a real estate licensee to his or her principal includes the duty to disclose that the buyer is a close personal friend.

A Licensee Acting Solely As a Principal. Typically, real estate law does not require that a licensee who is acting *solely* as a principal in a real estate transaction reveal his or her status as a licensee. However, the practical risk in not revealing the existence of his or her license almost surely outweighs any potential benefit to be gained from secrecy. If, after closing, the buyer (or seller, as the case may be) feels that something had been done wrong in the transaction and sues, the attorney handling the case may try to sway the jury by pointing out that the real estate licensee possessed much greater knowledge of real estate in general, and the subject property in particular, and "clearly took unfair advantage of my client!"

Responsibilities of Agent to Customers and Third Parties, Including Disclosure, Honesty, Integrity, Accounting for Money:

An agent has certain obligations of fair dealing and honesty to customers and third parties, even though the agent does not have a fiduciary relationship with such parties.

Disclose Agency Relationship. An agent must disclose to all parties involved in a transaction whom the agent represents. Laws differ as to exactly when this disclosure must be made, but generally this disclosure should be made as soon as possible.

Disclosure of Material Facts. An agent is responsible for disclosing numerous material facts bearing on the value or desirability of a property. The extent of these disclosures varies depending upon whether or not the property is residential or commercial. The subject of disclosures of property conditions will be discussed in detail in Chapter 5.

Making Any Substantial Misrepresentation. Misrepresentations can be either intentional or negligent. However, in real estate law even negligent misrepresentation is often characterized as fraudulent. Normally, to find fraudulent misrepresentation there must be a finding of an intention to deceive; however, even without bad intention and even believing his or her assertions to be true, a real estate agent may be guilty of fraudulent misrepresentation if the assertions are made in a manner not warranted by the information available to the agent.

Nondisclosures. Real estate agents have a duty to disclose any known defect in the property and, under the laws of most states, any defect that could have been discovered upon reasonable visual inspection. Nondisclosure can also result from an affirmative act of hiding defects in the property to prevent the buyer from discovering the defects. Such acts are referred to as *concealment*, and sometimes as *negative fraud.*

Accounting for Money. An agent is responsible for keeping careful records of all funds received from, or for, a customer, and, in nearly all states, must keep such funds in a trust account.

Secret Profits. An agent has a duty to be fair to everyone involved in a real estate transaction, not just to the principal. Most courts hold that this duty to be fair implies that agents must inform buyers of any agent interest in the transaction.

4. Conditions for Termination/Breach of Contract

When Contract Is Considered Performed/Discharged:

A contract is fully performed (executed) when each party to the contract has done (or not done) what that party agreed in the contract to do (or not to do). A contract can be *discharged* (i.e., canceled) in a number of ways:

- by being fully performed;

- by mutual agreement of the parties;

- by destruction of the subject matter of the contract;

- if the object or purpose of the contract becomes illegal;

- if by the time the purpose of the contract is to be performed, it is impossible to do so; and

- death or incapacity of the party whose performance is the object of the contract if the contract calls for specific performance (such as the performance of an artist).

Assignment and Novation:

Unless a contract calls for specific performance or otherwise prohibits assignment, a party to a contract may assign its rights and obligations under the contract to another. The party who assigns its rights is called the *assignor*; the party receiving the rights is called the *assignee*. An *assignment* does not typically relieve the assignor of liability under the contract, so that if the assignee fails to perform adequately, the assignor may be sued for damages.

A *novation* is the substitution of one party for another (in which case the first party is entirely excused from performing under the contract) or the substitution of one contract for another with the intent of extinguishing the original contract.

Breach of Contract and Remedies for Breach:

A *breach* is a failure to perform in accordance with the terms of a contract. A breach can be either material (also referred to as major) or non-material (also referred to as nominal). A *material breach* is often said to "reach to the heart of the contract" and deprives the non-breaching party of a substantial benefit of the bargain. A material breach may, depending on the circumstances, permit the injured party to recover damages, terminate the contract and cease performing his or her part of the bargain, rescind the contract, or seek specific performance or injunctive relief. A *non-material breach* allows the injured party to sue for damages (though they may be nominal or even nonexistent); however, as a general rule such an injured party must still perform his or her part of the bargain.

- **Rescission.** Rescission extinguishes a contract and returns each party to the position it was in immediately prior to the formation of the contract. Rescission is often sought in cases of fraud, duress, mistake, failure of consideration, or undue influence.

- **Damages.** An injured party to a contract may sue to recover monetary damages incurred by the other party's material breach. Generally, monetary damages are limited to damages foreseeably arising from the breach, whereas damages that could not have been foreseen are not recoverable.

  - *Liquidated Damages.* Parties may agree, usually in a building contract or in a contract to purchase real estate, that if a breach occurs, a specified amount of damages, referred to as liquidated damages, will be paid in lieu of any other remedy for the breach. As long as the amount is not excessive, and provided that it would be extremely difficult to determine actual damage amounts, courts normally will enforce such liquidated damages provisions.

- **Specific Performance and Injunctive Relief.** When monetary damages cannot provide an adequate remedy, the injured party may seek the equitable remedy of specific performance, whereby a court orders the breaching party to perform his or her part of the bargain (such as transferring the deed to a property), or injunctive relief, whereby a court orders a party to refrain from threatening to breach the contract if the breach would result in irreparable damage.

Monetary damages are often considered inadequate when the transaction involves unique items that cannot be replaced with an exchange of money. Examples include real estate (every property is unique), artwork, and family heirlooms. Personal service, though unique, cannot be compelled by specific performance.

5. Remuneration/Consideration/Fees

Compensation. The form of compensation must be set forth in the agency representation agreement. It is important to note that *all compensation is subject to negotiation — it is not* *fixed by law or custom.* Furthermore, an agent does not necessarily represent the person paying the commission; i.e., *the source of a real estate agent's compensation does not determine agency representation.* For example, an agent may represent only the buyer, but receive his or her entire commission as a commission split with the listing broker, in which case 100% of the buyer's agent commission would come (indirectly) from the seller.

6. Types of Service/Listing Contracts

There are three basic types of listing agreements: *open listing*; *exclusive agency listing*; and *exclusive right to sell listing.* The defining characteristics of these three types of listing agreements are summarized in Figure 1.

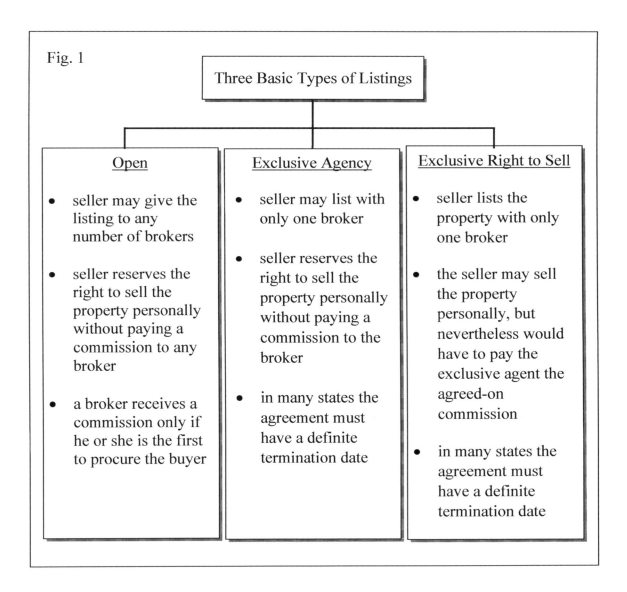

Fig. 1

Three Basic Types of Listings

Open	Exclusive Agency	Exclusive Right to Sell
• seller may give the listing to any number of brokers	• seller may list with only one broker	• seller lists the property with only one broker
• seller reserves the right to sell the property personally without paying a commission to any broker	• seller reserves the right to sell the property personally without paying a commission to the broker	• the seller may sell the property personally, but nevertheless would have to pay the exclusive agent the agreed-on commission
• a broker receives a commission only if he or she is the first to procure the buyer	• in many states the agreement must have a definite termination date	• in many states the agreement must have a definite termination date

Exclusive Agency Listing. In an exclusive agency listing, a specific broker is employed as the seller's exclusive agent. The exclusive agent may cooperate with other brokers with whom the exclusive agent may share any commission earned. However, the seller reserves the right to sell the property to a buyer the seller personally procures, without obligation to pay a commission to the exclusive agent. Many states require that an exclusive agency agreement must contain a specified date of termination.

Exclusive Right to Sell Listing. In an exclusive right to sell listing, the seller agrees to list the property with only one broker who will receive the agreed-on commission if, during the term of the listing, the property sells or if the broker procures a buyer who is ready, willing, and able to meet all of the terms of a sale contained in a listing agreement, regardless of who is responsible for procuring the buyer. Furthermore, under this type of listing, in most states the broker is entitled to a full commission if, during the term of the listing, the seller withdraws the property from the market or makes the property unmarketable. As with an exclusive agency listing, in order to be valid, most states require that an exclusive right to sell listing agreement must have a specified termination date.

Open Listing. An open listing agreement may be made by a seller to any number of brokers, though only one commission would be paid, going to the agent who first procurers an offer acceptable to the seller. The seller also reserves the right to sell the property to a buyer procured by the seller, without paying a commission to any broker. Furthermore, the sale of the property automatically terminates all outstanding open listing agreements for the property, without the need for notification on the part of the seller to the brokers to whom the seller gave an open listing. For these reasons, few agents are willing to spend time on open listings.

Other Types of Listings.

- **Net Listings.** A *net listing* can take the form of any of the three basic types of listings: open, exclusive agency, or exclusive right to sell. The unique feature of a net listing is that the seller demands to receive a certain amount from the sale, regardless of the price the property is ultimately sold for. In such a listing, the broker's compensation is not based upon a percentage of the sales price; rather the compensation would be the amount left over (if anything) after subtracting from the sales price all loan balances, liens, compensation to other brokers, closing costs, etc., and the net amount demanded by the seller.

   Example: Suppose a broker with a net listing finds a buyer who pays $500,000 for the property; the property had a loan balance of $400,000; closing costs were $5,000; the seller's specified net was $70,000; and there were no other claims against the property or its sale. The broker would then receive compensation of $25,000: $500,000 minus the sum of $400,000 plus $5,000 plus $70,000.

   Net listings are not legal in many states and are seldom used in others, because lurking in the background of every such listing is the potential that the broker may be subject to a charge of fraud, especially if the broker is successful in obtaining a high sales price for the property and, therefore, in obtaining what may appear to be excessive compensation. Because real estate agents owe fiduciary duties and obligations to their principals, a broker with a net listing must present all offers to the principal, even offers below the listing price, which, if accepted by the seller, would result in the broker's receiving no commission.

- **Flat Fee Listings.** One way that a seller who wishes to sell his or her home without paying a percentage commission to a listing broker, while still getting wide exposure for the seller's property, is to contact a broker who, for a flat fee (usually just a few hundred dollars), will list the home on the MLS. Flat fee brokers typically also provide additional (à la carte) services that the seller may want, including the composing of advertisements, furnishing of signs, filling out purchase contracts, and/or assisting with negotiations. Usually, the flat fee broker will recommend that the seller offer buyers' agents some form of compensation to encourage buyers' agents to bring the seller's property to the attention of the buyers' agents' clients.

- **MLS Listings.** A multiple listing service (MLS) is a service provided by groups of brokers affiliated with a real estate association. Such groups pool their listings and disseminate the listings to all members of the group, usually on the Internet. These listings offer subagency and/or compensation to other members. If a sale results, the commission is split between the brokers. A broker must obtain the seller's permission before submitting the listing to an MLS.

Buyer/Tenant Representation Agreements.

Although buyer/tenant representation agreements essentially mirror listing agreements, there are a few differences:

- A buyer/tenant agreement may take the form of an open buyer/tenant agreement, an exclusive buyer/tenant agency agreement, or an exclusive right to represent agreement. As with listing agreements, exclusive buyer/tenant agency agreements must, in most states, have a definite term period.

- The form of compensation must be set forth in a buyer/tenant representation agreement, and as with listing agreements, *all compensation is subject to negotiation — it is not fixed by law or custom.*

- The buyer/tenant agent may receive compensation either exclusively from the buyer/tenant or in the form of a commission split as with a cooperating agent; however, the form of compensation must be made explicit to both the buyer/tenant and to the seller/lessor as soon as possible.

- Because buyer/tenant representation by agents is relatively new, the law concerning buyer/tenant representation is not as developed as is the law of seller/lessor representation. One of the issues undecided in many states is whether a buyer/tenant agent may represent multiple buyers/tenants interested in the same property.

- In buyer/tenant agency representation, the buyer/tenant is the principal to whom the agent owes fiduciary duties.

- Unlike a listing agent or a cooperating agent whose primary goal is to get a sale of the listed property at the best price and best terms, the primary duty of a buyer/tenant agent is to protect the buyer/tenant by obtaining for the buyer/tenant the best property at the lowest price and best terms. In a (somewhat exaggerated) sense, *with respect to a specific property*, a listing agent can be viewed as a deal promoter; a buyer/tenant agent, as a deal killer, whose job it is to point out the merits of *other* properties.

25

Section E. Employment Agreements between Broker and other Licensees (including supervision)

Liability/Responsibility for Acts of Associated Licensees (Employees or Independent Contractors) and Unlicensed Employees:

Even though a broker may not be personally at fault, because the employees and associated licensees are agents of the broker, the broker can be held responsible for the negligent conduct of employees or agents who act within the scope of their employment or agency.

Responsibility to Train and Supervise Associated Licensees (Employees or Independent Contractors) and Unlicensed Employees:

An *employee* works for another person (the *employer*) who directs and controls the services rendered by the employee. An *independent contractor* is a person who performs work for someone, but does so independently in a private trade, business, or profession, with little or no supervision from the person for whom the work is performed. An agent also works for another person (sometimes referred to as the employer, but more often as the principal), but usually acts for and represents that principal in negotiating and/or creating narrowly defined, specific legal relationships with third parties.

Real estate licensees are categorized by different regulatory agencies differently: sometimes as an agent, sometimes as an independent contractor, sometimes as an employee — depending upon the context of with whom and under what circumstances the licensee is performing. Because real estate law requires the employing broker to supervise the activities of the salespersons employed by the broker, state real estate licensing authorities regulate the relationship between the broker and his or her employed licensees as *an employer-employee relationship.* As an employee of the broker, *a salesperson receives compensation from the broker and may not accept compensation from any other person, such as from a seller or a buyer, for any act that requires a real estate license.*

However, as a practical matter, a licensee who works for a broker works quite independently — for example, the employing broker does not, as a general rule, tell the licensee when to take lunch, how many hours to work, and so on. Therefore, a licensee for the most part appears to be an independent contractor vis-à-vis the employing broker — and the state and federal *taxing* authorities recognize a salesperson *as an independent contractor* by not requiring the employing broker to withhold from the salesperson's paychecks for items such as federal or state income taxes, Medicare, Social Security, or unemployment insurance, as long as there is a written contract between the broker and the salesperson that clearly states that the employment relationship between the broker and the salesperson is one between an employer and an independent contractor.

Finally, the salesperson is seen *as being an agent* of his or her employing broker, representing the broker vis-à-vis third parties; namely, with the buyers or sellers with whom the broker has an agency relationship. Though, as a general rule, both salespersons and brokers are referred to as real estate agents, only brokers are authorized by law to be the actual agents in a contractual relationship with sellers and/or buyers. Nevertheless, as agents for their employing brokers, *salespersons owe the same fiduciary obligations to the sellers and/or buyers with whom they work as do the brokers who technically are representing the sellers and/or buyers.*

A broker is responsible for training and supervising his or her salespersons, including any unlicensed personal assistants who work for salespersons. Regulatory agencies typically will take disciplinary action against a broker who fails to exercise reasonable supervision over the activities of his or her salespersons or unlicensed employees. In particular, the broker must take great care to ensure that unlicensed personal assistants do not perform acts that the law restricts to licensees.

CHAPTER 2: REAL PROPERTY OWNERSHIP/INTEREST

Bundle of Rights: Though historically the prevailing idea was that property existed independently of law and could not be taken away or substantially limited by law (the "natural rights doctrine"), the accepted modern view is that property is a creation of law. Property in this modern view is nothing more than a thing to which a ***bundle of rights***, created and protected by law, is attributed. This bundle of rights is all of the legal rights and privileges that attach to ownership of property, which may include the right to possess, use, enjoy, encumber, sell, and/or exclude from others. And because these rights are created by law, they can be changed or even abolished by law — sometimes with, sometimes without, compensation to their former owner(s).

Section A: Freehold estates (rights of ownership)

Buyers, renters, and lenders are concerned not only with what property (bundle of rights) they are acquiring an interest in; they are also concerned with the measure of the quality and the quantity of the rights they are obtaining. An ***estate*** refers to the degree, quantity, nature, duration, or extent of interest one has in real property.

The primary characteristic of an estate is its duration. If the estate's duration is potentially indefinite or for the length of someone's life (not necessarily for the estate holder's life), the estate is called a ***freehold estate***. Freehold estates include ***fee simple estates*** and ***fee simple defeasible estates*** as well as ***life estates*** and their future interests. All other estates are called ***leasehold estates***. Leasehold estates include ***estates for years***, ***estates from period to period***, ***estates at will***, and ***estates at sufferance***. (See Fig. 2)

Freehold Estates. The characteristic that distinguishes a freehold estate from a leasehold estate is its indefinite duration. How long an individual's freehold estate will last is unknown, because it may be transferred whenever the owner wishes. Freehold estates (other than life estates) are sometimes referred to as ***estates of inheritance*** because they always can be inherited. (See Fig. 3)

Fee Simple Absolute. The fee simple absolute estate is the greatest estate that the law permits in land. It is "the best you can get," and when a buyer purchases land, he or she generally purchases a fee simple absolute estate. Indeed, the law presumes that a fee simple absolute is being transferred unless specific words limiting the rights transferred are used at the time of conveyance.

The description "absolute" is perhaps a bit inflated, because the estate can still be subject to other restrictions, such as zoning codes and building restrictions. These governmental restrictions do not, however, affect title, and they are not found in the deed.

Fig. 2

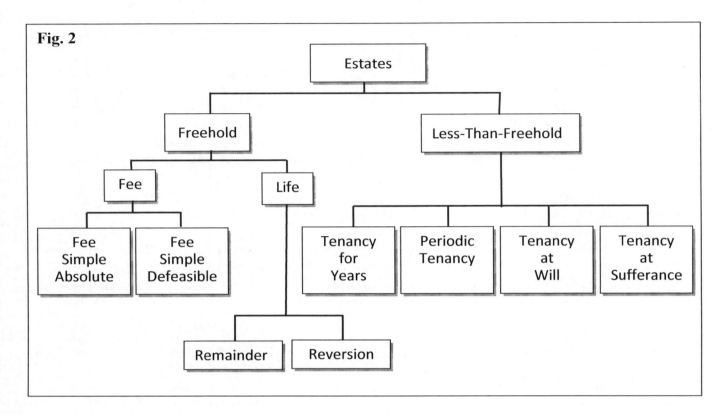

Fig. 3

Type of a freehold estate transferred by Grantor A	Words typically used in the deed to create	Future interest in the estate	Action needed to create the future interest
Fee simple absolute	Grant to B and his/her heirs	B has all present and future interests	N/A
Fee simple defeasible	To B on the condition that	B's estate may be terminated upon the happening of the condition	A may terminate B's estate but must do so timely
Life estate	To B for life	Reversion	Future interest automatically reverts to A
	To B (or A) for life, then to C	Remainder	All interests automatically go to C

Fee Simple Defeasible. Fee simple defeasible refers to a fee estate that is qualified by some condition that, if violated, may "defeat" the estate and lead to its loss and reversion to the grantor. Such conditions, called *conditions subsequent,* are infrequently used today as a means of private land restriction. Many attempts at private land restriction that were used in the past, such as transfer restrictions relating to race or ethnicity, are considered void by modern law, and the grantee of a deed containing such restrictions may petition courts to have such restrictions stricken from the deed.

A *life estate* is a freehold estate the duration of which is measured by the life of a natural person — either by the life of the person holding the estate, or by the life or lives of one or more other persons. There are two recognized categories of life estates. If, at the end of the estate, the future interest reverts to the grantor, the residue of the estate is called a *reversion*. If, at the end of the estate, the future interest arises in a third person C, the residue of the estate is called a *remainder* and C is called a *remainderman*. Probably the most common use of life estates is for Grantor A to keep a life estate interest in the property for his/her life, granting the remainder to an heir or heirs. (See Fig. 4)

Fig. 4

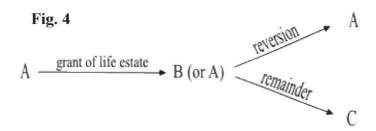

The owner of a life estate possesses most of the rights in the property as does an owner of a fee simple absolute estate. Unless expressly restrained in the grant of the life estate, the life tenant may rent, encumber, or sell his or her interest. Of course, once the life estate terminates, any such lease, encumbrance, or transfer of rights by the life tenant also terminates.

A life tenant has certain duties and obligations, such as the making of necessary repairs to structures and the paying of taxes. Additionally, a life tenant is obligated to act reasonably to avoid harming ("wasting") the value of the future interest of the property.

Forms of Ownership: When people acquire real property, they must decide in what legal form that ownership should be. This decision as to the form of ownership is important because it undoubtedly will have significant tax, inheritance, and liability consequences.

There are two general types of private ownership: *ownership in severalty* (the property is owned by one person only) and *joint ownership* or *co-ownership* (the property is owned by two or more persons).

Ownership in Severalty. When one person is the sole owner of property, the property is owned in severalty. "Severalty" is a term derived from "sever" and refers to keeping the bundle of rights that is this solely owned property entirely separate from the rights of others.

<u>Mineral, Air and Water Rights:</u> Ownership of land includes ownership of:

- *Airspace above the land.* Traditionally, a land owner could claim unlimited rights to the airspace above his or her property, no matter how high above the land. However, recognizing the need for air travel, contemporary law gives the landowner only a "reasonable" amount of airspace to use above his or her land. What constitutes "reasonable" in this context is often difficult to decide and is determined on a case-by-case basis whenever a lawsuit arises between parties. Airspace is also something that can be sold separate from the surface of one's land. Condominiums, for example, involve the selling of the exclusive ownership of a certain volume of airspace together with nonexclusive rights to common areas, such as halls, elevators, and recreational facilities.

- *Water.* Landowners' rights to water on, under, adjacent to, or near to the land are largely governed by state law. In general, states with ample supplies of water have adopted *riparian rights* laws that primarily address controversies that arise when two or more landowners attempt to use the same limited supply of water that lies or flows over or adjacent to their land. Today, riparian rights laws allow each riparian landowner the use the amount of water that does not unreasonably interfere with the beneficial use of water by other riparian landowners. On the other hand, states where water is scarce typically adopt water rights based on *prior appropriation theory*, which holds that the first person to appropriate water, regardless as to whether that person owns land adjacent to the water or over which the water flows, has priority over later users.

- *Mineral rights.* Landowners have certain rights in minerals that lie directly beneath the surface of their property and may sell their mineral rights separately from the rest of their property. As part of the purchase of such mineral rights, the buyer acquires the right to enter the land under which the minerals lie in order to extract the minerals. This automatically acquired right to enter the land for purposes of mineral extraction is an *implied easement* called a *profit á prendre*.
  - *Solid mineral rights.* Solid minerals, such as coal and metal ores, are owned by the landowner below whose property the minerals lie and are considered real property until they are extracted from the earth, at which time they become personal property. Upon the sale of real estate, the landowner's rights to the minerals that lie beneath the property automatically pass with the deed, unless specifically excluded.
  - *Liquid mineral rights.* When a reservoir of oil, gas, or geothermal steam is drilled into and pumping of the minerals to the surface begins, such liquid minerals begin to flow toward the pump, even from areas that do not lie directly below the land on which the drilling rights exist. States differ as to ownership of these liquid minerals. In states that recognize the *doctrine of capture*, such liquid minerals that lie in their natural state below the surface of land are not owned by the owner of the land — the owner of the land (or the owner of the drilling rights to these minerals beneath the land) merely has the right to drill from the surface of the land down to these types of minerals, which lie trapped in natural underground reservoirs. Only when these minerals are "captured" by being brought to the surface do they become property —

personal property, not real property. Other states have passed **utilization** or **pooling** statutes, under which landowners receive a fraction of the liquid minerals produced by a reservoir that extends under the owners' lands.

Section B: Types of Ownership (estates in land)

1. Joint Tenancy

A joint tenancy is one owned by two or more persons in equal shares with the right of survivorship. To establish a joint tenancy, it is necessary to state in the deed that the grantees will hold title as "joint tenants." Additionally, the following *four unities* must be obtain:

- *Unity of possession* — each of the joint tenants must have an equal, undivided right to possession of the entire property;
- *Unity of time* — each of the joint tenants must acquire his/her interest in the property at the same time;
- *Unity of interest* — the joint tenants must have equal interests in the property; and
- *Unity of title* — the joint tenants must receive their ownership in the property from the same deed.

The most important feature distinguishing a joint tenancy from a tenancy in common is the *right of survivorship*. On the death of one of the joint tenants, the surviving joint tenants receive in equal shares the decedent's interest in the property, free from probate; hence, the decedent's inclusion of his/her joint tenancy interest in a will would have no legal force and effect, provided that at least one joint tenant survives the decedent. This consequence is the result of the legal fiction that each joint tenant holds the (single) title to the entire property. An exception is that if a joint tenant murders another joint tenant, the murderer would not receive the decedent's interest in the joint tenancy.

A corporation may not be a joint tenant because the law regards a corporation as having potentially infinite duration, and infinite duration would result in the right of survivorship having no consequence.

Along with the right of survivorship, joint tenancy has another significant characteristic: any lien against a decedent's interest in a joint tenancy that was placed on the decedent's interest during joint tenancy is extinguished upon death, and the surviving joint tenant(s) receive the title unencumbered by the decedent's liens.

Transferring a joint tenancy interest. A joint tenant's interest may be severed from the joint tenancy either by voluntary or involuntary conveyance. The grantee of such a conveyance would take title as a tenant in common with the remaining tenants (if there had been more than one), who continue as joint tenants with respect to their interests among themselves.

Terminating a joint tenancy. A joint tenancy may be terminated either by agreement among the joint tenants through a *voluntary partition*, or, if no voluntary agreement can be reached, by a judicial determination after the filing of a *partition action* by one or more of the joint tenants. Of course, it is often impossible or impractical to divide real property into parts that are solely owned, so the termination of a joint tenancy through partition, whether voluntary or involuntary, usually requires the selling of the property.

2. Tenancy in Common

A tenancy in common is a form of co-ownership without the right of survivorship. Tenants in common may hold unequal interests; however, if the deed does not specify fractional interests among the tenants, the interests will be presumed to be equal.

Tenants in common are said to have an **undivided interest** in the property, which, as in joint tenancy, means that each owner has the right of possession of the entire property and may not exclude the other owners from any portion by claiming that any specific portion of the property is his or hers alone. All income and expenses related to the property are to be divided proportionally among all of the tenants in common.

Transferring a tenancy in common interest. A tenant in common may freely mortgage, sell, gift, or will his/her interest to another, who becomes a tenant in common with the others. There is no right of survivorship for tenants in common — the interest of a deceased tenant in common passes to the beneficiaries the decedent's estate, who take the decedent's place as tenant(s) in common with the other co-tenants.

Terminating a tenancy in common. As in the case of joint tenancy, a tenancy in common may be terminated either by agreement among the co-tenants by a voluntary partition, whereby each co-tenant receives an agreed-upon fraction of the property, or, if no voluntary agreement can be reached, by a judicial determination after the filing of a partition action by one or more of the co-tenants.

Tenancy by the Entirety. In approximately one-half of the states, a husband and wife can own property as tenants by the entirety. As with joint tenancy, tenancy by the entirety includes the right of survivorship. However, unlike a joint tenancy, neither the husband nor the wife may transfer his or her interest without the consent of the other. The theory of tenancy by the entirety is that a married couple owns the property as a single entity, not as separate individuals with equal interests in the property. A tenancy by the entirety may be terminated by divorce.

Community Property. In the nine states that have community property systems —Arizona, California, Idaho, Louisiana, Nevada, New Mexico, Texas, Washington, and Wisconsin — ownership of property acquired during marriage is considered **community property**. There is, however, a class of property called **separate property** that is excluded from community property. The separate property of a married person generally includes (1) all property owned by the person before marriage, (2) all property acquired by the person after marriage by gift, bequest, devise, or descent, and (3) all rents, issues, and profits from the separate property. Each spouse is considered to own half of the community property and may devise by will his or her interest to anyone. However, the sale of community property requires that both parties agree to the terms of the sale.

Tenancy in Partnership. A form of co-ownership called tenancy in partnership is created when two or more persons combine their assets and efforts in a business venture in exchange for a partnership interest in the venture. The corporate form of such business ventures can be **general partnerships** or **limited partnerships**.

The primary difference between a general partnership and a limited partnership is that each of the partners of a general partnership is personally liable for all of the debts of the partnership, whereas only the general partners of a limited partnership (there must be at least one) are personally liable for partnership debts — the limited partners have no liability beyond their investment in, and pledges to, the partnership.

3. Condominiums

Common Interest Ownership Properties: There are several types of common interest developments in which purchasers own or lease a separate lot, unit, or interest, and have an undivided interest or membership in a portion of the common area of the development.

- **Condominiums.** The modern trend in common interest developments is toward condominiums. Each of the 50 states has some form of condominium law, often referred to as a *horizontal property act*. A condominium is a residential unit owned in severalty, the boundaries of which are usually walls, floors, and ceilings, and an undivided interest in portions of the real property, such as halls, elevators, and recreational facilities. A *townhouse* is a form of condominium in which the individual units are connected by a common wall and, in general, (unlike in a high-rise condominium complex) a deed to the land beneath the townhouse is granted to the townhouse owner.

  Advantages of Condominium Ownership.

  o **Ease of maintenance**. An owner need not worry about mowing the lawn, shoveling snow, weeding, landscaping, cleaning the pool, taking care of the roof, etc. The burden of accomplishing these tasks is the responsibility of the condominium *homeowner's association* or management board.

  o **Tax benefits**. Condominium owners receive the same tax benefits (mortgage interest and property tax deductions, homeowner's exemption, homeowner's exclusion, etc.) as do owners of single-family residences.

  o **Appreciation**. Historically, homeowners, including condominium owners, have enjoyed significant long-term appreciation in their investments in their primary places of residence. Whether this long-term upward trend will continue is a matter of conjecture.

  Disadvantages of Condominium Ownership

  o **Homeowner's association fees**. All of that maintenance (mowing the lawn, cleaning the pool, etc.) that a condominium owner is free from performing must to be paid for — through homeowner's association fees. These fees must be high enough to also pay for electricity and insurance for common areas, professional management of the property, legal and audit fees, contributions to a reserve for maintenance and/or replacement of expensive property items such as elevators, roof, balconies, heating and air-conditioning systems, and so on.

  o **Restrictions**. Condominium projects are managed by homeowner's associations or management boards that place restrictions (*CC&Rs*, an abbreviation of "covenants, conditions, and restrictions") on the use of the property. Some of these restrictions might prohibit pets, renting or subletting, or limit the kinds of improvements owners can make to their units.

- o **Less privacy**. As compared to a single-family house, there is less privacy in the communal living of a condominium complex. Such close proximity to others often also comes with increased noise.

- o **Proximity to renters**. Most condominiums permit renting and some condominium projects have a high renter/owner ratio. As renters may not exercise the same degree of care of the property as do owners, prospective buyers should inquire as to the renter/owner ratio of any condominium complex in which they are considering investing.

- **Stock Cooperatives.** A stock cooperative is a corporation formed primarily for the purpose of holding title to improved real property either in fee simple or for a term of years. In a stock cooperative, all or substantially all of the shareholders of the corporation receive a right of exclusive occupancy in a portion of the real property (i.e., a leasehold interest), title to which is held by the corporation. Although the cooperative is responsible for paying all of the property taxes on the property, these taxes are collected by the cooperative from the stockholders, who are charged a pro rata fee based on the size or value of their units. Most stock cooperatives are of the apartment house type that include community recreational facilities and are governed by a homeowners' association.

- **Timeshares.** There are two basic types of timeshares:
    1. A timeshare that is a fee simple estate in real property coupled with the right of occupancy for only certain periods of time (such as for one month per year). Time-share estate interests are typically transferred by a grant deed.

    2. A timeshare that entitles the purchaser to a right to occupancy for certain periods time, not coupled to freehold estate in real property. This type of timeshare is typically transferred by license or membership agreement, not by grant deed.

Section C: Leasehold Interest

1. Basic Concepts and Terminology

The holder of a *leasehold estate* (also known as a less-than-freehold estate or nonfreehold estate) has the exclusive right to possession of land for a length of time. The holder of a leasehold estate is usually referred to as a *lessee* (or tenant); the owner of the property is referred to as the *lessor* (or landlord). When referring to leasehold estates, the terms "tenancy" and "estate" are used interchangeably. The four types of leasehold estates differ according to their characteristics, creation, duration, limitation on term, and termination.

An *estate for years* is a leasehold that continues for a fixed period of time. Unlike what the name implies, the lease need not be for a period measured in years — it only need be for a definite period, whether for days, months, or years.

An *estate from period to period* (commonly called a *periodic tenancy*) continues from period to period, whether by days, months, or years, until terminated by proper notice.

An *estate at will* is an estate (or tenancy) in which a person occupies a property with the permission of the owner; however, the tenancy has no specified duration, and, in most states, may be terminated at any time by either the tenant or the owner of the property upon giving proper notice.

An *estate at sufferance* arises when a lessee who legally obtained possession of a property remains on the property after the termination of the lease without the owner's consent. Such a *holdover tenant* can be evicted like a trespasser, but if the owner accepts rent, the estate usually becomes a periodic tenancy.

Dual Nature of a Lease. Whether written or oral, a lease has two distinct characteristics:

1. A lease transfers an estate in the real property leased. This transfer of a real property interest creates *privity of estate* between the landlord and tenant.

2. A lease also constitutes an executory bilateral contract between landlord and tenant that governs such matters as the landlord's maintenance of the property and the tenant's duty to make lease payments. This contract aspect of a lease creates *privity of contract* between landlord and tenant, which makes a leasehold estate a *chattel real* — an interest in land that is less than a freehold estate and is also a form of personal property governed by laws applicable to personal property.

2. Types of Leases

There are five major types of leases:

1. *Gross Lease.* Under a gross lease (also referred to as a *fixed lease*), the tenant pays a fixed rental amount, and the landlord pays all of the operating expenses for the premises.

2. *Net Lease.* Under a net lease, the tenant pays a fixed rental amount plus some of the landlord's operating expenses (such as a percent of property taxes). A common variation on the net lease is the *triple net lease*, under which the tenant pays a fixed rent plus the landlord's property taxes, hazard insurance, and all maintenance costs not specifically reserved for the landlord's maintenance (such as repairs to the roof).

3. *Graduated Lease.* A graduated lease (also referred to as a *step-up lease*) is similar to a gross lease except that it provides (in a lease provision referred to as an *escalator clause*) for periodic increases in the rent, often based on the Consumer Price Index.

4. *Percentage Lease.* Under a percentage lease, which is often used in shopping centers, the tenant typically pays a base rent amount plus a percentage of the gross receipts of the tenant's business. The percentage of gross charged is usually dependent on the percent markup used in the tenant's business. Thus, under a percentage lease the percentage of gross paid by a grocery store is likely to be much less than the percentage of gross paid by a parking lot.

5. *Ground Lease.* Under a ground lease, a tenant leases land and agrees to construct a building or to make other significant improvement on the land. At the end of the lease term, the improvement becomes the property of the landlord. These leases tend to be for long periods in order to make it economically viable for the tenant to incur the large expense of the construction.

Lease with an Obligation to Purchase. A *lease with an obligation to purchase* (also referred to as a *lease-purchase*) is typically used when the tenant-buyer wants to purchase a property but does not yet have the down payment or other ability to purchase the property at the present. Typically, a lease-purchase will provide that a portion of each rental payment will be applied to the purchase price, so that at some point the remaining amount necessary to complete the purchase is within the tenant's ability to do so. Because this agreement provides both for a lease and for a purchase, all legal requirements for both a lease and a purchase agreement must be satisfied.

Lease with an Option to Purchase. A *lease with an option to purchase* (also referred to as a *lease-option*) provides that the lessee has the right to purchase the property at the specified price and terms any time prior to a specified date, but has no obligation to do so. Typically in a lease-option the lessee pays both the agreed-upon rent and a fixed option price. Because, as with a lease-purchase agreement, a lease-option agreement contemplates both a lease and a purchase, all legal requirements for both a lease and a purchase agreement must be satisfied.

3. Basic Elements and Provisions of Leases

Though no standard pre-printed form or specific words are required, the terms of a valid, enforceable lease must:

1. establish a term for the lease, whether periodic or fixed;
2. identify the parties;
3. evidence the parties' intent to form a landlord-tenant relationship (e.g., by using such words as "lease" or "rent";
4. properly describe the leased property; and
5. specify the amount of rent, when due, and the manner in which the payments should be made.

Additional terms that are generally found in leases include:

Assignment; Subletting: Unless a lease expressly prohibits the tenant from transferring its interest in the premises, the tenant may *assign* (i.e., transfer the tenant's entire interest in the premises) or *sublease* (i.e., transfer the tenant's right to a portion of the premises or to the entire premises for less than the entire remaining lease term) its interest in the premises to any third party.

In an *assignment*, the original tenant remains secondarily liable under the lease through the lease term. The successor tenant (the *assignee*) becomes primarily liable to the landlord through the remainder of the lease term. If the assignee expressly assumed all obligations of the *assignor*, then the assignee will be fully liable under the lease. If, instead, the assignment was less than an express *assumption*, the assignee will be liable only for obligations that derive from its "privity of estate" or its occupancy of the premises, such as rent and duty to maintain, but will not be liable for certain other *purely contractual* obligations, such as an obligation to pay attorney fees in certain litigation outcomes with the landlord.

In a *sublease* the original tenant remains liable under the lease through the end of the lease term. However, because there is neither "privity of estate" nor "privity of contract" between the *subtenant* and the landlord, the subtenant has no direct lease obligations to the landlord. In a sublease situation, the subtenant is liable for the rent to the original tenant, and the original tenant is liable for the rent to the landlord. It is for this reason that a sublease is sometimes referred to as a *sandwich lease*, the original tenant being sandwiched between the subtenant and the landlord.

The landlord has no right to enforce the lease obligations against the subtenant but can enforce the obligations against the original tenant, regardless of whether it was the tenant or subtenant who performed an act or omission leading to a default. If, thereby, the original tenant's rights are extinguished, the subtenant's rights, which derive entirely from the original tenant, would also be extinguished. Nevertheless, if the landlord consents to a sublease, or a subtenant assumes certain obligations of the tenant, a sufficiently direct relationship may be found to enable the parties to enforce the terms of the lease against each other.

In addition to assignment and sublease, interests in the lease can be transferred through a *novation*, which occurs when the lease is replaced with a new one, or one party is replaced by another party. If a novation replaces the original tenant with another, then the liability of the original tenant under the lease would be terminated.

4. Rights and Duties of the Parties

Quiet Enjoyment. The essence of every leasehold interest is exclusive possession of the leased premises. Accordingly, in every lease, the law implies a covenant that the landlord will provide the tenant with possession and "quiet enjoyment" of the premises. Though this implied covenant protects the tenant from disturbances to a tenant's right to possession and quiet enjoyment from the landlord, it does not protect the tenant from acts of third parties over whom the landlord has no control. Examples of breaches of quiet enjoyment include the landlord's making extensive or unwarranted repairs, and the landlord's numerous or illegal entries.

Habitability. Landlords have responsibilities for maintaining dwelling units in a habitable condition, fit for tenants to live in; and tenants have responsibilities for keeping their dwelling clean and undamaged, thereby possessing and using the dwelling in a manner that maintains the landlord's reasonable expectation that his or her investment will be respected and responsibly cared for.

Before renting a dwelling, a landlord must ensure that the property meets certain structural, health, and safety standards necessary to make the unit fit to live in. Furthermore, after a tenant moves in, if problems arise that make the dwelling unfit to live in, the landlord is responsible for making the necessary repairs to return to the unit to a habitable condition. The tenant, on the other hand, must take reasonable care of the premises, keeping the dwelling clean and undamaged, and is responsible for repairs and damage caused by the tenant or by the tenant's family or guests.

Disclosures. As will be discussed later in this book, in particular in Section F of this chapter and in Chapter 5, federal and state laws mandate that landlords give residential tenants disclosures regarding such things as lead-based paint issues, and the availability of a website containing lists of sex offenders (Megan's Law).

Discrimination. Everyone has a rightful interest in not being arbitrarily discriminated against — and especially so when it comes to obtaining a basic necessity such as housing. Contemporary federal and state laws attempt to ensure that a tenant's basic right not to be discriminated against based merely upon personal characteristics, such as ethnicity or sex, is honored by landlords and by others, such as real estate agents, involved in the selling or renting of residential units. A more thorough discussion of anti-discrimination laws can be found in Section F of this chapter and in Chapter 5.

5. Remedies for Default/Non-Performance

If the tenant breaches the lease, the landlord may sue for damages. However, because of the severity of the remedy of termination, courts are unlikely to allow the landlord to terminate the lease for cause unless the breach is material and substantial. Such material and substantial breaches include failure to pay rent, material damage to the property, interference with other tenants' right to quiet enjoyment, breach of a covenant not to assign or sublease the premises, and illegal use of the premises.

Eviction. Eviction of a tenant is a three-step process, involving:

> 1. termination of the lease;

> 2. filing, serving, and succeeding in an unlawful detainer action; and

> 3. if the tenant has not already vacated, physical removal of the tenant by the sheriff.

Termination. A breach of a lease by a tenant, even nonpayment of rent, does not terminate the lease — the tenancy continues until the landlord gives proper notice, which typically is a 3-day, 30-day, 60-day, or 90-day notice, depending on the reason for termination and the type of tenancy involved.

Both tenants and landlords should be aware that because the law of most states (1) frowns on the forfeiture of leases, and (2) provides landlords with expedited eviction procedures, if the landlord makes even a small mistake in drafting or serving the required notice, the court may deny the eviction, thereby returning the landlord to step one: the drafting and serving of a new termination notice.

Illegal Retaliatory Eviction. A typical affirmative defense that a tenant might state in a written answer to an unlawful detainer complaint is that the landlord filed the eviction action in retaliation for the tenant's having exercised one of the tenant's rights, such as complaining to a governmental agency about the habitability of the premises.

Illegal Self-Help Evictions. It is illegal for a landlord to evict a tenant by any means other than by way of the unlawful detainer process as prescribed by state law. Even if the tenant is behind on rent, the landlord may not:

- physically remove the tenant (which may result in a civil action of forcible detainer, and criminal charges of assault, battery, and kidnapping);

- changing the locks or otherwise preventing the tenant from occupying the premises;

- removing any of the tenant's personal property;

- cutting off the utilities; or

- removing any outside doors or windows.

Section D: Forms of Business Ownership

1. Sole proprietorship

A sole proprietorship is defined as a business composed of one individual and that is not chartered as some other business entity, such as a trust, corporation, or LLC. A sole proprietorship is the simplest form of business ownership and has no existence apart from its owner. Any income earned by the sole proprietorship is passed through to the owner and taxed at the owner's personal income tax rates.

Sole proprietorship is also the most common form of business entity because it is very lightly regulated, ownership may be freely transferred, and it is easy and inexpensive to establish, usually requiring only a business license and/or some other license required due to the type of business conducted, such as a real estate broker license. This simplicity results in lower administrative and legal expenses than are to be expected if establishing a corporation, partnership, or LLC. The owner of a sole proprietorship also has the ease and flexibility of not having to answer to anyone regarding the business operations or having to disclose financial information to other persons financially interested in the business.

These considerable advantages do, however, come at a price:

- a sole proprietor is personally liable for all debts and actions of the business;

- a sole proprietor is limited to personal resources, so cannot purchase the expensive properties that require the pooling of resources of many persons; and

- a sole proprietorship is totally dependent on one person, so once that person dies, the sole proprietorship no longer exists.

2. General or Limited Partnership

There are two types of partnerships: *general partnerships* and *limited partnerships*. The primary difference between a general partnership and a limited partnership is that each of the partners of a general partnership is personally liable for all of the debts of the partnership, whereas only the general partners of a limited partnership (there must be at least one) are personally liable for partnership debts — the limited partners have no liability beyond their investment in, and pledges to, the partnership.

A partnership (either general or limited) is an association of two or more persons who carry on a business for profit. Partnerships are not separately taxed (though they must file partnership tax returns with the IRS and with many state taxing authorities); instead, income of the partnership flows to the partners.

Advantages to a partnership include:

- it does not require the formalities of a corporation;

- unlike a corporation, its income is not taxed before distribution to the partners (i.e., its income is not double-taxed);

- unlike a sole proprietorship, it allows for more than one owner;

- unlike a sole proprietorship, it allows for the pooling of resources from many individuals; and

- unlike a sole proprietorship, it will not necessarily cease to exist upon the death of one of the partners — rather, it will continue to exist as long as the partners agree it will and as long as there are at least two partners, one of whom is a general partner.

Partnerships do, however, have a significant disadvantage compared to corporations or LLC's: Each of the partnership's (general) partners has unlimited personal liability for the acts of the partnership.

For example, if a partnership consisting of 10 general partners incurs a judgment against it that exceeds the partnership's ability to pay, each general partner would be personally liable not merely for 1/10 of the amount unpaid, but for the full amount unpaid (i.e., the general partners would be "jointly and severally" liable.)

If property is acquired by the partnership:

- each partner has an equal right to possession of partnership property for partnership purposes; however, unless all of the partners agree, no partner has the right to use or possess partnership property for any other purpose;

- a partner's interest in partnership property is not assignable except in connection with the assignment of all partners' interests in the same property; and

- a partner's interest in partnership property is not subject to attachment or execution, except on a claim against the partnership.

When a partner dies, title to the partnership rests entirely in the surviving partners. The decedent's estate or heirs acquire no direct interest in the property of the partnership or in its management. The decedent's estate or heirs do, however, have a right to an accounting and a share of the partnership profits and value upon dissolution.

3. LLC

The ownership form of choice for many real estate investors is the limited liability company (LLC) because it combines many of the advantages of a partnership with the limited liability advantages of a corporation. Unless it elects to be treated as a corporation, its income passes through to its owners, who are referred to as "members."

The organization of an LLC is more flexible than a partnership because whereas all partners of the partnership must be natural persons, an LLC may have a combination of individuals and business entity owners, all of whom enjoy the limited liability of a corporation's shareholders.

Section E: Private Restrictions on Real Property/Land Use and Matters Affecting Ownership

Individuals who wish to limit the use of their land generally may do so unless such restrictions are against the law. Examples of private restrictions include the giving of land to a conservation group with the restriction that it not be developed, or an agreement between neighbors that neither will build a swimming pool on his or her land. Examples of unenforceable restrictions due to illegality include agreements to restrict the sale of property to persons of a particular race, ethnicity, or religion. If a private restriction and a zoning ordinance are at variance, whichever is more restrictive will, if it is legal, prevail.

1. Liens

An *encumbrance* is right or interest held by someone other than the owner of the property that affects or limits the ownership of the property, such as liens, easements, licenses, and encroachments.

A *lien* is an official charge against property as security for the payment of a debt or an obligation owed for services rendered. A lien can be either a *voluntary lien* or an *involuntary lien*. Liens are also classified as either specific or general. A *specific lien* is a lien that attaches only to specific property. Examples of specific liens include mechanic's liens, property tax liens, and liens created by mortgages. A *general lien* is a lien that attaches to all of a person's nonexempt property in the county or counties in which the lien is recorded. Examples include judgment liens and income tax liens.

   a. Voluntary: A voluntary lien is a lien voluntarily given by the owner of the land upon which the lien is placed, usually to secure repayment of long-term debt. In most states, voluntary liens include liens created by mortgages and deeds of trust.

   b. Involuntary: An involuntary lien is a lien created by operation of law, not by the voluntary acts of the debtor. Examples of involuntary liens include judgment liens, local property tax liens, general tax liens, and mechanic's liens.

- **Judgment Liens.** In many states, a judgment that includes a monetary award does not automatically create a lien; however, the winner of the monetary award may record the judgment, or a summary of the judgment, thereby creating a general lien against the (nonexempt) property (real or personal) of the loser (the debtor) in the county (or counties) in which the judgment or summary of judgment is recorded. Judgment liens are enforceable only for a number of years, usually no more than 10.

- **Property Tax Liens.** Real property taxes are the main source of revenue for most local governments. Property tax liens have priority over all other liens, but are specific liens, attaching only to the properties from which the property tax arose. Property taxes are *ad valorem* taxes, meaning that these taxes vary in proportion to the value of the property taxed. In most states, certain kinds of real property, such as property owned by governments, religious organizations, and educational institutions, are exempt from property taxation as long as the property is used for tax-exempt purposes.

- **Special Assessment Liens.** Certain laws lay the groundwork for significant increases in taxes on property by permitting local governments to tax property for "special benefits" conferred on properties in particular limited areas. There are many such *special assessments* for such items as streets, sewers, lighting, water service, parks, playgrounds, tree planting, landscaping, parking facilities, geologic hazard abatement, and so on. Special assessments attach special assessment liens only on the properties "benefited" in particular areas and are therefore specific liens.

- **Federal Tax Liens.** Federal tax liens, which are general liens, result from the failure to pay federal income taxes.

- **Mechanic's Liens.** Provided that certain requirements are met and strict procedures followed (which vary from state to state), persons who provide materials, labor, or other services that are used to improve property and who have not been fully paid for the work and/or materials may apply for a *mechanic's lien*, which are specific liens.

   c. Priority: At any given time, a piece of real property might have several liens recorded against it: a deed of trust, a mechanics lien, a tax lien, a judgment lien — all vying to obtain priority over the others in case of a default where the property is worth less than the sum of the existing valid liens. The order in which lien holders are paid is known as lien priority.

   As a general rule, the order of payment is determined by the order of lien recording; in other words, first to record, first in right. However, some types of liens are given special priority: property tax liens and special assessment liens have priority over all other liens against the property, even if another lien, such as a judgment lien, was recorded first.

   Regarding mechanic's liens, states vary considerably as to priority among mechanic's lien claimants. However, the majority of states follow the rule that all mechanic's liens related to a work of improvement are treated equally in terms of priority and relate back to the time when the work of improvement began, each mechanic's lien holder being entitled to collect his or her pro rata share of the work furnished.

2. Easements/Rights of Way/Licenses

   An easement is a non-possessory right to use a portion of another property owner's land for a specific purpose, as for a right-of-way, without paying rent or being considered a trespasser. Typical easements are right-of-way easements to access otherwise landlocked property and easements to lay power, cable, telephone, or water lines. The owner of an easement has the duty to maintain it.

   The land that is encumbered by an easement is called the *servient tenement* — it serves the purpose of the easement. If the easement benefits other land (as in the case of a right-of-way easement), the land benefited is called the *dominant tenement*, and such an easement is called an *easement appurtenant*— it is appurtenant to the dominant land and cannot be sold separately from it.

If the easement benefits not other land but a legal person (including a business entity), such as an easement to erect and maintain telephone poles and lines, the easement is called an *easement in gross*. Because an easement in gross is not appurtenant to any dominant land, it is considered personal in nature.

Easements can be created in many ways — some voluntarily on the part of the owner of the servient tenement, some involuntarily. The most important methods of easement creation are by:

- *express grant*: the owner of the servient tenement expressly grants someone else the right to use the servient land for some purpose;

- *express reservation*: the owner of the servient tenement expressly reserves the right to use a portion of the servient tenement (such as when the owner of the servient tenement sells the land but wishes to retain the right to use a private road);
- *implication*: an implied easement arises by implication, as when a buyer of a parcel of land discovers that the land he or she just purchased has no access except over the land of the person from whom the parcel was purchased;
- *necessity*: an easement by necessity arises as a creation of a court of law in certain cases were justice so demands, as in the case where a buyer of a parcel of land discovers that the land he or she just purchased has no access *except over the land of someone other than from the person from whom the parcel was purchased.*
- *prescription*: such as when, under certain circumstances, one uses another's land for a statutory period of time without permission.

Easements can be terminated in many ways, including

- by the person who benefits from the easement acquiring the servient tenement — a person cannot have an easement over his or her own estate;
- by the dominant tenement and servient tenement becoming owned by the same person (this is referred to as merger of titles or merger of estates);
- by the owner of the dominant tenement releasing the easement rights back to the owner of the servient tenement;
- by the destruction of the servient tenement; and
- in the case of a prescriptive easement, by nonuse.

A *license*, unlike a lease or an easement, is not a real property interest; it is a right to use that is merely personal to the licensee. A license is not considered an estate; it does not run with the land; and, unless otherwise agreed, it can be revoked at any time. If ownership of the property that the licensee has permission to use is transferred, the license is automatically revoked.

3. Pre-existing Leases

The law of pre-existing leases applies in several situations, including:

- if the landlord sells the leased property to a new owner, the new owner must honor the pre-existing lease;
- if A has a lease and wishes to sublease the property to B (and A's lease so permits), B would have no rights greater than A has under A's pre-existing lease.

4. Encroachment

An *encroachment* is a thing affixed under, on, or above the land of another without permission. Examples of encroachments include overhanging tree branches and roofs, or buildings or fences that cross a boundary line. The owner of the land encroached may seek either damages or removal of the encroachment.

5. Deed Conditions, Covenants, and Restrictions

Private restrictions (also referred to as deed restrictions) are either *covenants* or *conditions*. A covenant is a promise placed in a deed, stating that the owner will do something (an *affirmative covenant*, such a promise to maintain a party wall) or not do something (a *negative covenant*, such as a promise not to build a fence). Remedies for breach of a covenant are either monetary or injunctive relief.

Conditions (often called *conditions subsequent*) that are placed in a deed can have more serious consequences if breached; namely, forfeiture of title. An example would be where A sells to B a parcel of land "on the condition" that the land never be used for the sale of alcoholic beverages. If B subsequently uses that parcel of land to sell alcoholic beverages, a court may order a forfeiture of the parcel back to A. However, the law "abhors forfeiture" (an English common law maxim of equity). Therefore, unless there was a clear violation of an unambiguous condition, courts often will try to construe a restriction as being a covenant rather than a condition (such as in a case of ambiguous language) and impose monetary or injunctive relief for a breach rather than forfeiture of title.

6. Property Owner Associations

Most private restrictions are applied to entire subdivisions (including condominiums) and are known as *CC&Rs* ("covenants, conditions, and restrictions"). CC&Rs generally are negative covenants (not conditions) whereby persons agree to limit certain things, such as the color of paint on houses or the type of architecture used to build or remodel houses.

Section F: Government Powers and Control of Land Use

Federal, state, and local governments have broad powers that affect the use and value of real property.

1. Americans with Disabilities Act (ADA)

The *Americans with Disabilities Act (ADA)* prohibits discrimination against persons with disabilities, where "disability" is defined as "a physical or mental impairment that substantially limits a major life activity." Impairment due to substance abuse is not covered.

The Act applies to providers of public transportation and accommodations, which must make their facilities accessible to an extent that can be accomplished without unreasonable expense. As used in ADA, the term "public accommodation" includes hotels, motels, stores, care givers, property management firms, and places of dining, recreation, and education.

The Act also applies to employers engaging in interstate commerce and having 15 or more employees. Such employers must alter areas of their workplaces (e.g., entrances, waiting areas, and restrooms) in a manner to accommodate handicapped employees, unless such alterations would place an undue hardship on the business.

Enforcement of the Americans with Disabilities Act. ADA allows private individuals to receive back pay and injunctive relief for violations of its employment requirements and injunctive relief for violation of its public accommodation requirements, but does not provide for monetary damages.

2. Land Use Restrictions and Regulations (i.e., zoning)

Master Plans. All states now have laws mandating that a comprehensive, long-term master plan be created (usually by a municipal or county governmental body) for the physical development of the county or city, and of any land outside its boundaries which, in the planning agency's judgment, bears relation to its planning. These master plans are required to address transportation, housing, conservation, open spaces, noise, and safety.

Preparation of a Master Plan. Typically, master plans are prepared as follows:

1. data on the local economy, characteristics of the community, environmental conditions, and the capacity of public facilities and services are collected and analyzed;

2. a formulation of community goals and development policies based on the analysis of the above data is drafted;

3. diagrams that reflect and support the formulated development policies are prepared;

4. measures to implement the proposed general plan are prepared; and

5. once a proposed master plan is completed, the planning body usually holds at least one public hearing after which the proposed plan is forwarded to the relevant local legislative body, which may hold additional public hearings before adopting, amending, or rejecting the proposed plan.

After a master plan is adopted, the local government implements the plan by use of police power, eminent domain, taxation, and fiscal control.

Zoning laws. The primary purpose of zoning laws is to help implement the local master plan. Zoning laws split the jurisdiction into distinct land-use zones — residential, commercial, industrial, and rural being the basic zone-use categories. These main categories are often further refined into subcategories. For example, the residential category is often split into separate zones (generally referred to as R-zones) for single-family homes, duplexes, and condominiums and apartment buildings. Zoning laws also regulate many aspects of development, such as height, size, *setback*, and side-yard requirements to control population density and promote the aesthetic appeal of the community. Additionally, *buffer zones*, such as parks, may be created to separate residential zones from nonresidential zones. Additionally, buffer zones consisting of commercial or industrial zones may be established to separate residential zones from busy streets or highways.

Inclusionary zoning refers to city and county zoning ordinances that require builders to set aside a given portion of new construction for people of low to moderate incomes.

Zoning Exceptions and Changes.

Most locales have a *zoning appeal board*, which hears complaints about zoning regulations and entertains petitions for zoning exceptions and changes.

- *Nonconforming use* — refers to an exception for areas that are zoned for the first time or that are rezoned and where established property uses that previously were permitted do not conform to the new zoning requirements. As a general rule, such existing properties are "grandfathered in," allowing them to continue the old use but not to extend the old use to additional properties or to continue the old use after rebuilding or abandonment.

- *Conditional use* — refers to an exception for special uses such as for churches, schools, and hospitals that wish to locate to areas zoned exclusively for residential use. In these cases, the zoning authority may issue a *conditional use permit* to a limited number of such community service uses provided that they meet certain requirements for parking and security to minimize any negative impact on the neighborhood.

- *Variance* — refers to an exception that may be granted in cases where damage to the value of a property from the strict enforcement of zoning ordinances would far outweigh any benefit to be derived from enforcement. As a general rule, variances are given only for rather minor departures from zoning requirements, relating to such things as setbacks, building height, and parking.

- *Spot zoning* — refers to the zoning of isolated properties for use different from the uses specified by existing zoning laws. To spot zone a particular property may, in some cases, be a violation of the requirement that police power apply similarly to all property similarly situated, which in turn arises from the constitutional guarantee of equal protection under the law.

Building Codes: Building codes are federal, state, and local laws that govern all aspects of building construction, such as design, materials, electrical wiring, and plumbing. FHA and VA requirements regulate construction of housing that participate in their programs. Additionally, state laws and local ordinances provide for minimum construction and occupancy requirements. Building codes can be quite specific, applying to remodeling of existing structures and construction of walls and fences. Once construction of a structure intended for occupancy is completed, inspected, and found to be satisfactory, the appropriate official (such as a city inspector) will issue a certificate of occupancy.

Environmental Impact Reports: The environmental laws of federal, state, and local governments can have a significant impact on how property owners may use their properties.

The *National Environmental Policy Act* (*NEPA*) requires that federal agencies prepare an *Environmental Impact Statement* (*EIS*) for any development project that a federal agency could prohibit or regulate, and any development project for which any portion is federally financed. An EIS can include comments on the expected impact of a proposed development on such things as air quality, noise, population density, energy consumption, water use, wildlife, public health and safety, and vegetation.

State and local agencies also consider and respond to the environmental effects of private and public development projects. One of the first steps in analyzing a project is the preparation of an initial study that addresses the project's potential for significant adverse effects on the environment. As a general rule, if the public agency determines that the project will not have a significant adverse impact, the agency issues a negative declaration prior to making a final decision on the project. However, if the project is determined to have a possible negative environmental impact, the agency will prepare a draft environmental impact statement to be circulated and commented on. In response to a final environmental impact statement, the responsible agencies will attempt to mitigate any significant negative environmental impact by incorporating feasible changes into the project.

Regulation of Special Lands Types: Due to a growing awareness that we humans are part of a community that includes plants and animals and that our health is inextricably bound up with the health of all other living things, many laws been enacted at federal, state, and local levels aimed at protecting the environment that sustains us.

A *floodplain* is an area of low, flat, periodically flooded land near streams or rivers. Because of the relative abundance of water and the periodic depositing of nutrients carried by floods, floodplains are usually rich in diverse plant and animal life.

The federal *Flood Control Act* requires local communities to prepare plans to protect people living in floodplains, to discourage the building of new structures and the repairing of old structures in floodplains, and to repair flood control devices such as dams and levees.

The *Federal Insurance Agency* provides residents of communities that participate in the flood insurance program with flood insurance at rates that would not otherwise be affordable due to the high risk of flood damage.

The federal *Clean Water Act* (CWA) provides the statutory basis for regulating the discharge of pollutants into waters of the United States. The CWA requires that anyone discharging pollutants, or planning a development that would discharge pollutants, into waters obtain a permit, or else the discharge would be considered illegal. The CWA also allowed the *Environmental Protection Agency* (EPA) to authorize state governments to perform many of the permitting, administrative, and enforcement aspects of the Clean Water Act.

Although the term "wetlands" is not mentioned in the CWA, the EPA has taken the position that *wetlands* also come under its jurisdiction. The EPA defines wetlands as *"areas that are soaked or flooded by surface or groundwater frequently enough or for sufficient duration to support plants, birds, animals, and aquatic life. Wetlands generally include swamps, marshes, bogs, estuaries, and other inland and coastal areas, and are federally protected."* If an area is designated as a wetland, no development of the area is allowed, and no compensation to the owner of the wetland is provided for the resulting diminution in the value of the owner's land.

A *coastal zone* is a region where significant interaction of land and sea processes occurs. The federal *Coastal Zone Management Act* (CZMA) is intended to protect coastal zones, including the fish and wildlife that inhabit those zones, of the Atlantic, Pacific, and Arctic oceans, the Gulf of Mexico, Long Island Sound, and the Great Lakes from harmful effects due to residential, commercial, and industrial development.

Abatement, Mitigation, and Cleanup Requirements of Environmental Hazards:

The *Comprehensive Environmental Response, Compensation, and Liability Act* (CERCLA) (also referred to as the *Superfund Law*) is intended to clean up sites contaminated with pollutants and toxic wastes. CERCLA created the Hazardous Substances Response Fund, or Superfund, to pay for cleaning up hazardous waste sites. The Superfund is funded by taxes on industries, such as petroleum and chemical companies, and by Congressional appropriation. Many states have also enacted laws similar to CERCLA.

CERCLA was designed to ensure that the parties responsible for polluting a site would be held responsible for its cleanup. Unfortunately, the law can also impose liability for the cost of cleanup on unsuspecting landowners. CERCLA defines a **potentially responsible party** (PRP) as anyone who ever owned or operated the property, as well as anyone who produced the waste, transported the waste to the property, or disposed of the waste on the property. It is not necessary that a PRP have participated in, or even known about, the contamination to be held responsible for the cleanup and its cost. CERCLA provides for two types of actions in response to the discovery of contamination:

- *removal actions*, which are usually short-term responses to a perceived imminent threat that requires a prompt response, and

- *remedial actions*, which are usually long-term actions to permanently reduce or eliminate the contamination of a site.

CERCLA does, however, provide several limited exceptions to liability, known as the **innocent landowner defense**. For example, one who acquires a contaminated property by inheritance or bequest *after* it was contaminated is considered an innocent landowner. Also, a person who, before acquiring the property, undertook appropriate inquiry to ensure that the property was not contaminated may be considered an innocent landowner. Such appropriate inquiry would include checking government records, visual inspections, and obtaining an environmental assessment by a qualified professional.

Restrictions on Sale or Development of Contaminated Property:

Although it is the policy of regulatory agencies such as the EPA and its counterparts in the various states that, in general, the outright banning of the transfer of contaminated property is to be avoided unless necessary to achieve a statutory purpose, the development of a contaminated site is heavily regulated, requiring appropriate remedial action before proposed development may begin. Such regulation, of course, significantly impacts the ability of a landowner to find a buyer for contaminated property. Additionally, many states require that a transferee of real property who knows, or has reason to believe, that the property is contaminated must disclose this to any potential lessor or transferee.

Brownfields. The EPA defines **brownfields** as "real property, the expansion, redevelopment, or reuse of which may be complicated by the presence or potential presence of a hazardous substance, pollutant, or contaminant." Brownfields are typically abandoned or underutilized industrial sites in urban areas that are stigmatized due to their possible contamination. Because of the high cost and liabilities of acquiring such sites, businesses were reluctant to purchase such properties, or even to locate near such properties because of possible migration of contaminants due to the action of surface or underground water. To help reverse the continuing blight and the deterioration of brownfields and their neighborhoods, in 2002 the **Small Business Liability Relief and Revitalization Act** (also referred to as the **Brownfields Law**) was enacted to provide funds to assess and cleanup brownfields and to remove liability for for cleanup from owners who did not contribute to the contamination of their property. Many states also have policies that encourage the development and revitalization of abandoned or deteriorated urban properties.

3. Police Powers

One should be careful to distinguish eminent domain (see below), for which just compensation must be made, from **police power**, which is the power of a government to impose restrictions on private rights, including property rights, for the sake of public welfare, health, order, and security, for which no compensation need be made. Examples of the use of police power in regard to real property include the creation and enforcement of zoning codes, building codes, subdivision regulations, and property setbacks.

4. Eminent Domain

Eminent domain is a right of the state to take, through due process proceedings (often referred to as *condemnation proceedings*), private property for public use upon payment of just compensation. To exercise eminent domain, an appropriate governmental body must satisfy three basic requirements:

1. the property must be taken for the public good;

2. the property must be necessary for the public purpose for which it is supposedly being taken; and

3. the owner of the property must be paid just compensation, which is usually what a governmental agency or, ultimately, a court determines is the fair market value of the property.

When land is taken by eminent domain, in addition to just compensation for the value of the land taken, the owner may be able to receive *severance damages* if the owner's remaining land is reduced in value due to the severance of the condemned land from the owner's remaining property. A typical case is where an interstate bisects a farmer's land, making it much more difficult and costly for the farmer to farm his or her land.

In certain cases, condemned land or land used for public purposes (such as for noisy airports) may severely reduced in value nearby land. In such cases, an owner whose property has been severely reduced in value may sue to force condemnation of the property by using a judicial or administrative action called *inverse condemnation*. However, zoning that merely reduces the value of a property does not give the owner the right of inverse condemnation as long as the property still has viable economic use.

Escheat is a process whereby property passes to the state (or in some cases to the county) if a person owning the property dies intestate without heirs. If no heirs of a decedent can readily be found, publication is made to locate heirs, but if none comes forward to claim the property within a statutorily mandated time, the court will order an escheat of the property to the state. The right to escheat also applies to property found to be abandoned. The primary purpose of escheat is to prevent property from remaining ownerless or abandoned.

5. Property Taxation

Property Taxes. Property taxes are the main source of revenue for most local governments. Property taxes are *ad valorem* taxes, meaning that these taxes vary in proportion to the value of the property taxed. The Sixteenth Amendment to the U.S. Constitution prohibits the federal government from taxing land. In most states, certain kinds of real property, such as property owned by governments, religious organizations, and educational institutions, are exempt from property taxation as long as the property is used for tax-exempt purposes.

Special Assessment Liens. Certain laws lay the groundwork for significant increases in taxes on property by permitting local governments to tax property for "special benefits" conferred on properties in particular limited areas. There are many such *special assessments* for such items as streets, sewers, lighting, water service, parks, playgrounds, tree planting, landscaping, parking facilities, geologic hazard abatement, and so on. These assessments attach special assessment liens only on the properties "benefited" in particular areas and are therefore specific liens.

6. Subdivision/Planned Unit Development Regulations

A *subdivision* is what results when a parcel of land is divided into two or more parcels for sale. State and local governments control land use by regulating how improved or unimproved land is divided for the purpose of sale, lease, or financing. These regulations concern street construction, sidewalks, sewers, maximum and minimum lot size, fire hydrants, and the like. In addition to large parcels of land developed into many single-family homes, examples of subdivisions include condominiums, stock cooperatives, and timeshares.

A subdivider must draw up plans to comply with all of the many subdivision regulations applicable to the land the subdivider intends to develop. The subdivider will prepare a *plat*, which is a detailed map showing the boundaries of the individual parcels, streets, easements, engineering data, and, often, the environmental impact of the development.

The subdivision plat map is reviewed by numerous local agencies, including the planning department, health department, parks and recreation department, and others who may have an interest in regulating the development. These agencies try to ensure that the subdivision conforms to the county and/or city *master plan*, which addresses such issues as transportation, housing, conservation, open spaces, noise, and safety on a county- or city-wide scale.

For most subdivisions, an area of land is first designated as a block and then divided into lots using the lot, block, and tract system (also called the recorded map or recorded plat system).

In addition to the public regulations controlling a subdivision, many subdividers also impose private restrictions on the subdivision to control and maintain the quality and appearance of the subdivision. These private restrictions take the form of *covenants*, *conditions*, and *restrictions* (CC&Rs), which are typically concerned with the height, size, and architectural styles of buildings, lot size, land use, and setbacks. CC&Rs are typically enforced by homeowners associations.

Interstate Land Sales Full Disclosure Act. The federal *Interstate Land Sales Full Disclosure Act* is a consumer protection act intended to prevent unscrupulous subdividers from taking advantage of the public (e.g., by selling swamp land in Florida for residential development). This Act requires that certain land developers register with the Consumer Financial Protection Bureau if they offer across state lines parcels in subdivisions containing 100 or more lots. Subdivisions where each lot in the subdivision contains at least 20 acres are exempt from this registration requirement. A developer must provide each prospective buyer with a *Property Report* that contains pertinent information about the subdivision and that discloses to the prospective buyer that he or she has a minimum of 7 days in which to rescind the purchase agreement.

CHAPTER 3: FINANCE

Section A: Basic Concepts and Terminology

A buyer's having access to financing is critical to nearly all real estate transactions. Even the few buyers who accumulate enough cash to make an all-cash purchase of real property often choose to *leverage* their money by financing the bulk of the purchase with borrowed funds. Leverage results in multiplying gains (or losses) on investments by using borrowed money to acquire the investments. A significant risk of leveraging is that if property values fall, rental values will fall, possibly resulting in *negative cash flow* to the leveraged investor.

1. Equity

Equity is the difference between the current fair market value of a property and the total indebtedness against the property.

2. Loan-to-Value Ratio

The *loan-to-value ratio (LTV)* is an important risk factor lenders use to assess the viability of a proposed loan. LTV is defined as the amount of a first mortgage divided by the lesser of (1) the appraised value of the property or (2) the purchase price of the property. As a general rule, a high LTV (usually seen as over 80%) will either cause the loan to be denied, the lender to increase the cost of the loan to the borrower, or the lender to require that the borrower pay for private mortgage insurance.

3. Term and Payment

Term refers to a length of time something (e.g., an agency contract, a lease lease, an option, or a loan) lasts or is valid. A *payment* is the amount paid at a particular time, such as a monthly payment on a mortgage loan.

4. Principal and Interest

In financing, *principal* is the amount at risk on a real estate investment, or the amount outstanding on a loan. *Interest* is the amount paid for the use of another's money, usually expressed as an annual rate.

5. Direct and Indirect Costs (points, discounts)

Points. In finance, a point is equal to 1% of the loan amount. The term is used by lenders to measure discount charges and other costs such as origination fees and private mortgage insurance premiums.

Origination Fees. An origination fee is the fee a lender charges to cover expenses of processing a loan, such as purchasing credit reports, inspection reports and appraisals, and paying office expenses and salaries of personnel who interview borrowers and analyze the reports and appraisals.

Discounts. Discount points are a form of prepaid interest paid to a lender by a borrower to increase the lender's yield on loans that yield lower rates than investors currently demand, which is why discount points are sometimes referred to as *loan equalization factors*. One discount point is equal to 1% of the loan amount (not the purchase price). For example, if a borrower wished to obtain a loan rate 1% less than current market, a lender would charge the borrower a certain number discount points in order to make such a loan.

Broker Commissions. A broker's commission is the compensation earned (usually expressed as a percentage of the selling price) by a broker for the broker's representation of a seller or buyer in a property transaction. Unless the listing agreement specifies otherwise, if a broker who has been hired to sell a property procures a buyer who is ready, willing, and able to perform pursuant to the terms of the listing agreement, the broker will have earned the full agreed-upon commission. On the other hand, if a broker procurers an offer from a buyer ready, willing, and able to purchase at variance from the terms of the listing agreement, the broker would be entitled to the commission only if the seller accepts the counteroffer.

Private mortgage insurance (PMI). PMI is insurance that lenders often require for loans with an LTV more than 80%. PMI *insurers the lender*, not the borrower, and covers the top amount of the loan in case of default.

> **EXAMPLE:** A property with a purchase price and an appraised value of $100,000 and a loan of $90,000 would have an LTV of 90%. If the lender required PMI to cover the top 20% of the loan, the PMI coverage for the lender would be 20% of $90,000 = $18,000.

In the past, lenders usually honored a borrower's request to cancel PMI once the borrower's equity in the home reached 80% of the value of the property and the borrower had a good payment history. However, many homeowners did not know, or did not remember, that they could make this request, so they continued paying unnecessary PMI premiums. The ***Homeowner's Protection Act (HPA)*** of 1998 requires lenders to provide borrowers with certain disclosures, including when the balance of the loan is scheduled to reach 80% of the property value. [Note: HPA does not apply to FHA-insured or VA-guaranteed loans.] HPA also requires that PMI be canceled when the mortgage balance reaches 78% of the property value (77% for "high risk loans") and the borrower is current on the loan.

6. Return on Investment/Rate of Return

Return on investment (ROI) is an investor's cash flow (net income minus financing charges) divided by the investor's actual cash investment (as distinct from the purchase price).

Section B: Types of Financing

1. Amortized Loan

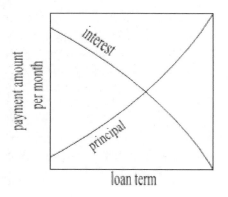

loan term

Installment loans require periodic payments that include some repayment of principal as well as interest. Installment loans are the most common type of loan used to finance real estate, and the most frequently used installment loan is the ***level payment loan*** — a loan under which all periodic installment payments are equal, though the amount allocated to principal and interest may vary over the term of the loan. A loan wherein the payments are sufficient to pay off the entire loan by the end of the loan term is referred to as a ***fully amortized loan***. The diagram to the left shows that with a level payment, fully amortized loan, during the first years of the loan term most of each month's payment goes to interest, but during the final years of the loan term most of each month's payment goes to reducing the principal. For a 30-year loan, the breakeven point occurs at 222 months (18.5 years) into the loan term.

There are many variations in installment loans. One such variation, called a ***partially amortized loan***, is to have the monthly payments pay all of the interest due but not enough of the principal to fully pay off the loan at the end of the loan term. In such a case, a ***balloon payment*** (generally considered to be any payment — most likely the final payment — that is more than twice the lowest installment payment) would be due at the end of the loan term.

Another type of loan, referred to as a ***negative amortized loan*** (or a "NegAm" loan), has been used by some borrowers. Under a negative amortized loan, the monthly installment payments do not cover all of the interest due— the unpaid part of the interest due being tacked onto the principal, thereby causing the principal to grow and grow as each month goes by. During housing booms, such loans may look appealing, but if housing prices do not continue to rise as fast as the outstanding principal rises under negative amortized loans, the buyers will eventually be stuck with loan balances greater than the value of their property — they will, in other words, be "underwater."

2. Interest Only Loan

An ***interest-only loan*** (also referred to as a ***straight loan*** or a ***term loan*** or) is a loan under which periodic payments consist of interest only — the full amount of the principal being due at the end of the loan term in one lump sum.

3. ARM Loan

Interest rates on certain loans, referred to as ***adjustable-rate loans*** or ***adjustable-rate mortgages (ARMs),*** vary over the term of the loan. Under an adjustable-rate loan, the interest rate remains fixed during certain time intervals, referred to as the ***adjustment periods***, such as 3 months or 6 months, and then at the end of each adjustment period the rate increases or decreases according to some set ***index*** beyond the control of the lender. The most common indexes used are Treasury securities (T-bills), the 11th District cost of funds of the Federal Home Loan Bank Board, and the London inter-bank offered rate (LIBOR).

The ***fully indexed rate*** on an ARM is the index plus a ***margin*** (also referred to as a *spread*), which is a predetermined number of percentage points. In other words,

ARM fully indexed rate = index + margin.

The margin is negotiated between each borrower and lender and, though the index varies over the term of the loan, the margin usually remains fixed over the loan term. Sometimes a lender will give a few months initial interest rate on an ARM that is less than the fully indexed rate. Such an initial rate is called a ***discounted rate*** (also referred to as a *teaser rate*). Discounted rates are usually accompanied by higher initial loan fees, called *points*, and with higher rates after the initial discounted rate expires. Therefore, though the loan payments may remain low for a short time, any savings during the discount period may (and likely will) be offset by higher cumulative payments over the remaining life of the loan.

Many lenders place ***interest-rate caps*** on ARMs. The most common two types of interest rate caps are:

1. a periodic adjustment cap, which limits the rate increase or decrease from one adjustment period to the next; and

2. a lifetime cap, which limits the interest rate increase over the entire loan term.

It is important to note that with some ARMs that have interest-rate caps, the cap may hold the interest rate below the fully indexed rate. Any increase in the interest rate not imposed because of the interest-rate cap might carry over to later rate adjustments. This increase in future rate adjustments is called a *carryover*. In a situation where there is a carryover, future monthly payments may actually increase even though actual interest rates remain the same or decline.

In addition to interest-rate caps, some ARMs limit the amount of installment payment increases. Under ARMs with *payment caps*, any interest not paid because of the payment cap will be added to the balance of the loan, thereby resulting in negative amortization.

4. Construction Loan

A construction loan is a short-term or interim loan given for the purpose of constructing a building or developing a property. The loan is usually given in incremental amounts (called *draws*) as the construction project progresses. Construction loans are typically written so that when construction is complete, the construction loan is replaced by a "take-out" loan.

5. Home Equity Loan

Equity Loans. Equity is the difference between the current fair market value of a property and the total indebtedness against the property. A loan based on the equity of a property is referred to as an *equity loan*.

A *home equity mortgage* is a security instrument used to provide the borrower with a loan based on the amount of equity in the borrower's home. Compared to a usual second mortgage, which provides the borrower with a lump sum payment (as does a typical home equity loan), a *home equity line of credit* (referred to as a *HELOC*) allows borrowers to borrow only what they need as they need it (for example, to purchase a refrigerator or to remodel the kitchen).

Typically, lenders set the credit limit on a HELOC by first taking a percentage of the appraised value of the home and then subtracting any balance owed on existing liens against the home.

Example: If the appraised value of the home is $700,000, the only lien against the home is a first mortgage with balance outstanding of $300,000, and the percentage the lender is willing to lend on the appraised value of the home is 80%, then the lender would establish a HELOC with credit limit equal to $260,000 (($700,000 × .8) - $300,000).

Reverse Mortgages. A *reverse mortgage* is a security instrument for a loan for homeowners 62 of age or older who have a large amount of equity in their homes. The reverse loan is usually designed to provide such homeowners with monthly payments, often over the lifetime of the last surviving homeowner or until such person either permanently leaves the home or dies, at which time the outstanding balance must be repaid or the house sold. The estate is not liable for any deficiency should the house sell for less than the outstanding balance of the loan.

If the reverse mortgage is insured by the FHA, it is called a ***Home Equity Conversion Mortgage (HECM)***. For an HECM, the definition of "permanently leaves the home" is 365 days of continuous absence. Under an HECM, homeowners can receive a percentage of the value of their equity in one lump sum, as monthly payments (either for a fixed term or for life), or as a line of credit.

A homeowner with a reverse mortgage continues to be responsible for paying property taxes; paying homeowners insurance premiums; paying any homeowners association assessment fees; and maintaining the home in good repair.

Section C: Methods of Financing

1. Government Programs (e.g., FHA, VA)

FHA. The FHA was created by the National Housing Act of 1934 in order to make housing more affordable by increasing home construction, reducing unemployment, and making home mortgages more available and affordable. The FHA does not make loans; it insures loans that approved lenders make for residential properties of 1 to 4 dwelling units. The availability of FHA-insured loans is particularly helpful for people who cannot afford a conventional down payment or do not qualify for PMI.

The benefits of FHA-insured loans include:

- relatively high LTVs, with down payments as little as 3.5%;
- down payments can be gifted by a relative;
- the loans cannot have a prepayment penalty;
- lower FICO scores are required than are required by conventional loans;
- the loans are assumable upon approval by the FHA; and
- relatively lenient front-end debt-to-income (PITI) ratios (the standard guideline is 29%; 31% max) and back-end debt-to-income ratios (the standard guideline is 41%; 43% max).

The disadvantages of FHA-insured loans include:

- relatively low loan amounts: FHA-insured loans have caps that the FHA will insure of varying amounts depending upon the relative value of homes in various areas.;
- upfront mortgage insurance premium (upfront MIP) and annual MIP premiums;
- requires that properties meet certain minimum standards as determined by an FHA-approved appraiser.

VA: The ***VA-guaranteed loan*** program is designed to help veterans obtain affordable loans. Like the FHA, the VA does not make loans — approved lenders make the loans. The VA guarantee works much like PMI in that the VA will reimburse the lender for part of the lender's loss in case of default and foreclosure.

Eligibility. Eligibility for a VA-guaranteed loan depends upon the length of active service in the United States armed forces. Periods are longer for peacetime service (181 days) than for wartime service (90 days). Persons who served in the National Guard or Selected Services are also eligible, usually with six years service. Persons dishonorably discharged are not eligible.

Application. Eligible persons must apply to the VA for a *Certificate of Eligibility* (can be done online), which the applicant must present to the lender. The property must be appraised pursuant to VA guidelines. The appraisal value is presented in a *Certificate of Reasonable Value (CRV)*.

Advantages of a VA-Guaranteed Loan

Reasons why VA-guaranteed loans are attractive include:

- do not require a down payment (so long as the loan does not exceed certain limits, see example below), so LTV can be 100%;
- underwriting standards are less stringent than for FHA or conventional loans;
- no mortgage insurance required; and
- loans are assumable if approved by the VA.

Other VA-Guaranteed Loan Features

Although the VA loan guarantee program does not set a maximum amount that an eligible veteran may borrow using a VA-guaranteed loan, the maximum amount of the guarantee for a veteran with full entitlement is 25% of the VA-determined county loan limit, the appraised value, or the purchase price whichever is less.

Example: If the county loan limit is $625,000 and the lower of the purchase price and appraised value is $500,000, the maximum guarantee would be 25% of $500,000 = $125,000. If the appraised value and the loan amount are greater than the county limit, the lender may require a down payment.

The VA does not dictate the interest rate charged by the lender. However, if the rate the lender requires is not acceptable to the borrower, a motivated seller may sweeten the deal by paying a *discount fee* to the lender.

Other Federal Programs: In addition to the FHA-insured and VA-guaranteed loan programs, the federal government also plays a significant role in the secondary mortgage market through the government-sponsored enterprises (GSEs) Fannie Mae and Freddie Mac, and through the government-owned corporation Ginnie Mae.

The FHA was established in 1934 to help alleviate the housing crisis caused by the 1930's economic depression. The FHA did this by insuring certain loans. The continuing depression demonstrated the need for still more government assistance, and in 1938 the *Federal National Mortgage Association (Fannie Mae)* was established to purchase mortgages from primary lenders, thereby (1) transferring the risks of these loans from the primary lenders to Fannie Mae, and (2) freeing up funds for the lenders to make more loans.

In 1968 Fannie Mae was effectively split into two entities: a privately held corporation that retained the name Fannie Mae, and a wholly owned government corporation within the Department of Housing and Urban Development (HUD) called the *Government National Mortgage Association (Ginnie Mae)*. Whereas Fannie Mae continued to purchase mortgages, Ginnie Mae's role was to guarantee pools of eligible loans that primary lenders issued as Ginnie Mae mortgage-backed securities. Also in 1968, the *Federal Home Loan*

Mortgage Corporation (Freddie Mac) was created, also as a privately held corporation, essentially to compete with Fannie Mae in the purchasing of eligible loans.

Though both Fannie Mae and Freddie Mac were private corporations, there was widespread belief that they were impliedly government backed, which helped to drive down their borrowing costs, drive up their stock prices, and lower concern about the extent of risks they were incurring in many of the loans they purchased. And, of course, the more questionable the loans that Fannie Mae and Freddie Mac were willing to purchase at a profit to primary lenders, the more questionable loans the primary lenders were willing to make.

As the housing crisis that began in late 2007 worsened, concern mounted that Fannie Mae and Freddie Mac might go bankrupt, and their stock plummeted. Fearing that Fannie Mae and Freddie Mac might take the entire financial system down with them, in September 2008 Fannie Mae and Freddie Mac were put into government conservatorship under the *Federal Housing Finance Agency (FHFA)*.

As government conservatorships, Fannie Mae and Freddie Mac still play a major role in the secondary market, purchasing FHA-insured, VA-guaranteed, and conventional loans on residential properties of 1 to 4 dwelling units, condominiums, and planned unit developments (PUDs) that have been created in conformance with FHFA guidelines. Maximum conforming loan limit for loans originated in 2014 for one-unit properties is $417,000 for most of the country. In the District of Columbia and all of the U.S. states except Alaska and Hawaii, the highest-possible local area loan limit for one-unit properties is $625,500.

Down Payment Assistance Programs.

Down payment assistance programs are offered by many state housing authorities. These programs can take the form of outright grants, interest-free seconds, and other special loan programs. The *Housing and Economic Recovery Act of 2008 (HERA)* prohibited anyone with a financial interest in the sale to fund any down payment assistance program for any loan insured by the FHA. However HERA does permit down payment assistance from family members of the buyer.

2. Conventional

Conventional loans are loans that are not FHA insured or VA guaranteed. Insured loans are loans in which the lender is insured against some portion of the loan in case of default by the borrower. Loans can be insured by private mortgage insurance (PMI), by the FHA, or by certain state-government entities.

Loans created in conformance with the Federal Housing Finance Agency guidelines are called *conforming loans*. Loans that are not conforming loans are called *nonconforming loans*, which are more difficult to sell into the secondary market and usually cost borrowers 1/4% to 1/2% more.

A *subprime loan* is a loan made to a borrower who has a relatively high-risk profile (such as a low credit score). Subprime loans usually carry interest rates that are 1% to 5% higher than loans made to borrowers with good credit standing.

3. Owner-financed

A seller of real estate may finance the purchase of the seller's real property for the buyer with a note secured by a mortgage or deed of trust. Such loans (or "sales on credit") by sellers of real property are referred to as *seller carry back loans*.

4. Land Contract

Seller/owner financing can also take the form of a *land installment contract* (also referred to simply as a *land contract*), whereby the seller (referred to as the *vendor*), rather than receiving the full purchase price immediately, sells the property on an installment basis, thereby becoming in essence the lender. Upon the closing of a land installment contract, the buyer takes immediate possession of the property, but the seller does not convey legal title to the buyer (referred to as the *vendee*) until all installments are paid.

Section D: Financing Instruments (Mortgages, Deeds of Trust, Promissory notes)

1. Basic Elements and Provisions of Financing Instruments

While there is no standard form used for all mortgages or deeds of trust, most contain certain important provisions either in the promissory note or the security instrument, or in both.

Acceleration Clause. An *acceleration clause* states that, upon default (such as failure to make payments as agreed) or a violation of other conditions (such as failure to maintain proper insurance), the lender has the option of declaring the entire balance of outstanding principal and interest due and payable immediately.

Due-On-Sale Clause. A *due-on-sale clause* (also referred to as an *alienation clause*) states that the lender has the right to accelerate the loan — declare the entire outstanding principal and interest due and payable immediately — if the secured property is sold or some other interest in the property is transferred. Without an alienation clause in the loan, the property would be freely transferable. With an alienation clause, the property can still be sold, but only if the existing loan is paid off in full.

Until 1982, enforceability of due-on-sale clauses was a matter of state law. But the *Garn-St. Germain Act* made the enforceability of due-on-sale provisions a federal issue. This act provides that due-on-sale provisions are enforceable except for certain transfers, such as transfers:

1. by devise, descent, or operation of law on the death of a joint tenant
2. granting a leasehold interest of three years or less not containing an option to purchase
3. to a relative resulting from the death of the borrower
4. where the spouse or a child of the borrower becomes an owner of the property
5. resulting from a decree of dissolution of marriage or legal separation
6. to a family trust

Regardless of whether the loan contains a due-on-sale clause, the sale of the secured property does not extinguish the lien that the lender obtained through the loan's security instrument. In such a case, if the loan is not paid off in full when the property is sold, the new owner can either assume the outstanding mortgage or deed of trust, or take title subject to the mortgage or deed of trust.

Partial Release Clause. A *blanket mortgage* is a mortgage used to finance two or more parcels of real estate. Blanket loans are used by borrowers in case one property does not provide sufficient equity to obtain the amount of funds the borrower needs, in which case the borrower may offer another property in which she or he has equity as additional collateral.

Blanket mortgages are also commonly used by developers who buy large tracts of land with the intention of subdividing them into many individual parcels to be sold individually over a period of time. Such a blanket mortgage would probably contain a *partial release clause*, which would allow the developer to sell off individual parcels and pay back, according to a release schedule, only a proportionate amount of the blanket loan. Note that with a normal due-on-sale clause, the sale of any interest in a property would require a repayment of the entire loan.

Assumption Clause. In an *assumption*, the purchaser agrees to be primarily liable on the loan, but the original borrower remains secondarily liable in case the purchaser defaults, unless there is a complete novation, in which case the seller would be relieved of all responsibility. If, on the other hand, the purchaser takes title *subject to* an existing loan, the original borrower remains fully liable for the debt, not the purchaser, but in the event of a default, the property can be foreclosed on.

The distinction between a buyer's assuming a loan versus taking the property subject to a loan becomes important in a case where the proceeds of a foreclosure sale of the property are insufficient to satisfy the amount due on the mortgage or deed of trust, in which case the lender might seek to recover the deficiency from whoever is liable for the loan payments. Such a recovery, if permitted by law, is called a *deficiency judgment*. Under an assumption, the buyer commits to being personally liable for the loan payments, so any deficiency judgment obtained would be a judgment against the buyer. If, on the other hand, the buyer purchased the property subject to the underlying loan, the seller remained personally liable, and the deficiency action would be brought against the seller.

Prepayment Clause. A prepayment clause states the terms by which a loan may be paid off faster than the agreed-upon schedule of payments without incurring a *prepayment penalty*. Without a prepayment clause, the borrower may prepay the whole or any part of the balance due, together with accrued interest, at any time without penalty.

The federal government has prohibited prepayment penalties from being imposed on loans secured by owner-occupied dwellings if the loan has been accelerated by a due-on-sale clause. FHA-insured and VA-guaranteed loans do not have prepayment penalties of any kind.

Subordination Clause. A *subordination clause* states that the mortgage or deed of trust will have lower priority than a mortgage or deed of trust recorded later. This clause is common in mortgages securing unimproved land, making it far easier for the borrower to obtain a construction loan to improve the property. Because lien priority is usually determined by recording date, a subordination clause allows a construction lender to take a first lien position even though the construction lender's lien is recorded later.

Defeasance Clause. A *defeasance clause* states that when the loan debt has been fully paid, the lender must release the property from the lien so that legal title free from the lien will be owned by the borrower. Under a deed of trust, the formal process of transferring legal title is by way of having the trustee sign a ***release deed*** (also referred to as a ***deed of reconveyance***). In the case of a mortgage (under which legal title has remained with the borrower), the lender executes a ***satisfaction*** (also referred to as a *release* or *discharge*), which the borrower may record to remove the lien.

Mortgages/Deeds of Trust and Note As Separate Documents:

Deeds of trust are three-party instruments, involving the trustor (the borrower), the beneficiary (the lender), and a neutral third party (the trustee). Under a deed of trust, the borrower retains equitable title to the property, but legal title is held by the trustee, who has a power of sale. See Figure 5 below.

A mortgage, on the other hand, typically is a two-party instrument, by which the legal title remains with the borrower. Because legal title remains with the borrower, a foreclosure by the lender requires the lender to wrest legal title from the borrower, which involves a cumbersome, time-consuming court action — a court action that is not necessary to pursue when foreclosing on a deed of trust. *The most significant benefit of a deed of trust over a mortgage to either a third-party lender or to a seller who lends part of the purchase price is that foreclosure is usually a simpler, faster, and less expensive process.*

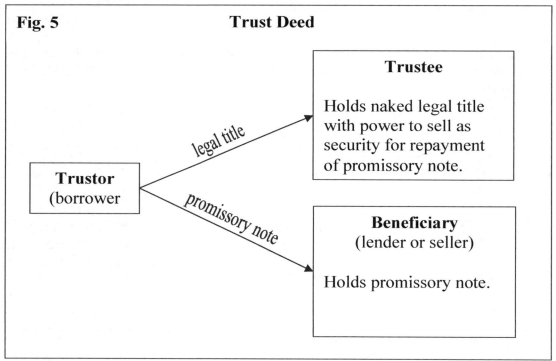

Fig. 5   **Trust Deed**

Trustor (borrower

— legal title → **Trustee**
Holds naked legal title with power to sell as security for repayment of promissory note.

— promissory note → **Beneficiary** (lender or seller)
Holds promissory note.

2. Legal Principles

Historically, two main theories concerning the legal effect of a mortgage have arisen: title theory and lien theory.

Title theory. Under title theory, a mortgage transfers legal title to the mortgagee (the lender) while the mortgagor (the borrower) retains equitable title to the property, which permits the mortgagor exclusive possession and use of the property. Upon default, the mortgagee is entitled to immediate possession and use (such as to collect rents) of the property.

Lien theory. Under lien theory, the mortgagor retains both legal and equitable title, including exclusive possession and use of the property. The mortgagee simply possesses a lien against the property (usually a lien of higher priority than certain other liens, such as judgment liens). Upon default, the mortgagee must go through a formal (judicial) foreclosure proceeding to obtain legal title and possession.

In reality, few states subscribe exclusively to either the lien theory or the title theory, but have developed some mixture of both. Such states are often referred to as *intermediate or modified lien theory states*. Some modified lien theory states make a distinction between a mortgage and a deed of trust, treating a mortgage as a two-party transaction — in which the mortgagor retains both equitable and legal title — and a deed of trust, which is viewed as a three-party transaction, legal title being held by a trustee; equitable title (and therefore exclusive possession and use) being held by the mortgagor; and a promissory note being held by the mortgagee. Upon default, the lender may initiate foreclosure by having the trustee foreclose on, and sell the property, without court action.

Primary Market.

The *primary mortgage market* consists of the market wherein mortgage loans are originated. Lenders that create these mortgages include institutional lenders such as commercial banks, savings and loan associations, and life insurance companies, as well as noninstitutional lenders, such as credit unions, pension funds, mortgage companies, private individuals, and real estate investment trusts (REITs).

Secondary Market.

The *secondary mortgage market* is the market wherein mortgages are sold by primary mortgage lenders to investors, such as pension funds and insurance companies.

3. Non-Performance

Foreclosure/Short Sale. Foreclosure is a legal process by which a lender, in an attempt to recover the balance of a loan from a borrower who has defaulted on the loan, forces the sale of the collateral that secured the loan. The two primary purposes of a security instrument, be it a mortgage or a deed of trust, are (1) to create the legal groundwork for the lender's right to foreclose and (2) to establish the lender's priority among creditors. Unless timely cured, defaults leading to foreclosure can result from a variety of breaches of loan agreements, such as failure to make installment payments, to maintain fire insurance, or to pay property taxes.

A *nonjudicial foreclosure* is a foreclosure that does not involve the judicial process. The right to pursue a nonjudicial foreclosure is contained in the power-of-sale clause of a mortgage or deed of trust, which, upon borrower default and the beneficiary's request, empowers the trustee to sell the secured property at a public auction.

A *judicial foreclosure* is a foreclosure carried out not by way of a power-of-sale clause in a security instrument, but under the supervision of a court. At the end of the judicial foreclosure process, a public sale is advertised, and the property is sold to the highest bidder, usually at a public auction. A holder of a mortgage or deed of trust with a power-of-sale clause may, if so desired, use judicial foreclosure; however, many states have a *one-action rule*, under which a choice of either judicial or non-judicial foreclosure must be made.

A few states permit **strict foreclosure**, through which the lender may foreclose upon default of a debtor without going through the process of a public sale. In a strict foreclosure, the lender merely gives the debtor proper notice and prepares the proper papers; a court sets a period of time for the debtor to redeem the property by paying all past-due payments; and if the debtor fails to so redeem the property, title passes to the lender and the debtor loses all rights and interests (including equity) in the property.

Alternatives to Foreclosure. If a borrower cannot make payments on his or her loan, or, if because of a steep decline in property values the borrower simply wants to stop making payments on a property in which the borrower has negative equity, the borrower has several possible alternatives to foreclosure, including:

Loan modification is a restructuring or modification of a mortgage or deed of trust on terms more favorable to the borrower's ability (or desire) to continue making loan payments.

A **short sale** is a pre-foreclosure sale made by the borrower (usually with the help of a real estate agent) with lender approval of real estate for less than the balance due on the mortgage loan.

Surrendering a **deed in lieu of foreclosure** is a method of avoiding foreclosure by conveying to a lender title to a property in lieu of the lender's foreclosing on the property. This is a quick way out from under a mortgage and is likely to be less damaging to the borrower's credit than a foreclosure. The lender need not accept a deed in lieu of foreclosure, but it is less expensive than a foreclosure proceeding and it permits the lender to take over the property immediately rather than letting the borrower live rent free for months on end during a foreclosure proceeding.

Real Estate Owned (REO).

One of the negative effects of the upsurge in foreclosures in recent years has been a downward spiral of home values in neighborhoods, caused in part by the unkempt, deteriorating condition of many foreclosed properties, which leads to decreased desirability and value of neighboring properties and to increased crime. To help break this vicious cycle, many states and local governments have passed laws or ordinances that impose civil fines and penalties for failure to maintain foreclosed properties.

Of course, the sale of most foreclosed properties results in no bids other than the secured creditor's bid, because if there had been enough equity in the property to fully satisfy the loan, the owner likely would have sold the property and prevented foreclosure. Such bank-owned properties acquired through foreclosure are called **real estate owned (REO)** properties. The laws discussed above prohibiting blight on foreclosed properties were designed in part to force lenders to maintain their REOs.

Section E: Government Oversight

Financing for home loans is a process that has greatly increased in complexity in recent years due to extensive federal and state legislation that attempts to address lending practices that are considered to be unfair, deceptive, or fraudulent.

1. RESPA

Enacted in 1974, the **Real Estate Settlement Procedures Act (RESPA)** is a federal law designed to prevent lenders, real estate agents, developers, title insurance companies, and other persons (such as appraisers and inspectors) who service the real estate settlement process from providing kickbacks or referral fees to each other, and from facilitating bait-and-switch tactics. RESPA applies to all purchases of owner-occupied residences of 4 or fewer dwelling units that use funds from institutional lenders regulated by the federal government.

RESPA requires lenders to provide an applicant within *3 business days* of receiving a loan application the following information:

1. a **good-faith estimate (GFE)** of all costs related to a loan;

2. an information booklet entitled *Shopping for Your Home Loan: HUD's Settlement Cost Booklet*, which summarizes RESPA, closing costs, and the settlement statement; and

3. a mortgage servicing statement that discloses whether the lender will service the loan or transfer the servicing of the loan to another entity.

Violation of RESPA's prohibitions on kickbacks and referral fees can result in criminal penalties up to $10,000 and a 1-year prison sentence.

2. Regulation Z

One of the most important aspects of Regulation Z (which implements the **Truth-in-Lending Act (TILA)**, see below) is that the **annual percentage rate (APR)**, the terms of the loan, and the total costs to the borrower must be disclosed before the loan is consummated. The APR expresses the effective annual rate of the cost of borrowing, which includes all finance charges, such as interest, prepaid finance charges, prepaid interest, and service fees. A disclosure of the APR is helpful in providing consumer information and protection because simply looking at interest rate quotes for a loan can be deceptive, as other costs incurred in closing a loan can vary significantly from lender to lender. The APR, by contrast, gives the prospective borrower a way to compare "apples to apples."

Regulation Z also provides for a 3-day right of rescission for certain types of refinancing loans and junior deeds of trust, but not for seller carry back loans or first trust deeds. Additionally, prepayment penalties, if any, and late charges must be disclosed.

Another important mandate of Regulation Z is that any advertising that contains a **triggering term** must disclose a number of other credit terms, including the APR. A Regulation Z triggering term is any specific term that states one or more of the following:

- the amount or percentage of any down payment;
- the number of payments or period of repayment;
- the amount of any payment;
- the amount of any finance charge.

An advertisement that contains a trigger term must also state the following terms:

- the amount or percentage of any down payment;

- the terms of repayment, which reflect the repayment obligations over the full term of the loan, including any balloon payment;
- the annual percentage rate, using that term, and, if the rate may be increased after consummation, that fact.

Stating only the APR in an advertisement does not trigger the requirement for additional financial term disclosures.

TILA's advertising rules apply to any advertisement that promotes consumer credit for either real or personal property, and to consumer leases. All advertisers, including real estate brokers and developers, as well as lenders and lessors, must comply with TILA's advertising rules.

TILA has been amended numerous times since its inception in 1968 when the power to issue implementing regulations was given to the Federal Reserve Board. In July 2011, TILA's regulatory making authority was transferred to the Consumer Financial Protection Bureau.

3. Truth-in-Lending Act

The *Truth-in-Lending Act (TILA)* is a federal consumer protection law that was enacted in 1968 with the intention of helping borrowers understand the costs of borrowing money by requiring certain disclosures about loan terms and costs and to standardize the way in which certain costs related to the loan are calculated and disclosed. The set of regulations that implemented TILA is known as *Regulation Z*.

4. Antitrust

Antitrust laws, which are intended to safeguard competitive free enterprise, impose restrictions on real estate agents' conduct toward competitors, clients, and customers. Having a firm grasp of the basics of how antitrust laws impact a real estate agent's behavior is very important because:

- it is easy to unintentionally violate antitrust laws; and
- the penalties, both criminal and civil, can be very severe.

The basic federal antitrust law is the *Sherman Act* passed in 1890, which prohibits agreements, verbal or written, that have the effect of restraining free trade, including conspiracies. An antitrust *conspiracy* occurs when

1. two or more persons agree to act (referred to as "group action"); and
2. the agreed-upon action has the effect of restraining trade.

It is important to note that *such an agreement need not be express* — the mere appearance of an *implied* agreement between or among competitors is likely to be deemed a conspiracy to fix prices, to boycott a competitor, or to allocate market shares, if, subsequent to communication between or among the parties, the parties act as if such an agreement had been reached.

Every state has its own antitrust laws, which usually closely parallel federal law.

Antitrust Violations in Real Estate.

The prohibited activities that a real estate agent must be aware of can be grouped into four main categories:

- Price Fixing;
- Group Boycotts;
- Tying Arrangements; and
- Market Allocation.

Price Fixing. Price fixing is an agreement between competitors to set prices or price ranges. It is immaterial whether the price fixed is a maximum price, a minimum price, a fair price, or a reasonable price — *all* agreements to fix prices between competitors are criminal acts according to federal law. Note that because of this federal anti-price-fixing law, it would be illegal for any state agency or any trade organization to set commission rates for real estate transactions — in other words, commission rates must remain freely negotiable between the client and the client's agent.

MLS organizations and other professional real estate organizations may *not* set fees or commission splits; nor may they refuse membership to a broker because of the fees (such as discount fees or flat fees) that the broker charges.

To avoid price fixing, real estate agents should avoid discussing prices (commission rates or referral fees) or pricing strategy with a competitor. Exceptions to this rule include that a broker may offer a competing broker a referral fee and discuss the amount of that fee, and may discuss with a cooperating broker how to split a commission or referral fee when negotiating regarding a particular transaction. Competing brokers may also receive compensation from the buyer, the seller, or from both.

Group Boycotts. A group boycott occurs when two or more brokers agree not to deal with another broker or brokers. It is important when thinking about group boycotts to understand the distinction between individual action and group action. A broker may choose not to do business with another broker if he or she so wishes (e.g., if the broker feels that the other broker is dishonest), but the broker may not encourage other brokers to do likewise.

Tying Arrangements. A tying arrangement (also referred to as a tied-in arrangement) occurs when a seller conditions the sale of one product on the purchase of another (the tied) product. Not all tying arrangements are illegal, but the analysis of what is permissible and what is impermissible tying involves a complex analysis of whether the seller has such an advantage as to coerce the buyer to purchase the tied product. In real estate agency, a typical case of an *impermissible* tying arrangement occurs when the sale of a property is conditioned upon the agent's obtaining the listing for future sales.

Market Allocation. Market allocation occurs when competitors agree to divide up geographic areas or types of products or services they offer to customers. Market allocations are actually a form of price fixing, in that they reduce competition and therefore tend to raise prices. However, it should be noted that *because a real estate office is usually considered to be an individual entity for antitrust purposes*, a real estate office may assign salespersons to work specific areas — a practice called "farming."

Penalties. The Sherman Act provides for both civil and criminal penalties, both of which can be severe. Criminal penalties can be up to $100 million for a corporation and up to $1 million for an individual, along with up to 10 years in prison.

5. Mortgage Fraud

Mortgage Fraud. Mortgage fraud consists of deceit or dishonest practices related to mortgages that are intended to take advantage of borrowers, lenders, or investors in the secondary market. Mortgage fraud against lenders typically involves a conspiracy between a loan originator or seller and an appraiser who gives an inflated valuation of a property. Mortgage fraud against investors in the secondary market typically involves selling loans for which proper due diligence in loan processing is lacking, resulting in a loan that carries much more risk than is apparent.

Predatory Lending Practices (Risks to Clients). *Predatory lending* is the imposition of unfair, deceptive, abusive, or fraudulent loan terms on borrowers, such as:

- refinancing that results in loss of loan terms beneficial to the borrower;
- frequently refinancing loans, resulting in little more than the generation of loan fees — a practice called *loan flipping*;
- steering borrowers to lenders with higher rates than the borrower could obtain elsewhere;
- inadequately disclosing loan costs and risks;
- making loans to borrowers who most likely will not be able to avoid defaulting; and
- employing bait-and-switch tactics that involve offering a loan with one set of terms but then pressuring the borrower to accept less beneficial terms at the time of closing.

Usury Lending Laws. *Interest* is the compensation fixed by the parties for the use of money. *Usury* is the charging of interest in excess of that allowed by law. Most states have statutes that prohibit lenders from charging excessive interest rates. However, the *Depository Institutions Deregulation and Monetary Control Act (DIDMC)* exempts from state usury laws interest paid on residential mortgage loans.

Appropriate Cautions to Clients Seeking Financing. Licensees should caution clients who are seeking financing to be wary of the following red flags:

- you are asked to pay a real estate agent the purchase price directly;
- you are asked to pay something "on the side" or "outside of escrow" to obtain a special deal;
- you are working with an "attorney-backed" business or with a "law office" that refuses to provide an attorney's name and state license number;
- you are not provided with the required state and federal disclosures early in the transaction process;
- you are asked to transfer title to someone other than to the purchaser; or
- you are encouraged to make mortgage payments to anyone other than the mortgage servicer.

6. Equal Credit Opportunity Act

Enacted in 1974, the *Equal Credit Opportunity Act (ECOA)* is a federal law that prohibits a lender from discriminating against any applicant for credit on the basis of race, color, religion, national origin, sex, marital status, age (unless a minor), or on the grounds that some of the applicant's income derives from a public assistance program. The law applies to all persons who regularly participate in decisions involving the extending of credit, including retailers, credit card companies, banks and other mortgage lenders. As of July 2011, the **Consumer Financial Protection Bureau** became the authority for promulgating regulations to implement and enforce ECOA.

Some of the most important provisions of ECOA are that lenders may not:

- ask if the applicant is divorced or widowed; but may ask if the applicant is married, unmarried (meaning single, divorced, or widowed), or separated;

- ask about birth-control practices, child-bearing capacity or expectations, or whether a woman of child-bearing age will stop working to raise children;

- ask about the applicant's receipt of alimony or child support unless the applicant is first notified that such information need not be given; however, such questions may be asked if the applicant requests that income from such sources be used to qualify for a loan. Lenders may ask whether the applicant has any obligations to pay alimony or child support; or

- discount income based on sex or marital status.

Under ECOA, an applicant has the right to receive notification from the lender within 30 days as to what action the lender has taken on a loan application. If an adverse action was taken, the lender must send the applicant an ECOA notice about prohibitions against lending discrimination, the name of the federal agency that enforces compliance with ECOA, and the specific reasons for the denial of credit.

From its inception in 1974, ECOA has been particularly instrumental in helping women obtain credit on an equal footing with men. Failure to comply with the provisions of ECOA can result in punitive damages up to $10,000 for an individual action and up to the lesser of $500,000 or 1% of the creditor's net worth in class actions.

Section F: Lending Process

1. Pre-approval and Pre-qualification (e.g., debt ratios, credit scoring, and history)

The Loan Process. The loan process consists of (1) application, (2) loan processing, (3) underwriting analysis, and (4) loan approval, funding, and closing.

Application. There are two approaches to beginning the loan process: *loan prequalification* and *loan preapproval*. To obtain a prequalification letter, a prospective purchaser simply has to call a lender or mortgage broker, provide some information on income, assets, debts, and potential down payment. The lender or mortgage broker will probably get back to the prospect by fax or e-mail within a few minutes with a prequalification letter that gives an estimate of the amount of loan for which the prospect might be able to qualify. There is no cost, no verification, and no commitment involved. Today, all of this can even be done on various websites, with an instant response generated by a computer program. The only value of obtaining a prequalification letter is that (assuming the information provided was accurate) it gives the prospective purchaser an idea as to the price range of a house for which the purchaser might be able to obtain a loan. Obtaining a preapproval letter, on the other hand, involves verification of the information provided and may require an application fee.

Loan Processing. Once a prospective borrower has submitted a completed application with the supporting documentation required to make a credit decision, the lender must make numerous disclosures required by RESPA, ECOA, TILA, and other federal and state laws. The application form that has become standard for residential loans is often referred to as *Form 1003*.

Loan processing consists of assembling all of the information necessary for a lender to assess the risk of the proposed loan. There are two broad categories of information to be assembled to determine a borrower's ability and willingness to repay the debt: borrower information and property information. Investigation and analysis of borrower information and property information, in turn, exposes what is often spoken of as the *three Cs of credit*: capacity, character, and collateral.

Borrower Information. The loan processor gathers information and verifies that information to help the lender assess the borrower's *character* and *capacity*.

Character. In loan processing, character refers to a borrower's willingness/desire to make payments and fulfill other obligations under a mortgage loan.

Purpose of the Loan. The borrower's intended purpose for using the loan funds is important for assessing risk. There are five common categories of loan purpose:

1. to purchase an owner-occupied residence — considered to be the loan purpose with the lowest risk — or a second home;

2. to purchase investment property;

3. to obtain a loan with a better interest rate or more favorable terms;

4. to obtain an equity loan to finance home improvements or other financial need, such as tuition for college; or

5. for the purpose of "cashing out," where the new loan is large enough to pay off an old loan in full plus give the borrower extra cash. Cash-out refinances are considered to have a higher risk than other loans and usually carry a .25% to .50% increase in the interest rate.

Credit History. Lenders place considerable emphasis on the borrower's ability/willingness to fulfill financial obligations as evidenced by the borrower's track record of repaying past debt obligations in a timely manner. To help make this assessment, lenders rely on credit scores and reports by the large credit reporting agencies and on a *FICO (Fair Isaac Corporation) score*, which ranges from 300 to 850 (median ≈ 720), where a higher score indicates less risk. Probably the second most significant credit report qualifier is the borrower's history of making timely payments on an existing mortgage or, if renting, on lease payments. Delinquencies during the past couple of years are usually considered unacceptable.

Capacity to Repay. Capacity refers to the borrower's ability to repay the loan in accordance with loan terms. The main components of capacity are source of income, assets, and liabilities.

Source of Income. Data on the borrower's historical income, length of employment, future trends of such employment, investment income, and income from other sources are important for proper analysis of future ability to make mortgage payments. W-2 statements for wage earners, tax returns for self-employed persons, and eligibility to receive pension or Social Security income for retired persons are generally required.

Assets. The amount of assets owned by a borrower and the liquidity of those assets are important determinants as to whether the borrower has the ability to make the down payment as well as to overcome interruptions in income. Having equity in assets, such as other real estate, stocks, or insurance policies, also demonstrates the owner's overall financial substance.

Liabilities. Prior to approving a loan, a loan processor must obtain information on monthly housing expenses, which the underwriter will use to establish a ratio of monthly housing expenses to monthly gross income, and information on total monthly recurring debt obligations, which the underwriter will use to establish a ratio of total monthly expenses to monthly gross income. Monthly housing expenses include principal, interest, taxes, and insurance (referred to as *PITI*). Total monthly expenses include housing expenses plus additional long-term monthly debt service, such as for car payments, credit card payments, child support, and alimony. In this context, "long-term debt" typically refers to debt that is not scheduled to be retired within 9 months. Monthly housing expenses divided by the monthly gross income is referred to as the *PITI ratio* or *front-end ratio*). Total monthly expenses divided by monthly gross income is referred to as the *LTD ratio* or *back-end ratio*). See Chapter 10, Section 4, Part H, for an example how to calculate PITI.

Property Information. After a lender has granted a loan on a property, the lender has to rely for many years or decades on the value of the property — the *collateral* — as security for the loan. Therefore, the lender will want from the loan processor information sufficient to qualify the property as well as the borrower. To obtain this information the loan processor will order the following reports:

1. *Preliminary Title Report*: A preliminary title report

   a) identifies the property with an assessor's parcel number, street address, and legal description;

   b) identifies the current owner of the residence; and

   c) reveals title policy exceptions, such as property taxes, assessments, encumbrances, liens, and easements.

2. *Appraisal*: To determine the value of a property an appraiser will be engaged to inspect the property to ascertain such things as current market value, conditions of the land and of property improvements, the appeal and amenities of the neighborhood, and market conditions, such as sales of similar homes of neighboring properties.

3. *Property Due Diligence*: The loan processor should also determine whether there is an occupant of the residence (such as a long-term guest) who is asserting a claim, whether there are any assessments against the property not disclosed on the preliminary title report, and whether there has been any work done on the property within the last 90 days that might result in mechanics' liens against the property.

Borrower's Capacity. In analyzing the borrower's capacity for repaying the loan, the underwriter calculates the front-end and back-end ratios and compares them to the underwriting guidelines established for the type of loan the borrower is applying for. For **conventional loans** (loans that are not FHA insured or VA guaranteed) the current Federal National Mortgage Association ("Fannie Mae") guideline is that the back-end ratio (referred to by Fannie Mae as "maximum DTI" (debt-to-income ratio)) should be no greater than 36%, with allowable ratios up to 45% if specific criteria of Fannie Mae's Eligibility Matrix are met.

Security of the Property. In analyzing the amount of security the lender should have in the property used to secure the loan, the underwriter will consider the property appraisal and other property information, as described above, the type of property, the loan-to-value ratio, and private mortgage insurance (PMI).

Type of Property. Owner-occupied homes are considered to have the least risk. Duplexes, townhouses, condominiums, and investment properties have higher rates of default.

2. Parties to the Lending Process (e.g., loan originator, underwriter, mortgage broker)

A residential loan typically begins with the potential borrower contacting an MLO, who may be a real estate broker who has an MLO endorsement. Effective January 1, 2011, all real estate licensed salespersons, brokers, and companies must obtain an MLO license endorsement before soliciting, offering, or participating in negotiations for residential loans. The SAFE Act, which established the **Nationwide Mortgage Licensing System and Registry (NMLS)**, requires state-licensed MLOs to complete 20 hours of pre-license education, pass both a National and a state MLO examination, and submit fingerprints and an authorization to obtain a credit report. Yearly renewal of the MLO license endorsement is required. To obtain the annual renewal, the MLO must complete 8 hours of continuing education. MLOs employed by an insured depository institution (such as a bank or savings and loan) must register with the NMLS but do not need to be licensed under state law.

Many different kinds of lenders operate in the primary mortgage market. While institutional lenders such as state banks, national banks, and savings and loans create many residential loans, life insurance companies operating in the primary mortgage market create mortgages mainly for large commercial and industrial properties.

Many noninstitutional lender mortgages are created by mortgage companies, which can be either **mortgage bankers** (who lend their own money, either selling the loan to another lender or keeping the loan as an investment) or **mortgage brokers**, who find borrowers and match them with lenders for a fee.

Underwriting Analysis. When the loan processor has completed assembling and verifying the borrower and the property information, all of this data is sent to a loan underwriter who analyzes the risk of, and recommends whether to approve, the proposed loan. Today, the process of underwriting a mortgage loan is increasingly being performed by computerized underwriting systems such as Desktop Underwriter® rather than by the traditional manual system. Such automated underwriting increases objectivity and reduces underwriting time from weeks to minutes.

CHAPTER 4: REAL PROPERTY

Section A: Methods of Legal Description of Land

A land description (also known as a "legal description") is a description that properly delineates and identifies a piece of property and which describes no other piece of property. A requirement of a transfer of real property is that the instrument of conveyance (the deed) includes a legal description of the property.

There are three main systems of describing real property:

1. Metes and Bounds

Metes and Bounds System. The oldest method of surveying in the United States is the metes and bounds system, which describes a parcel of land by using physical features of the locale, along with directions and distances, to define the boundaries of the parcel. The original 13 states were surveyed using this method.

Metes is a term referring to the measurement of length, in units such as feet, meters, and miles. *Bounds* refer to boundaries such as rivers and roads. Starting with a *point of beginning*, such as an iron stake, an old oak tree, or the intersection of two walls, the boundaries of a parcel are described, working in sequence around the parcel, and finally ending at the beginning point.

The metes and bounds method of describing land may be used when the property is not covered by a recorded map or has irregular contours, such as in mountainous areas. A difficulty with this method of describing land is that old oak trees can be cut down, walls can be removed, and even rivers can change course.

2. Rectangular Survey

Rectangular survey system (also referred to as the *U.S. government survey system*). This method is based on first establishing principal east-west *base line(s)* and north-south *meridian(s)*. Extending these principal base line(s) and meridian(s), a grid of horizontal lines, referred to as *tier lines*, running parallel to the principal base line(s) and vertical lines, referred to as *range lines*, is established. The tier lines are 6 miles apart, as are the range lines.

A *section* is an area one square mile, containing 640 acres. Creating sections of 640 acres makes for ease of dividing into halves, quarters, and so on through seven divisions, down to 5 acres. A township is a six mile square parcel of land consisting of 36 sections. The sections in each township are uniformly numbered from 1 to 36, with Section 1 located in the northeast corner and the Section 36 located in the southeast corner. See, Figure 6 below.

Example: The description "township 3 north, range 2 east, Stonyfield Base Line and Meridian" (typically abbreviated as "T3N, R2E, SBL&M") is a description of the township that is 3 townships north from the Stonyfield Base Line and 2 townships east from the Stonyfield Meridian.

Fig. 6	A theoretical township showing numbered sections (large bold type) and adjacent township sections (smaller regular type).						
36	31	32	33	34	35	36	31
1	**6**	**5**	**4**	**3**	**2**	**1**	6
12	**7**	**8**	**9**	**10**	**11**	**12**	7
13	**18**	**17**	**16**	**15**	**14**	**13**	18
24	**19**	**20**	**21**	**22**	**23**	**24**	19
25	**30**	**29**	**28**	**27**	**26**	**25**	30
36	**31**	**32**	**33**	**34**	**35**	**36**	31
1	6	5	4	3	2	1	6

When working with land measurements, it is often helpful to remember the following:

- 1 acre = 43,560 square feet
- 1 square acre ≈ 208.7 ft. × 208.7 ft.
- 1 mile = 5,280 feet or 320 rods
- 1 rod = 16½ ft.
- 1 township = 6 mi. × 6 mi. = 36 sections
- 1 section = 1 mi. × 1 mi. = 640 acres

Because a section contains 640 acres, a quarter section contains 160 acres. Parts of a section are often described using direction abbreviations and fractions. For example, the 40-acre southeast quarter of the southwest quarter of Section 15 would be described as "the SE¼ of the SW¼ of Section 15."

3. Lot and Block

The *lot, block, and tract system* (also called the "*recorded map or recorded plat system*") is the most recently developed method of land description and is the simplest of the three land description methods to understand. A *subdivision* is what results when a large parcel of land is divided into smaller parcels. The subdivision map describes the subdivision by reference to a particular lot and block in a particular city and county.

Example: "All of Lot 6 of Block A of Tract number 355 in the city of Take Your Pick, County of Some, State of Any, as per map recorded in Book 23, page 67, of maps in the office of the county recorder of said county."

Certain properties, such as individual condominium units, require additional legal descriptions; namely, vertical or airspace descriptions. Such descriptions usually refer to a unit number, such as a Condo Declaration Recording Number, in a building that has been given a subdivision description.

Usage of Legal Property Descriptions:

In order for a claim of ownership of property to be enforceable in a court of law (and therefore valuable to a seller or purchaser), the property claimed must have a verifiable, legally sufficient description. Hence, the ***primary use of legal property descriptions is to delineate and unambiguously identify the property***.

Physical Descriptions of Property and Improvements:

The descriptions of property described above serve only to identify the situs of a property for legal and jurisdictional purposes. Other forms of description serve to identify the physical characteristics of real property for such purposes as valuation and a determination of the best use of the property. Such descriptions of land include size and shape, corner influence, topography, accessibility, and natural hazards. Additionally, descriptions of limitations of use are important, and include zoning restrictions, set-back restrictions, and the existence of easements or other encumbrances. Probably the most important physical aspect of a property that affects its value is its location, some areas being in greater demand than others due to such factors as low crime rates and the proximity of good schools, roads, and recreational facilities

Descriptions of improvements are also important, and include such items as architectural style, building components, construction materials, the availability of utilities such as water and sewers, and the condition of roofs, exterior and interior walls, and heating and air-conditioning systems.

Physical Characteristics of Land:

It is generally understood that land has ***three fundamental physical characteristics***:

- ***Immobility***. Though a certain amount of the constituents of land — such as soil, rocks, and minerals — can be moved, land has a fixed geographical location.
- ***Indestructibility***. Land can be altered by natural processes, such as by erosion, landslides, and earthquakes, and by human activities, such as by mining, road building, and landfill, and its value can go up and down, but as a geographical location land cannot be destroyed.
- ***Uniqueness*** (also referred to as ***heterogeneity*** or ***non-homogeneity***). Because each parcel of land has a unique location, no two parcels of land are the same — each has different neighbors, different views, different access, different natural vegetation, and so on.

Economic Characteristics of Land:

Four economic characteristics of land affect its value:

- *Area preference (situs)* — refers to the degree to which people desire a particular location to live, work, or invest in.
- *Scarcity* — refers to the relationship of the supply of land to its demand in a particular location.
- *Improvements* — refer to the ability of improvements to modify the value not only of the land modified but also the value of neighboring properties.
- *Permanence of investment (fixity)* — refers to the fact that land and improvements to land are usually long-term investments, requiring large amounts of capital and long periods of time to recoup the investments.

Section B: Methods of Measurement

1. Structures (space and volume)

The space or floor area of a building is expressed in square feet, square yards, or square meters. There are three primary floor area designations:

- *gross floor area* is the area of the building found by measuring the faces of the exterior walls;
- *gross internal area* is the area found by measuring the interior faces of the exterior walls;
- *net internal area* (also referred to as *usable floor area*) is generally referred to as the gross internal area minus the floor areas taken up by such spaces as lobbies, stairs, escalators, and elevators.

The volume of a building is the volume between the faces of the exterior walls from the level of the lowest storey to the roof of the building.

2. Livable Area

The *livable area* of standalone residential structures is calculated using the *outside* dimensions of the structure, including laundry rooms and storage areas if they are located on the same level(s) as the main living areas. Items excluded from livable area typically include garages, carports, decks, and patios.

The livable areas of condominiums and townhouses, however, are calculated by measuring the interior of each room and adding 5 inches to each measurement to accommodate the interior and exterior walls.

3. Land Measurement

Here some land measurement correspondences that you should know for the AMP exam:

- 1 mile = 5,280 feet or 320 rods
- 1 rod = 16½ ft.
- 1 township = 6 mi.× 6 mi. = 36 sections
- 1 section = 1 mi. × 1 mi. = 640 acres

- 1 acre = 43,560 square feet

Section C: Property Valuation

1. Basic Concepts and Terminology

One of the most important characteristics of property, real or personal, is its value. Value has many forms: monetary, sentimental, cultural, educational, etc. In this chapter, we will consider the monetary value of real property and the appraisal process as one method of determining that value.

Because the value of property lies at the heart of the real estate business, real estate agents should have a good grasp of the theoretical concepts of value and of the appraisal process. As a real estate agent, you will constantly be asked by clients what you think is the market value or rental value of their property.

Market Value and Market Price:

Market value is defined for appraisal purposes by HUD/FHA as: *"The most probable price which a property should bring in a competitive and open market under all conditions requisite to a fair sale, the buyer and seller each acting prudently, knowledgeably and assuming the price is not affected by undue stimulus."*

Market value is a distinct concept from market price. *Market price* is the price actually paid for a particular property, which might not have been the "most probable price" that the property "should bring" in a competitive and open market with buyers and sellers acting "knowledgeably" and "prudently."

Value:

Value is the present worth to typical users or investors of all rights to future benefits arising out of property ownership.

(i) Types and Characteristics of Value. Value is not something intrinsic to property; rather, it is a creation in the minds of people based on certain external circumstances, generally accepted as being the *four characteristics (or elements) of value*:

- *Utility* (also referred to as *functional utility*) refers to the usefulness of property — its ability to satisfy a potential buyer's need or desire, such as to provide shelter or income.

- *Scarcity* refers to a lack of abundance and is a key component of the theory that supply and demand drive market prices.

- *Demand* refers to the level of desire for a product. *Effective demand* refers to demand coupled with purchasing power sufficient to acquire the property from a willing seller in a free market.

- *Transferability* refers to the ability to transfer (such as by sale, gift, or lease) some interest in property to another.

If the property is to have monetary value, it must possess all four of the elements of value to some degree. **Example:** An item might be scarce, but with no demand, in which case the scarce item would be essentially worthless (except perhaps in a nonmonetary sense). Or, if an item is not transferable, it will command no market price even if there is high demand for the item.

Although market value is the type of value most often considered in the real estate context, there are other types of value:

Assessed value is the value a taxing authority places on the property, which may differ significantly from the property's market value.

Loan value (also referred to as *mortgage value*) is the value at which a lender is willing to make a loan on the property.

Appraised value is of the value placed on a property by an appraiser, and is usually intended to estimate the market value of the property.

Investment value is the value attributed to the use of a property for a certain period of time.

Insurance value is the value at which an insurance company is willing to ensure the property to build it from the ground up in case of destruction.

Replacement value is the value measured by the cost of building the property with current materials and labor.

Estate tax value is the value placed on a decedent's property for purposes of determining estate tax.

Salvage value (also referred to as *residual value* or *scrap value*) is the value of a property at the end of the property's useful life.

Book value is the value at which a property is carried on the owner's balance sheet, consisting of cost minus book depreciation.

Condemnation value is the value that is paid for property acquired by eminent domain.

Subjective value (also referred to as *value in use*) is value placed on the amenities of a property by a specific person. **Example:** If an owner builds a house for his or her specific needs and desires without due concern for resale value (such as a large house with only one bedroom), such a house would likely have more subjective value to the original owner than for most other potential future owners.

2. Influences and Characteristics Affecting Value

Principles of Value. As we shall see later in this chapter, there are several methods of appraisal (sales comparison approach, cost approach, and income approach); however, regardless of the appraisal method being used, the appraiser takes into account numerous principles of valuation that have been developed by appraisers over the years:

- *Principle of supply and demand* — states that the value of property in a competitive market is influenced by the relative levels of supply and demand: the greater level of demand in relation to the level of supply, the greater the value.

- *Principle of the highest and best use* — states that the best use of a property in terms of value is the use most likely to produce the greatest net return (in terms of money or other valued items, such as amenities) over a given period of time.

- *Principle of conformity* — states that the maximum value of land is achieved when there is a reasonable degree of social, economic, and architectural conformity in the area. For a particular property, however, nonconformity may benefit or reduce the property's value.

> **Example:** If a smaller, lower-quality home is in a neighborhood of larger, higher-quality homes, the value of the lesser home will be raised simply due to its proximity to more valuable properties. This rise in value is referred to as the *principle of progression*. Conversely, the value of a large, high-quality home will be lessened by proximity to smaller, lower-quality homes by the *principle of regression.*

- *Principle of plottage* — states that assembling two or more parcels of land into one parcel may result in the larger parcel having a greater value than the sum of the values of the smaller parcels. The process of gathering together two or more parcels to make the whole more valuable than the sum of its parts is called *assemblage*. The resulting added value is called *plottage value*.

- *Principle of change* — states that property values are in a constant state of flux due to economic, environmental, political, social, and physical forces in the area. Closely associated with the principle of change are the concepts of the *economic life* and *physical life* of a property. A property's economic life (also referred to as *useful life*) is the period of time that the property is useful or profitable to the average owner or investor. The physical life of the property is the period of time that the property lasts with normal maintenance. The economic life of a property almost always ends before its physical life ends.

- *Principle of four-stage life cycle* — states that property goes through a process of development, stability, and eventual wearing out. Property is often seen as being in one of four phases of change:
  - *growth* (also referred to as *integration)* is the development stage of the property;
  - *stability* (also referred to as *equilibrium)* is the period of stability when the property changes very little;
  - *decline* (also referred to as *disintegration)* is the phase when the property's usefulness is in decline and constant upkeep is necessary;
  - *revitalization* (also referred to as *rejuvenation)* is the phase when the property is rebuilt, remodeled, or otherwise revitalized to a new highest and best use.

- *Principle of substitution* — states that the value of a property will tend toward the cost of a comparable, or of an equally desirable, substitute property.

- *Principle of contribution* (also referred to as the *principle of diminishing marginal returns*) states that improvements made to a property will contribute to its value or that, conversely, the lack of a needed improvement will detract from the value of the property. Of course, to maximize net return, the cost of the improvement should be less than the improvement's increase in value to the property as a whole.

- *Principle of anticipation* — states that value is derived from a calculation of anticipated future benefits to be derived from the property, not from past benefits, though past benefits may inform as to what might be expected in the future.

- *Principle of competition* — states that increased competition results in increased supply in relation to demand, and thereby to lower profit margins. Furthermore, where substantial profits are being made, competition likely will follow, reducing the margin of profits and thereby reducing the value of (especially income) properties.

- *Principle of balance* — states that the maximum value of property, its highest and best use, is created and maintained when land use by interacting elements of production is in equilibrium or balance.

  <u>Example:</u> If a property is over-improved, too much has been invested in relation to the value of the property, and the property's return on investment will be lower than — out of equilibrium with — the return on investment of other properties in the area.

Market cycles. Like other types of free markets, the real estate market tends to go through recurrent cycles. These cycles typically go through four main stages:

1. *Recovery.* Recovery typically begins when the market "bottoms out," that is, when the market stops declining. Signals that the real estate market may be set for recovery include decreasing vacancy rates due to little supply coming onto the market, and the unemployment rate plateauing and beginning to fall.

2. *Expansion.* Expansion is the exciting part of the market cycle when property values increase. Such expansion is highly correlated with growth in new construction, falling unemployment rates, and a continuing fall in vacancy rates.

3. *Oversupply.* Oversupply is a time during a market cycle when the supply of new construction begins to overtake demand. Typical signs of this period in a market cycle include slowing construction, rising vacancy rates, and a leveling off of job growth.

4. *Recession.* The last stage of a market cycle is typified by high vacancy rates, high unemployment, stalled construction of new housing, and a rise in the rate of foreclosures.

Other factors affecting property value. Once established, the value of real estate can be increased, decreased, or even destroyed by the interplay of four main types of external forces:

1. *environmental and physical characteristics*, such as climate, earthquakes, typography, the availability of shopping centers and other amenities, and the quality of nearby schools and transportation systems;

2. *social forces, ideals, and standards*, such as population growth, divorce rates, and attitudes toward education, recreation or ideal family size;

3. *economic influences*, such as unemployment rates, interest rates, availability of credit, and rental costs; and

4. *political forces and governmental regulations*, such as zoning laws, which affect use and demand for property, rent controls, environmental legislation controlling development, governmental fiscal policy, government guaranteed loans, and government housing.

These four forces constantly interweave to affect, positively or negatively, the value of property. Together, they largely determine the advantages or disadvantages of a particular location — "location, location, location," which are popularly thought of as being the three most important determinants of real property value.

3. Comparative Market Analysis (performed by a real estate licensee)

Selecting and Adjusting Comparables:

The uniqueness of real property implies that the value of a property cannot be determined simply by looking at the value of exact equivalents, as one can in determining the value of an ounce of gold or the value of a Swiss franc. However, the value of nearby properties that have recently been sold and that are reasonably similar to a subject property can be highly probative as to the value of the subject property.

The primary factors for which adjustments in comparable properties must be made include:

- *Physical features*, such as fireplaces, swimming pools, decks, patios, built-in appliances, detached guesthouses, landscaping, walls, gates, and other special amenities.
- *Quality of construction.*
- *Lot size.*
- *Age.*
- *Location:* Similar properties quite near to each other may require adjustment because location preferences can change dramatically within just a block or two. For example, a house with a great ocean view might be right next door to a house with a peekaboo ocean view.
- *Property rights:* Land consists of a bundle of rights, and adjustments must be made if the subject property or a comparable property is not fee simple, has a lease, easement, deed restriction, or encroachment.
- *Change of market conditions.* Sometimes market conditions can change quickly, so that even sales completed within the past six months or year may need to be adjusted due to change in market conditions.
- *Number of bedrooms and baths.*
- *Financing.* The sales price of a property can be significantly affected by financing terms, and proper adjustments for differences in financing between a subject property and comparables must be made.
- *Aesthetic appeal.* Commonly referred to as "curb appeal," aesthetic factors may need to be considered if the subject property or a comparable has a unique architectural design.

Contrast CMA and Appraisal:

Although a *comparative market analysis* (also referred to as a *competitive market analysis*) (CMA) is similar to the market comparison approach to appraisal, a CMA differs from an appraisal in important ways:

- *Who prepares:* A CMA is prepared by a real estate broker; an appraisal is prepared by a licensed, professional appraiser.
- *How used.* A CMA is used primarily to help licensees and their clients determine list prices, and to help licensees decide whether to accept listings (e.g., from clients who have an unrealistically high opinion of the value of their property). An appraisal is

typically used to obtain financing, but may also be used for legal purposes, such as to determine a valuation for taxation, eminent domain, and insurance.

- *Data used to prepare:* A CMA typically will include data on three types of properties: (1) similar properties that have recently sold, (2) similar properties currently on the market, and (3) similar properties that have been on the market but whose listings have expired. A CMA often will also include selling costs, such as brokerage fee, points, prepayment penalty, inspections, and repairs that should be made before listing. An appraisal will only consider data on properties that have actually been sold. Additionally, an appraisal often involves estimating value by the income approach and the cost approach, as well as by the market comparison approach, then reconciling the value estimate of the three approaches.

(i) Price Per Square Foot.

Appraisers determine the square footage of a property by using the *outside* measurement of the property. The price per square foot of a specific property is determined by dividing the price (either selling or listing) by the property's square footage.

In addition to the ***price per square foot*** of a specific property, property analyses often refer to median or average price per square foot. The ***average price per square foot*** for a given set of properties is arrived at by adding the per-square-foot cost of each property in the set by the number of properties in the set. The ***median price per square foot*** of a set of properties is the price per square foot of the property whose price per square foot is such that half of the properties in the set have an equal or lower price per square foot and half have an equal or higher price per square foot.

It is important to be aware that for a given area, the price per square foot of smaller homes is generally higher than the price per square foot of larger homes.

(ii) Gross Rent and Gross Income Multipliers.

As we have seen, the income approach uses capitalization of *net* income to arrive at the valuation of a property. However, some investors, especially of single-family homes, use a simpler method of determining value: capitalization of *gross* income. If only gross rents are capitalized, this approach to value is called the ***gross rent multiplier (GRM)*** approach; if additional income is involved (such as from parking fees), the method is called the ***gross income multiplier (GIM)*** approach.

> **Example:** Using the gross rent multiplier approach, suppose the sales price of a house is $500,000 and the monthly gross rent is $2,000. In this case the sales price is $500,000 ÷ $2,000 = 250 times the monthly rental; i.e., the monthly gross rent multiplier is 250.

Suppose now that other comparable homes in the area have a monthly gross rent multiplier similar to the home in the prior example. Further, suppose that a comparable home in the area with a fair market value of $800,000 is to be rented. Using the gross rent multiplier approach, we can simply determine the monthly rent for this subject property by dividing the value ($800,000) by the monthly gross rent multiplier (250) to get a rent of $3,200 per month.

(iii) Capitalization Rate.

The *capitalization rate* (also referred to as the *cap rate*) is the rate that an appraiser estimates is the yield rate expected by investors from comparable properties in current market conditions. To estimate the capitalization rate of a certain property, an appraiser will collect data on the market value of comparable properties, on the vacancies and uncollectible rents of these comparable properties, and on the operating expenses of these comparable properties. Then, because value = net income ÷ capitalization rate, the capitalization rate can be calculated for these comparable properties as net income ÷ market value.

> **Example:** If the net annual income of a property is $20,000 and the capitalization rate is 8.5% per year, then the income approach valuation of the property would be $20,000 ÷ 8.5% = $235,294 (rounded).

The above example might also take the following form: if an investor purchased a property for $235,294 and derives an annual net income from the property of $20,000, what is the property's capitalization rate? Answer: $20,000 ÷ $235,294 = 8.5%.

A finance concept closely related to the capitalization rate is *return on investment (ROI)*, which is the investor's cash flow (net income minus financing charges) divided by the investor's *actual cash investment* (as distinct from the purchase price). *Note that the capitalization rate and the ROI would be the same if the investor had paid all cash for the property because in such a case there would be no finance charges and the initial investment would be equal to the sale price.*

4. Broker Price Opinion

A *broker price opinion (BPO)* is an estimate of the value of a property as determined by a real estate broker, usually for the purpose of setting a selling price of the property. BPOs are often used when lenders feel that they do not need an appraisal. Factors often considered by a broker in making a BPO include sales of comparable properties, neighborhood conditions, and the amount of repairs necessary to put the property up for sale. *Some states do not permit brokers to charge for giving price evaluations.*

5. Real Property (e.g., fixtures vs. personal property (e.g., chattel)

Property comes in two mutually exclusive kinds: real and personal. Each kind of property can, under certain circumstances, be transformed into the other kind. A wood board being carried by a carpenter toward a house that is being built is personal property. Moments later, once the carpenter permanently affixes it to the house as part of a wall or floor, the board becomes real property. If sometime later during remodeling the board is removed from the house, it again becomes personal property. As a general rule, the distinction boils down to this: *real property is fixed and immovable*; *personal property is movable*. Examples of personal property include furniture, cars, jewelry, annual crops (emblements), and stock in a corporation. Knowing the distinction between real property and personal property is important because the laws relating to the acquisition and transfer of real property differ considerably from the laws relating to the acquisition and transfer of personal property.

The *three broad categories of real property* are (1) *land*, (2) *appurtenances*, and (3) *things affixed to the land*.

(1) Land is the material of the earth, such as soil and rock.

(2) Appurtenances are objects, rights, or interests that are incidental to the land and go with or pertain to the land. A thing is deemed to be appurtenant to land when it is by right used with the land for its benefit. Appurtenances include:

- *Support rights*. Every piece of land is supported by land beneath and to the sides of it. A landowner has the right to have maintained both *lateral support* from adjacent properties and *subjacent support* from the ground below. Anyone who excavates land, as for the purpose of leveling the land to build upon or for the purpose of building underground parking, must take care not to reduce the lateral support of a neighbor's land to such a degree as to cause damage to the neighbor's property. A property owner must also be careful that his or her improvements or buildings do not cause or contribute damage through subsidence to a neighbor's land or buildings by reducing the subjacent ground support of that neighbor's land.

- *Easements*. An easement is a non-possessory right to use a portion of another property owner's land for a specific purpose. Easements were considered in greater detail in Chapter 2.

- Appurtenances also include *airspace above the land*, *water rights*, and *mineral rights*, all of which were discussed in Chapter 2.

(3) Things affixed to the land. The third broad category of real property is that which is affixed to the land, including (1) things attached to the land by roots, such as trees; (2) things embedded in the land, such as walls; (3) things permanently resting upon the land, such as buildings; and (4) fixtures, which are things permanently attached to what is otherwise permanent, as by means of cement, plaster, nails, or screws.

Natural attachments, such as natural trees and vines that are attached to the earth by roots, are considered to be part of the land. However, once such natural vegetation is severed from the land or harvested it becomes personal property. Trees, shrubs, vines, and other plantings by humans are also considered real property, but the crops growing on such plantings are treated as personal property.

Growing crops, such as grapes, avocados, and apples that are produced seasonally through a tenant farmer's labor and industry, are called *emblements*. Emblements are considered the personal property of the tenant farmer, and the *doctrine of emblements* holds that even if the tenancy expires before harvest, the tenant may harvest and remove the crops he or she had planted. Unless otherwise specified, upon transfer of the land, growing plants, natural or human-planted, would transfer with the land, but a tenant farmer would still be able to remove that season's crops.

Defining Fixtures: A *fixture* is a thing that starts out as personal property but then is attached to the land in such a manner as to be considered real property. For example, lumber, which is personal property, becomes a fixture when it is used to build a pergola. That same lumber can be changed back to personal property through an act of *severance* — detaching an item from real property that changes the item to personal property.

Sometimes — as with lumber being used to construct shelving — it is not altogether clear whether the item has become a fixture or remains personal property. Courts have established five tests of the degree of *attachment* (also referred to as the degree of *annexation*) of a fixture to determine whether an item of personal property is a fixture. It might be of help to remember these five tests by the mnemonic, "MARIA": method of attachment, adaptability, relationship of the parties, intent, and agreement between the parties.

- *Method of attachment*. The degree of permanence of the fixed item is significant. An item attached by cement or plaster, for example, is likely to be classified as a fixture. Thus, a bookcase built into a wall and securely nailed or bolted thereto is a fixture; but a freestanding bookcase remains personal property. Also, fixtures that have been temporarily removed for repair remain fixtures — as, for example, a built-in dishwasher that has been sent out for repairs.

- *Adaptability of the attached item*. If an item of personal property is attached to real property and is well adapted for use with that real property, the item is probably a fixture. Wall-to-wall carpeting, for example, is cut specifically for a room or rooms of a specific property, is well adapted for use on that property, and would, therefore, be a fixture. Even an item of personal property that is not physically attached to real property may be so well and specifically suited for use on the property as to be considered "constructively attached" and therefore a fixture of the real property — as, for example, a key to the front door.

- *Relationship of the parties*. Also of significance is the relationship between the person who installs an item of personal property on real property and the person with whom a dispute arises as to whether the installed item is a fixture. Such a situation would usually involve a tenant and landlord or a seller and buyer. All other considerations being equal, it is generally held that a tenant who installs an item, such as a chandelier, intends to remove the item at the expiration of the lease. However, an owner who installs the same chandelier likely did so with the intention of improving the property, thus making this chandelier a fixture. Following similar reasoning, buyers are usually favored over sellers and lenders are favored over borrowers when it comes to deciding whether an item is a fixture.

- *Intent of the person attaching the item*. The intention of the person incorporating an item into the land is considered to be the most significant test for determining whether the item is a fixture. Each of the other tests of a fixture is used as evidence of the incorporator's intention. For example, cementing a bench into the foundation of an outdoor patio would be evidence that the owner intended to make the bench a permanent fixture, whereas merely setting a bench out onto the patio would not.

- *Agreement between the parties*. Courts look to any agreement between the parties involved to determine the nature of items affixed to the land. Such agreements are typically manifested in real estate listings and in purchase or lease contracts.

It is important to keep in mind the difference between a fixture and a **trade fixture**. A trade fixture — often called a "chattel" fixture — is an object that a tenant attaches to real property for use in the tenant's trade or business. Trade fixtures differ from other fixtures in that, even though they are attached with some permanence to real property, they may be removed at the end of the tenancy of the business, and, therefore, *trade fixtures are personal property*. Examples include store shelves, display counters, and machining equipment, even if cemented into the property's foundation.

Section D: Methods of Valuation (Performed by an Appraiser)

1. Sales Comparison (Market Data) Approach

The *sales comparison approach* (also known as the *market data approach*) is the best method for appraising land, residences, and other properties for which there is a ready market of similar properties. It is based on what is referred to as the ***principle of substitution***, which holds that buyers are generally unwilling to pay more for a property than for a substitute property in the area. Using this method, the appraiser gathers data on recent sales (if sold at fair market value) of comparable properties in the area and makes comparisons of each of the features of the comparable properties to arrive at an estimate of the current market value of the subject property.

Once these data are collected, the appraiser adjusts the sales price of the comparable properties by *estimating what these properties would have sold for if they had had the same features as the subject property*. A ***comparable property*** is a property similar to the subject property that recently sold at arm's length, where neither the buyer nor the seller was acting under significant financial pressure. Note that it is the value of the similar features of the comparable properties that are adjusted, not the value of the features of the subject property. If a feature of a comparable property is *superior* to the same type of feature of the subject property, then an adjustment equal to the estimated difference in value of the feature of the comparable property to the feature of the subject property is *subtracted* from the comparable. If, on the other hand, the feature of the comparable property is *inferior* to the same type of feature of the subject property, then the estimated difference between the value of that feature of the subject property and the feature of the comparable is *added* to the comparable. See Figure 7 below.

Fig. 7	Example of Sales Comparison Approach			
Assume that the subject property is a 2,200 ft.², 10-year-old, single-family home in good condition, with a good view, 3 bedrooms, 3 baths, and a 2-car garage. Assume also that there has been no appreciation in home values since the dates of the sales of the three comparables.				
	Comparable 1	**Comparable 2**	**Comparable 3**	**Subject**
sales price	$850,000	$920,000	$880,000	?
condition	equal	equal	equal	good
view	inferior*	superior*	equal	good
adjustment	+ $5,000	- $2,000		
age	equal	equal	equal	10 years old
square footage	equal	superior*(2,250)	equal	2,200
adjustment		- $50,000		
bedrooms	equal	equal	equal	3
baths	inferior*(2 ½)	equal	superior*(3½)	3
adjustment	+ $5,000		- $5,000	
garage	equal	equal	equal	2
Net adjustment	+ $10,000	- $52,000	- $5,000	
Adjusted sale price	$860,000	$868,000	$875,000	
Indicated value				$870,000

*Inferior means that the comparable's feature is inferior to the same feature of the subject property. Superior means the opposite. A subtraction of value is estimated if the comparable feature is superior; an addition of value if inferior.

Reconciliation: Comparable 3 is the most similar to the subject property, so its adjusted value is given slightly more weight. Indicated value: $870,000.

2. Cost Approach

The *cost or summation approach* calculates the value of a subject property by:

1. **Estimating the value of the land as if vacant.** This step is usually performed using the sales comparison approach.

2. **Estimating the cost of replacing (or reproducing) the improvements.** This step involves first deciding whether to use replacement cost or reproduction cost. *Reproduction cost* is the cost of replacing the improvements with exact replicas at current prices. *Replacement cost* is the cost of replacing the improvements with those having equivalent utility, but constructed with modern materials, designs, and workmanship. If a building is quite old, it likely was built with materials that are now quite expensive and that were installed with detailed hand-labor. In such a case, reproduction cost would not, in general, represent the current market value of the building, so the appraiser would use replacement cost in the appraisal.

There are four primary methods used to estimate reproduction or replacement cost:

*   the most widely used method is the *square-foot method*, which involves collecting cost data on recently constructed similar buildings and dividing the total cost by the square footage to obtain cost per square foot;

*   the *quantity survey method* is the most detailed method, in which an estimate is made of the cost of all of the raw materials needed to replace the building. Such material-cost information is available in construction cost handbooks;

*   the *unit-in-place method* estimates the unit cost of components of the structure;

*   the *cubic-foot method* is much like the square-foot method except that it uses the volume of recently constructed similar buildings. This method often is used for warehouses and other industrial buildings.

3. **Subtracting the accrued depreciation of the improvements.** *Accrued depreciation* is depreciation that has happened prior to the date of valuation. By contrast, *remainder depreciation* is depreciation that will occur after the date of valuation. The two most used methods of calculating accrued depreciation are the straight-line method and the cost-to-cure method.

*   **Straight-line method of calculating depreciation.** The *straight-line method* (also referred to as the *age-life method*) calculates the amount of annual depreciation by dividing the cost of the improvement by the estimated *useful life* (*economic life*) of a typical such improvement. Once the cost and the useful life of an improvement have been determined, calculating the straight-line depreciation is easy, as illustrated in the following example.

    Example: If an improvement had a cost of $1,000,000 and a typical such improvement had a useful life of 50 years (with no residual value), the straight-line method would determine the annual depreciation to be $1,000,000 ÷ 50 = $20,000, which is a depreciation rate of 2% per year. Next, the appraiser would estimate the *effective age* of the improvement, which is defined as the age that is indicated by the condition of the structure, as distinct from its chronological age. If, in this example, the appraiser determined that the effective age of the improvement was 10 years rather than its chronological age of 20 years (perhaps because of greater than average care and upkeep) then the accrued depreciation would be $20,000 × 10 = $200,000 (rather than $20,000 × 20).

- **Cost-to-cure method of calculating depreciation.** The *cost-to-cure method* calculates depreciation by estimating the cost of curing the curable depreciation and adding to it the value of the incurable depreciation.

The cost approach is likely to be the approach of choice if (1) there are few if any comparables in the area (thus eliminating the sales-comparison approach) and the income approach is inappropriate, or (2) the improvements are quite new so that data on precise current costs can be gathered. The older the improvement, the less likely it is that an estimate of replacement cost can be made with precision. Furthermore, replacement cost would not take into consideration changes in the neighborhood, zoning laws, etc. that would have occurred in the meanwhile. Therefore, appraising a 50-year old house using the cost method would likely result in an unrealistic appraisal. See Figure 8 below.

3. Income Analysis Approach

The *income approach* (also referred to as the *capitalization approach*) estimates the value of an income-producing property as being worth the present value of the future income of the property through a three-step process:

1. determine the net annual income,

2. determine an appropriate capitalization rate, and

3. divide the net income by the capitalization rate to obtain the estimate of value; i.e., value = net income ÷ capitalization rate.

Net operating income (NOI) is determined as follows:

a) estimate the potential annual gross income the property;

b) deduct from the gross income an annual allowance for vacancies and uncollectible rents to arrive at the *effective gross income*; and

c) deduct from the effective gross income the estimate of annual operating expenses, including fixed expenses (such as hazard insurance and real estate taxes), maintenance, and reserves for replacements of building components. See Figure 9 below.

Not all expenses are deducted from effective gross income to obtain net income. Examples of such expenses include mortgage payments and taxes on income.

Fig. 8   **Example of Cost Approach**

Assume that the subject property is a 50 ft. x 40 ft. rectangular single-story house with an attached 20 ft. x 20 ft. garage. Suppose also that

- the land value is $200,000,
- the replacement cost of the house is $150 per square foot,
- the replacement cost of the garage is $40 per square foot,
- the estimated useful life of similar houses and garages is 50 years, and
- the effective age of this house and garage is 20 years.

Problem: What is the estimated value of the subject property?

Cost Approach Solution:

Subject value = land value + replacement cost - accrued depreciation.

Replacement cost of the house = 50 ft. x 40 ft. x $150/ ft.^{2} = $300,000
Replacement cost of the garage = 20 ft. x 20 ft. x $40/ ft.^{2} = $16,000
Total replacement cost = $300,000 + $16,000 = $316,000

Because the useful life is 50 years, using the straight-line method the rate of depreciation is 100% ÷ 50 years = 2% per year.
The effective age is 20 years, so the accrued depreciation percent in this case would be 20 years x 2% per year = 40%
40% of $316,000 = $126,400 = the accrued depreciation.

   $316,000 replacement cost
- $126,400 accrued depreciation
   $189,600 present value of the house and garage
+$200,000 land value
   $389,600 estimated of value of subject property

Fig. 9 **Example of Income Approach**

Assume that an apartment building has the following:

- 10 rental units each having fair market rent of $2,000 per month
- estimated loss for vacancies and uncollectible rents is 10%
- annual fixed expenses (property tax, insurance, etc.) are $30,000
- annual maintenance expense is $45,000
- annual reserve for replacements is $20,000
- the appraiser's capitalization rate is 8%

Problem: What is the value of the apartment building?

Solution

gross income ($2,000/unit x 10 units x 12 months)	$240,000
less vacancies & collection loss (10% of $240,000):	- $24,000
effective gross income :	$216,000
less annual expenses and replacement reserves:	- $95,000
net operating income:	$121,000

value = $121,000 ÷ 8% = $1,512,500

---

4. Appraisal Process/Procedure

While there is no official order in which the appraisal process is carried out, the following are steps that appraisers typically follow in the process of developing an appraisal report:

Step 1: Define the appraisal problem.

    a) Identify the client and the intended users of the appraisal.

    b) Identify the intended use of the appraisal. Clients have different appraisal problems they want to solve, such as determining the value for sale, the value for insurance, etc.

    c) Identify the relevant characteristics of the property, such as land, improvements, and rights.

Step 2: Determine the scope of work necessary to achieve the purpose of the appraisal.

    a) What data specific to the property are needed?

    b) What data concerning the neighborhood are needed?

    c) Where is this data to be found?

Step 3: Collect, verify, and analyze the data.

Step 4: Apply the pertinent approaches to value: cost, sales comparison, and/or income.

Step 5 Reconciliation: perform a reconciliation of value indications and determine a final opinion of value.

Step 6: Issue the appraisal report.

Uses of Appraisals. The basic purpose of an appraisal is to estimate the value of a property for a particular use. Appraisals are used for many reasons, including:

1. *Transfer of ownership.*

   a) to help sellers determine an asking price;

   b) to help buyers determine an offering price;

   c) to help listing agents decide whether to accept a listing from an owner (who may have unrealistic expectations) and to help listing agents assist their clients in arriving at realistic expectations regarding the sales price of their clients' properties; and

   d) to determine valuation for distribution of estate properties to heirs.

2. *Financing, credit, and insurance.*

   a) to help lenders decide whether a property provides sufficient security for a loan or for an extension of credit;

   b) to help evaluate the amount of insurance coverage for a property; and

   c) to help evaluate the cost of replacement and the settling of claims.

3. *Taxation.*

   a) to establish value of improvements for real estate taxes;

   b) to help ascertain estate and gift taxes; and

   c) to help ascertain the basis for depreciation in regard to income-producing properties.

4. *Miscellaneous appraisal purposes.*

   a) to help establish a price the government must pay in eminent domain proceedings;

   b) to help establish rents; and

   c) to help establish the value of traded properties.

Situations Requiring Appraisal by a Certified Appraiser. Because obtaining an accurate estimate of the value of real estate is vital to the mortgage process, most lenders require a licensed or certified appraiser for properties of substantial value. *Federal rules require the use of a state licensed or certified appraiser for any federally related residential loan when the transaction value is $250,000 or more.*

Basic Appraisal Terminology:

We have already discussed replacement cost, reproduction cost, and some aspects of depreciation in our discussion above regarding the replacement cost or summation approach to estimating the value of a subject property. For appraisal purposes, *depreciation* is defined as the loss in value due to any cause. *Appreciation*, on the other hand, is an increase in value due to any cause (such as inflation or increased demand). The appraisal concept of depreciation ("*actual depreciation*") is distinct from the income tax concept of depreciation ("*book depreciation*" or "*cost recovery*"), which is a mathematical calculation used by tax authorities and accountants to determine a depreciation deduction from gross income. In this chapter, we will only consider depreciation as applied in the appraisal process.

There are three main causes of depreciation:

1. *Physical deterioration* results from wear and tear of use and from natural causes such as water damage or termites. A closely related concept, referred to as *deferred maintenance*, is any type of depreciation that has not been corrected by diligent maintenance.

2. *Functional obsolescence* results (1) from deficiencies arising from poor architectural design, out-dated style or equipment, and changes in utility demand, such as for larger houses with more garage space, or (2) from over-improvements, where the cost of the improvements was more than the addition to market value.

3. *External obsolescence* (also referred to as *economic obsolescence*) results from things such as (1) changes in zoning laws or other government restrictions, (2) proximity to undesirable influences such as traffic, airport flight patterns, or power lines, and (3) general neighborhood deterioration, as might result from increased crime.

Depreciation can be either curable or incurable. *Curable depreciation* is physical deterioration or functional obsolescence that can be repaired or replaced by a prudent property owner at a cost that is less than or equal to the value added to the property. *Incurable depreciation* is (1) physical deterioration or functional obsolescence that cannot be repaired at a cost that is less than or equal to the value added to the property and (2) economic obsolescence (which is beyond the control of the property owner).

Reconciliation. If the subject property is an older single-family home that has never been rented and is located in an area where few if any homes are being rented, then the only reasonable approach to value is the sales comparison approach. But suppose instead that the subject property is a relatively new single-family home in an area where a significant number of comparable newly built homes are being rented. In this case, all three approaches (sales comparison, cost, and income) may contribute insight into the value of the property, and all three approaches likely would be investigated by an appraiser. Of course, the three approaches probably would give different valuations, in which case the appraiser must use his or her expert experience and judgment to arrive at a final estimate of value. This process of ascertaining value by comparing and evaluating values obtained from different valuation approaches is called *reconciliation*. Note that the reconciliation of estimated values is *not* simply an averaging of those values.

Section E: Conveyance of Real Property

1. Definition of Clear (Marketable) Title

A clear (marketable) title is a title free of any defects, liens, and encumbrances. However, many properties are transferred (in other words, can be sold) if the title is free of any defects, liens, and encumbrances *except* for encumbrances (such as a mortgage that the purchaser is assuming) that the buyer and lender agree are acceptable.

2. Matters Affecting Title

Matters affecting title include: deeds, wills, mortgages and the age, marital status, residence, capacity, and homestead status of the persons named in such documents. Other matters affecting title are court decrees, bankruptcies, liens, easements, and any knowledge of surveys, inspections, adverse possession, and occupants (such as long-term guests) who may claim an interest in the property.

3. Recordation

Every state has a recording system that provides a person who has acquired real property with a method of protecting his or her interests in the property by recording the document of conveyance, usually with the county recorder. Recording provides access to information regarding ownership of the property and imparts *constructive notice* to subsequent purchasers or encumbrancers. Constructive notice (as distinct from *actual notice*, which is express notice of information given in fact) refers to notice given to the public by the records available to the public.

Most states require that a deed be acknowledged for it to be recorded. An *acknowledgment* is a formal declaration made by the grantor before a duly authorized public official (such as a notary public), that states that the grantor voluntarily signed the deed and that the signature on the deed is the grantor's.

In most states there is no requirement of a valid deed that it be recorded; however, if the conveyance is not recorded, it will be considered void as against subsequent purchasers or encumbrancers who act in good faith without actual knowledge of the prior, unrecorded conveyance.

4. Title Insurance

What Is Insured Against:

Real estate is expensive, and real estate transactions are complex, so it behooves a property buyer to obtain a complete chronological history of all of the documents affecting title to the property and have it examined by an attorney. But even a thorough examination and analysis of the chain of title would not offer protection to the buyer against latent or undiscovered defects in the documents affecting title (for example, a forged deed).

In most real estate transactions, the lender requires that the buyer pay for a *lender's policy* of title insurance that protects the lender up to the amount of principal outstanding on the loan. As for the *owner's policy*, which insurers the title of the buyer, either the seller or the buyer pays for the title policy — a point of negotiation between them.

There are many ways in which title may be adversely affected, and, consequently, there are different policies of title insurance to cover various possible defects. The two main title insurance policies are the *standard coverage* and the *extended coverage* (sometimes called an *ALTA policy*, after the American Land Title Association). A lender's policy can be transferred if the loan is sold. An owner's policy is canceled upon the sale of the property.

A standard coverage policy typically ensures against title defects found in public records plus latent defects in title such as:

- forged deeds;
- incompetent grantor documents;
- legal delivery problems; and
- incorrect marital settlements.

An extended coverage insures everything covered by a standard coverage policy, plus:

- rights of parties in possession, such as tenants and adverse possessors;
- matters that a survey would disclose, such as encroachments and boundary lines;
- unrecorded physical easements and mechanics liens; and
- certain mining and water claims.

Neither the standard coverage nor the extended coverage offers protection regarding governmental regulations concerning occupancy and use (which affect the condition of the property rather than the condition of the title) or regarding defects that the buyer knew as of the date of policy issuance.

When a title insurance company makes payments due to defects in the title of an insured property, the insurance company acquires, by right of *subrogation*, all rights the insured would have against any third party due to the defect (such as a forged deed).

Title Searches, Title Abstracts, Chain of Title: A *title search* is an examination of all relevant public documents to determine whether there exist any potential defects (such as judicial liens, lis pendens, or other encumbrances, including tax liens and special assessments) against the title. When requested to provide title insurance on a property, a title insurance company usually utilizes their own set of records (called *title plants*) to examine the condition of title before issuing a *preliminary report*, which is a statement by the title insurance company of the condition of the title and of the terms and conditions upon which it is willing to issue a policy.

A *chain of title* is a complete chronological history of all documents affecting the title to a property. An *abstract of title* is a chronological summary of all grants, liens, wills, judicial proceedings, and other records that affect the property's title. An *abstractor* is the person who prepares an abstract of title. In many real estate transactions, the abstract of title is sent to an attorney who examines the abstract and renders an *opinion of title* on the condition of ownership. However, examining an abstract of title would likely not uncover latent defects in the title (such as a forged deed) — thus the need for title insurance.

Cloud on Title, Suit to Quiet Title: A *cloud on title* is any document, claim, lien, or other encumbrance that may impair the title to real property or cast doubt on the validity of the title. A *suit to quiet title* (also referred to as a *quiet title action*) is a court proceeding intended to establish the true ownership of a property, thereby eliminating any cloud on title.

5. Deeds

A *deed* is a written document that conveys some right, title, or interest in real property from a *grantor* to a *grantee*. Title passes when all essential elements of a deed have been incorporated into the deed, the deed is signed by all the grantors, and the deed is delivered to, and accepted by, the grantee. Deeds can also be transferred involuntarily, such as by eminent domain, escheat, or upon the death of the owner.

Types of Deeds: A deed can take many forms, regulated by the laws of the state in which the property is located.

General Warranty Deed. A general warranty deed provides the greatest deed-warranty protections to a grantee. In some states, the warranties are implied by words in the deed such as "convey and warrant." In other states, the warranties must be expressly stated in the deed. The following are the five basic warranties in a general warranty deed:

- **Covenant of seisin.** The grantors warrant that they are the owners of the property and have the right to convey title.
- **Covenant of warranty.** The grantors promise to compensate the grantee for any losses that the grantee may incur due to the failure of the grantors to convey title.
- **Covenant against encumbrances.** The grantors warrant that the title is free from defects other than those explicitly disclosed in the deed.
- **Covenant of quiet enjoyment.** The grantors warrant that the grantor will compensate the grantee for any expenses and losses if the grantee's title is found to be inferior to the title as represented in the deed.
- **Covenant of further assurance.** The grantors promise to execute documents and to initiate legal actions to protect any defects in the title that are found in the future.

Note that unlike in a special warranty deed (see immediately below), the covenants in a general warranty are not restricted to the time during which the grantor owned the property, but extend all the way back to the title's origin.

Special Warranty Deed. In a special warranty deed, the grantors warrant that they own the property and have the right to convey it, and that the property was not encumbered during the period of their ownership. The primary difference between a general warranty deed and a special warranty deed is that a special warranty deed only covers the period of time of the grantors' ownership, whereas a general warranty deed covers all time. A special warranty deed is typically used by fiduciaries (trustees, executors, and corporations) and by grantors who acquired the property in a tax sale, because they cannot warrant the actions of prior holders of the title.

Quitclaim Deed. A *quitclaim deed* contains no warranties of any kind. It merely provides that any interest (if there is any) that the grantor has in the property is transferred to the grantee. Typically, a quitclaim deed is used to clear some "cloud on the title" to the property, such as to eliminate a presumption of community property if the grantee is married, or to remove an easement.

Grant Deed. In a few states (primarily in the West, such as California), a *grant deed* is the most commonly used deed. It has three implied warranties that are enforced whether or not they are expressly stated in the deed:

1. the grantor has not transferred title to anyone else;
2. the property at the time of execution is free from any encumbrances made by the grantor, except for those disclosed; and
3. the grantor will convey all *after-acquired title* (all interests in the property acquired by the grantor subsequent to the conveyance of the deed automatically pass to the

grantee).

Note that these implied warranties do *not* warrant that the grantor is the owner of the property or that there are no other liens or encumbrances that exist against the property — good reasons why the grantee of a grant deed should insist upon the acquisition of title insurance as a condition of closing.

Sheriff's Deed. A *sheriff's deed* is a deed given at the foreclosure of a property, subsequent to a judgment for foreclosure of a money judgment against the owner or of a mortgage against the property. A sheriff's deed contains no warranties and transfers only the former owner's interest, if any, in the property.

Gift Deed. A *gift deed* is used to convey title when no tangible consideration (other than "affection") is given. The gift deed is valid unless it was used to defraud creditors, in which case such creditors may bring an action to void the deed.

Essential Elements of Deeds: There are several essential elements to a valid deed:

In Writing. Because a deed transfers an interest in real property, a deed falls under the statute of frauds and, therefore, must be in writing to be enforceable.

Signed by the Grantors. The deed must be signed by all of the grantors named on the deed, who, in most states, must use the same names as they did when they took title, or must use both their original names and current names. For example, a person who used a different name before marriage and took title in that name must use that prior name when signing the deed or, in some states, use both names — such as, "Mary Smith, now known as Mary Jones." If a grantor's signature is forged, the deed is void.

Recital of Consideration. The recital of consideration is usually in the form of some dollar amount; however, for gift deeds the recital of "love and affection" may be sufficient, though it is best to add something as "and for $1 and other good and valuable consideration."

Grantor must be Competent. The grantors must have legal capacity to sign the deed. Unemancipated minors and incompetents are not competent to sign deeds. If an unemancipated minor enters into a contract to purchase or sell real property, the minor may rescind the contract at any time while still a minor and for a reasonable time after attaining majority. If a mentally incompetent person enters into a contract to purchase or sell real property, the transfer is void, or voidable by that person or his or her guardian or heirs, depending on state law.

Grantee must be Capable of Holding Title. All grantees must be living (or existing in the case of legally established business organizations) and all such existing legal persons may hold title to real property.

Parties must be Properly Described. The identities of the grantors and grantees must be adequately described. To ensure that there will be no confusion in the future as to the identity of the grantees, their identities must be designated so as to be determined with certainty.

Property must be Adequately Described. The property must be described specifically enough so that it can be located with certainty. As a general rule, one of the legal land descriptions discussed above is used.

Granting Clause. The deed must contain a clause with operative words of conveyance, such as "I hereby transfer," "I hereby grant," or "I hereby convey."

Abendum Clause. Following the granting clause and usually beginning with the words "to have and to hold," a deed must state the type of estate being transferred — for example, fee simple, life estate, or easement.

Delivered to the Grantee. A deed is not effective until it is legally delivered to the grantee. Delivery of a deed in this context is a legal, not a physical, concept. Actual physical delivery is not sufficient; there must be an unconditional intent on the part of the grantor to pass title *immediately* to the grantee. Therefore, physical delivery of the deed to escrow is not effective to transfer title because there is no intention on the part of the grantor to pass title immediately. Nor would the physical delivery to a grantee of a deed properly filled out in every way be effective if the intention of the grantor were that the grantee would not take title until some future date, such as upon the grantor's death — a deed cannot take the place of a will. Because the past intention of a party is often difficult to determine, legal delivery is probably the most litigated issue concerning the validity of deeds.

The law in most states provides certain (rebuttable) presumptions as to the legal delivery of a deed. Typically, legal delivery is presumed if:

- the deed is found in the possession of the grantee; or

- the deed is recorded, unless it was recorded after the grantor's death.

Conversely, finding the deed in the grantor's possession raises the (also rebuttable) presumption of nondelivery.

Accepted by the Grantee. Acceptance must be voluntary, unconditional, and accomplished during the grantor's lifetime. Acceptance by the grantee can be evidenced by acts, words, or by conduct such as by recording a deed.

6. Will

Transfers of a decedent's property can either be by ***will*** or by ***intestate succession***. The maker of a will is called a ***testator***, the real property transferred by will is called a ***devise***, and the receiver of real property by will is known as a ***devisee***. The transfer by will of personal property is known as a ***bequest***, and the person who receives personal property by will is known as a ***legatee***. The three types of recognized wills are (1) ***formal or witnessed wills***, (2) ***holographic wills***, which are handwritten wills, and (3) ***nuncupative wills***, which are oral wills and which are no longer considered valid in most states.

Property owned by a decedent who does not leave a will (i.e., dies intestate) is distributed according to the resident state's ***statute of descent***. Persons who receive property by way of intestate succession are referred to as heirs.

Probate is the legal procedure whereby a court oversees the distribution of a decedent's property in accordance with the will or, if no will, the laws of intestate succession.

7. Court-Ordered Sale (e.g., foreclosure)

A ***nonjudicial foreclosure*** is a foreclosure that does not involve the judicial process. The right to pursue a nonjudicial foreclosure is contained in the power-of-sale clause of a mortgage or deed of trust, which, upon borrower default and the beneficiary's request, empowers the trustee to sell the secured property at a public auction.

A *judicial foreclosure* is a foreclosure carried out not by way of a power-of-sale clause in a security instrument, but under the supervision of a court. At the end of the judicial foreclosure process, a public sale is advertised, and the property is sold to the highest bidder, usually at a public auction. A holder of a mortgage or deed of trust with a power-of-sale clause may, if so desired, use judicial foreclosure; however, many states have a *one-action rule*, under which a choice of either judicial or non-judicial foreclosure must be made.

A few states permit *strict foreclosure*, through which the lender may foreclose upon default of a debtor without going through the process of a public sale. In a strict foreclosure, the lender merely gives the debtor proper notice and prepares the proper papers; a court sets a period of time for the debtor to redeem the property by paying all past-due payments; and if the debtor fails to so redeem the property, title passes to the lender and the debtor loses all rights and interests (including equity) in the property.

8. Adverse Possession

Adverse possession is the process by which unauthorized possession and use of another's property can ripen into ownership of that other's property without compensation. Certain conditions must be met before legal title through adverse possession can be acquired. These conditions vary among the states, but typically include:

1. There must be *actual, open, and the notorious possession*. This means that the possession must not be kept secret; it must be of a kind such that the true owner of the property could discover the unauthorized possession if he or she used due diligence to inspect the property occasionally. This requirement of possession does not imply the necessity of residence on the land; exclusive use, such as by fencing off the property or by the use of the property for the cultivation of crops, will suffice.

2. The possession must be *exclusive and hostile* to the owner. As the word is used in adverse possession law, "hostile" does not imply physical or verbal confrontation; it means that the possession is adverse to the owner's rights or interests in the property. Therefore, permission by the owner would defeat this second requirement for adverse possession.

3. There must be a *claim of right or color of title*. If, in good faith, the possessor claims the land because of a forged or otherwise defective document, the possession is under *color of title*. Possession is by *claim of right* if the possessor, perhaps even knowing that he or she is trespassing, possesses the property with the intent to claim ownership of it and can establish evidence through action of that intention.

4. The possession must be *continuous and uninterrupted for a certain statutory number of years, usually 5 to 30 years*.

5. In some states the possessor must *pay all real property taxes* during the statutory period of continuous and uninterrupted possession — a requirement that makes acquisition of property by adverse possession an uncommon occurrence.

It is not possible to acquire title to government property or to property owned by an incompetent through adverse possession.

9. Settlement Procedures (closing the transaction)

Responsibilities of Escrow Agent:

A real estate *closing* (also referred to as a *settlement*) is a process leading up to, and concluding with, a buyer's receiving the deed to the property and the seller's receiving the purchase money (or other consideration, pursuant to the terms of the sale agreement).

For a real estate transaction, every valid escrow must have four basic elements:

1. a binding contract between buyer and seller;

2. an escrow agent;

3. irrevocable delivery of transfer instruments and deposits called for in the contract; and

4. instructions to the escrow agent that impose conditions as to the delivery of instruments and funds on the performance of the stipulated conditions.

An *escrow agent* (also referred to as an *escrow holder*) is an impartial agent who holds possession of written instruments and deposits until all of the conditions of escrow have been fully performed. An escrow agent is a special agent whose only authority is to see to it that all of the escrow instructions are fully performed. Who will serve as escrow agent and which party or parties will pay the escrow fees are matters to be negotiated between the buyer and the seller; neither the real estate broker nor the lender may dictate either of these matters.

Prorated Items:

As a general rule, at the close of escrow in a real estate transaction certain allocations of expenses incurred in the ordinary course of property ownership must be made. For example, if the escrow closes midyear or midmonth, the seller may have prepaid taxes, insurance, or association dues, in which case credit to the seller's account should be made. Conversely, if the seller is behind on paying taxes or insurance, etc., the seller's account should be debited. Such an adjustment of expenses that either have been paid or are in arrears in proportion to actual time of ownership as of the closing or other agreed-upon date is called *proration*.

Rent *is typically paid in advance*, in which case the buyer would be credited for the portion of the month remaining after closing. On the other hand, mortgage interest *is usually paid in arrears*, in which case a seller would be debited for the portion of the month before closing. Special assessments *are often not prorated*, though this is a subject to be negotiated between the buyer and seller.

To compute proration, follow these steps:

1. determine which, if any, expenses are to be prorated;

2. determine to whom the expenses should be credited or debited;

3. determine how many days the expenses are to be prorated;

4. calculate the per day proration amount; and

5. multiply the number of days by the per day proration amount.

> **Example:** *Susan purchased a condo that had been rented from Bob at $1,500 a month. Escrow closed on September 16. Who pays whom in regard to proration of the rent if the day of closing belongs to the buyer?*

Rent is normally collected *in advance* on the first day of the month, so unless stated otherwise one should make this assumption in proration of rent problems. Under this assumption, Bob received $1,500 on or about September 1, but only deserved to keep half of the month's rent because Susan acquired ownership of the condo on September 16. Therefore, Susan should be credited $750 at the close of escrow.

Closing Statements/HUD-1:

At the close of escrow, a settlement statement is prepared that itemizes all charges and credits for both the seller and the buyer. The HUD Settlement Statement (HUD-1) is the settlement statement required in all federally related real estate loans, including refinancing. The HUD-1 has become so popular that it is also widely used as the settlement statement for other loans.

Preparing the settlement statement involves determining what **credits** (items payable *to* a party) and **debits** (items payable *by* a party) apply to the transaction and taking care that each is allocated to the correct party. In making this allocation, the escrow agent acts pursuant to the escrow instructions. Certain costs of home ownership such as prepaid rents or prepaid taxes typically are allocated partially to one party and partially to the other.

Estimating Closing Costs:

A good-faith estimate (GFE) of closing costs must be provided by any mortgage lender for a loan under RESPA. The GFE itemizes all fees and costs related to closing and must be provided to a potential borrower within three days after submission of a mortgage loan application. There are three GFE tolerance levels for settlement charges that must be included on the HUD-1 form:

- *Charges that cannot increase* (lender's origination charge; points for the specific interest rate; adjusted origination charges (after the rate is locked); and transfer taxes)

- *Charges that in aggregate cannot increase more than 10%* (title services and lender's title insurance; appraisals, credit reports, tax service, flood certification — only where lender selects or identifies; mortgage insurance premium; and county recording charges)

- *Charges that can change* (initial deposits for escrow services; daily interest charges; homeowners insurance; lender-required services where the borrower shops for and selects their own third-party provider (i.e., closing services and lender's and owner's title insurance)

Property and Income Taxes:

1099-S Reporting. The IRS requires escrow agents to report every sale of real estate on Form 1099-S, giving the seller's name, Social Security number, and the gross sale proceeds. If the escrow agent fails to perform this reporting duty, the obligation becomes the lender's. If the lender also fails to report the sale, the obligation becomes the broker's.

Foreign Investment in Real Property Tax Act (FIRPTA). After becoming concerned that foreign investors may have been evading their income tax liabilities, Congress passed FIRPTA, which requires the buyer to determine whether the seller is a non-resident alien; and if so, the buyer has the responsibility of withholding 10% of the amount realized from the sale and sending that 10% to the IRS. In practice, the obligation to check the seller's residency status and, if appropriate, withhold the 10% and send it to the IRS is given to the escrow agent in the escrow instructions. As not all real estate transactions are subject to

FIRPTA, current IRS regulations should be consulted in any real estate transaction involving a non-resident alien. Some states also have withholding laws similar to FIRPTA for sales of nonexempt real estate.

Property Taxes. Property taxes that are due or that have been paid in advance are among the items that an escrow agent will be required to prorate prior to closing.

Income Taxes. Transfers of real estate can have significant federal and state income tax consequences. Income taxes are ***progressive***, meaning that the greater an individual's income, the higher the tax rate on that individual's income. Rental income is taxed at the individual's regular income tax rate, but gains on the sale of ***capital assets*** are taxed at a ***capital gain rate***. What constitutes a capital asset is a technical question often hinging on how the asset is used or held. In very general terms, capital assets are non-inventory assets held by individuals or businesses for personal or investment purposes, and include homeowners' homes, household furnishings, stocks, bonds, land, buildings, and machinery.

Capital gain rates vary depending on whether the gain is a ***short-term capital gain*** or a ***long-term capital gain***. Short-term rates are typically applicable to investments held for one year or less and have often been equal to the individual's regular income tax rate; long-term rates are typically applicable to investments held for more than 12 months and are usually lower than short-term rates. Income tax rules and rates for both regular income and capital gain income are constantly changing; therefore, *before* entering into a real estate transaction, it is prudent to seek the advice of an attorney or accountant who is an income tax specialist.

Income Tax Ramifications of Homeownership.

IMPORTANT CAUTIONARY NOTE: Real estate licensees should never dispense tax advice to their clients. Instead, they should refer clients who have tax issues to an attorney or to an accountant who is competent in tax matters. On the other hand, it is important that real estate licensees be aware of the kinds of tax issues that may arise in a real estate transaction so that they are knowledgeable enough to be able to make proper referrals in situations that may call for tax expertise.

Homeowners are eligible for certain federal income tax benefits, including:

1. Interest paid on a mortgage secured by a principal residence or by a second home is deductible from personal income. There is a limit on how much interest can be deducted, which limit currently is the interest on the portion of a loan that does not exceed $1 million. The mortgage interest deduction can only be taken on a principal residence and one second home.

2. Property taxes paid on a homeowner's residence are also deductible from personal income.

3. Pursuant to the ***Taxpayer Relief Act of 1997***, an individual of any age who sells a property that has been his or her principal place of residence for at least 2 out of the 5 years prior to the sale may exclude $250,000 from capital gains on the sale. For married couples who have both lived in the residence for the requisite 2-year period, the exclusion is $500,000. These exclusions can only be taken once every two years. If the home was not the principal residence for the requisite 2-year period, individuals and married couples can still obtain a partial exclusion if the sale was necessitated by

a change of employment, health problems, or other unforeseen circumstances, such as divorce or a death in the family. In such cases, an exclusion based on the portion of the requisite 2-year period can be taken. For example, if because of a change of employment a married couple moves and sells their home, having lived there only one year, the exclusion would be ½ of $500,000, or $250,000.

4. Loan discount points on new loans are deductible if they are clearly identifiable as prepaid interest and not as service fees.

5. Mortgage loan prepayment penalties are also deductible.

Compared to ownership of investment properties (see below), there are a few negative tax consequences of home ownership. For example, loss on the sale of a taxpayer's personal residence is not tax deductible. Repairs, maintenance, and other operating expenses of owning a principal place of residence are also not tax deductible, nor are private mortgage insurance premiums.

Tax issues regarding investment property. Though property taxes and interest on real estate loans are in general deductible, there are numerous regulations limiting such deductions.

Passive income. As a general rule, passive losses are deductible only to the extent of passive income. There are only two sources of *passive income*: (1) rental activity and (2) a business in which the taxpayer does not materially participate. Salaries, wages, interest, dividends, royalties, annuities, and gains on stocks and bonds are not considered passive income and, therefore, income from such sources may not be used to offset passive losses.

An exception to the passive loss limitation rules exists for an active investor. An *active investor* is someone who actively participates in the activities of a business invested in (for example, an individual who manages his or her own rental properties), as distinguished from a *passive investor*, who is someone who does not actively participate in the activities of a business invested in. Under this exception, an active investor who has adjusted gross income of $100,000 or less may deduct up to $25,000 of losses from passive rental real estate activities from personal income. If the taxpayer's adjusted gross income is between $100,000 and $150,000, the taxpayer loses $1 of their $25,000 maximum for every $2 above the $100,000. Passive losses that are unused in one tax year may be carried forward for possible use in subsequent years.

Investors who qualify as "real estate professionals" can benefit even further than the $25,000 exception discussed above. A *real estate professional* for this purpose is a real estate investor who (1) materially participates for at least 750 hours during the tax year in the real estate business and (2) spends more than 50% of his or her personal services performed in all businesses during the tax year in the real estate business that he or she materially participates in. An individual who so qualifies as a real estate professional would not have their rental income automatically treated as passive income, so the full amount of losses from rental income could be deducted from personal income.

Depreciation. Depreciation in the tax context is a method of book accounting that in some sense reflects anticipated wear resulting from the use of improvements to property. Because depreciation is an accounting vehicle for reflecting replacement cost, it is technically referred to as *cost recovery*. Depreciation can only be used to benefit the improvements to investment or income property; it cannot be taken on owner-occupied residences or on the value of the portion of property attributable to land.

A *depreciation deduction* is an annual allowance for the depreciation of property. As a general rule, real estate is depreciated in equal annual amounts over the depreciable life of the property (i.e., straight-line depreciation), which for residential rental properties is 27½ years, and for nonresidential properties is 39 years. As an alternative, both residential rental properties and nonresidential properties may elect to use 40 years as their depreciable lives. The depreciation deduction can be used to reduce a taxpayer's ordinary income. However, numerous tax regulations (which we will not pursue here) place restrictions on how much depreciation can be taken to shelter non-rent income. *It is important to note that only the cost of improvements is subject to a depreciation deduction — the cost of land is not.*

Installment Sales. An installment sale is a sale in which the seller receives at least one payment in a later tax period and may report part of the gain from the sale (as well as any interest received) for the year in which a payment is received. An installment sale can confer tax benefits on the seller by spreading tax on the gain from the sale out over a number of years. This may be particularly beneficial to a seller who anticipates being in a lower tax bracket in the year or years subsequent to the sale.

The installment sales method cannot be used for the regular sale of inventory of personal property, sales of stock or securities traded on established securities markets, or dealer sales (sales of real property held for sale to customers in the ordinary course of a trade or business, or regular sales of the same type of personal property) even if the sale is made in installments.

1031 Exchange. A *1031 exchange* is a tax-deferred exchange (often misleadingly called a tax-free exchange) of "like kind" property held for productive use. In general, this means that any property held for business use or investment can be exchanged for any other like-kind property held for business use or investment (for example, a farm can be exchanged for an apartment building), though rules for exchanges of personal property (such as office furniture) are a bit more involved than are exchanges of real property. *A personal residence does not qualify for a 1031 exchange, nor do vacation or second homes, unless they are held as rentals for sufficient periods of time pursuant to IRS Rev Proc 2008-16.*

If a 1031 exchange has been properly structured, neither gain nor loss is recognized at the time of the exchange. If, on the other hand, a like-kind property is received in exchange along with *boot* (cash or other not like-kind property), gain is recognized on the value of the boot at the time of the exchange, but losses are still excluded from recognition at the time of the exchange.

> **Example:** If an apartment building with a adjusted cost basis of $2 million is exchanged for an office building worth $2.3 million plus $100,000 cash (resulting in a $400,000 gain to the apartment building owner), the boot is $100,000 and will be recognized as taxable income at the time of the exchange. The $300,000 additional gain the apartment owner received due to the greater value of the like-kind property received will not be recognized at the time of the exchange, but the cost basis of the $2.3 million office building will be lowered to $2 million, so that the additional $300,000 gain will be recognized when the newly acquired property is eventually sold.

Trust/Escrow Accounts:

A *trust account* (*escrow account*) is an account set up by a broker in a bank or other

103

recognized depository in the state where the broker is doing business, into which the broker deposits all funds entrusted to the broker by principles or others. Many states require that separate trust accounts be maintained for sales transactions and for rents received from property management accounts. Most states also require that a trust account be non-interest-bearing unless the beneficiaries request otherwise. Trust fund accounts are audited by most states, and violations of trust fund accounting is one of the most common reasons for suspension or revocation of real estate licenses.

Trust funds may be cash or any other thing of value, such as a check, a note payable to the seller, or even a pearl necklace. Other examples of trust funds include:

- **earnest money deposits** (the deposit, usually a check, that a prospective purchaser gives to a broker as good-faith evidence of intention to complete the transaction);

- advance fees paid by a seller to an agent to cover expected cash outlays of the agent, such as advertising expenses;

- proceeds from a sale of real estate or other property owned by a broker's client;

- rent or lease payments made by a client's tenants;

- security deposits made by a client's tenants;

- funding for a loan; and

- interest (if any) paid on a trust fund account.

By contrast, examples of non-trust funds include:

- a broker's real estate commissions;

- rent and security deposits from a broker's own real estate; and

- any other funds personally owned by a broker.

Responsibility for Earnest Money and Other Trust Monies, Including Co-Mingling/Conversion:

Funds on deposit in a broker's trust account must always equal the amount of funds received from or for the benefit of a principal. The process of comparing what is in the account with what should be in the account is called **reconciliation**. If, after reconciliation, it is found that the account balance is less than it should be, there is a **trust fund shortage**.

Having a trust fund shortage is a violation of trust account regulations. The most serious kind of trust fund shortage results from a licensee's misuse of trust funds for his or her own purposes. This violation of real estate law is called **conversion**, and is a criminal offense, punishable by fines and/or jail time.

If the trust fund account balance is greater than it should be, there is a **trust fund overage**, which is also a violation of trust account regulations. **Commingling** results from the failure to properly segregate the funds belonging to the agent from the funds received and held on behalf of the seller or buyer. Commingling of funds is strictly prohibited, and is grounds for suspension or revocation of a real estate license.

CHAPTER 5: MARKETING REGULATIONS (PURCHASE AND RENTAL)

Section A: Property Advertising (including Fair Housing) Disclosures

1. Environmental Concern (e.g., led-based paint; radon)

Material facts related to the property that are known, or that reasonably should have been known through diligent discovery, by the seller or agent must be disclosed to potential purchasers. *A material fact is any fact that is likely to affect the decision of a party as to whether to enter into a transaction on the specified terms.* Material facts regarding property condition or location include:

Land/Soil Conditions: Land and soil conditions that may affect the value or desirability of the property include stability of landfill in earthquake prone areas, stability of ground on hill or mountain sides, possible contamination of soil or groundwater, and composition of soil and suitability for growing crops in agricultural areas. Because of the potential for astronomical damages, care must be taken to disclose known or suspected dumping of hazardous material on the property. *See,* discussion of *the Comprehensive Environmental Response, Compensation, and Liability Act* (CERCLA) in Chapter 2, Section 3, Part A.

Accuracy of Representation of Lot or Improvement Size, Encroachments or Easements Affecting Use: One of the most litigated issues in real estate representation is misrepresentation of lot size, the size of homes, or the size other improvements. The most accurate way of determining lot size is to have a professional survey performed. Appraisers determine the square footage of homes by taking the home's outside measurements.

Agents should be careful to verify the square footage of properties they list, not relying without verification on information on lot size or improvement size given to them by sellers, who often have an incorrect (inflated) assessment of those sizes. In fact, with regard to any client statement about property condition, it is best to "trust, but verify," as President Reagan said about negotiations with the Soviets on the INF Treaty.

Encroachments and easements affecting use can be discovered by examining title and other public records, and by having a surveyor determine the exact boundaries of the property.

Pest Infestation, Toxic Mold and Other Interior Environmental Hazards: Interior environmental hazards include pest infestation, toxic mold, radon, lead-based paint, urea formaldehyde insulation, and asbestos. Increasingly, states are requiring sellers, lessors, and their agents to disclose to potential purchasers or tenants such known interior environmental hazards.

Pursuant to the federal *Residential Lead-Based Paint Hazard Reduction Act* rule, a seller (or lessor) of a residential dwelling unit built before 1978 must notify a buyer (or tenant) in writing about required disclosures for lead-based paint. The seller (or lessor) must disclose any knowledge he or she has about whether lead-based paint was used in the dwelling unit and must provide the buyer (or tenant) with an EPA pamphlet titled *Protect Your Family From Lead In Your Home,* which describes ways to recognize and reduce lead hazards. The seller must deliver this pamphlet to a prospective buyer before the contract is completed. The seller must also offer a prospective buyer 10 days to inspect for lead-based paint and lead-based paint hazards. The seller is not required to pay for this inspection.

Structural Issues Such As Roof, Gutters, Downspouts, Doors, Windows, Foundation: Buyers agents should recommend that structural inspections of homes be performed. Such inspections should include roofs, gutters, downspouts, doors, windows, and foundations. In the states that require sellers, lessors, and their agents to disclose known material facts about homes, such disclosures must be made on appropriate forms.

Condition of Electrical and Plumbing Systems, and of Equipment or Appliances That Are Fixtures: The condition of electrical and plumbing systems (such as defective or poorly working water heaters, air-conditioning units, and furnaces), and other equipment or appliances that are being transferred as part of the sale to the purchaser (such as fixtures) should also be inspected for defects and to obtain an estimate of remaining useful life.

Location within Natural Hazard or Specifically Regulated Area, Potentially Uninsurable Property: Natural hazard areas include flood hazard areas, fire hazard areas, and earthquake zone areas. Many states require sellers, lessors, and their agents to disclose to potential purchasers (or tenants) whether the subject property lies in any of these known natural hazard zones. Mortgages that involve the federal government (such as FHA-insured or VA-guaranteed loans) require proof that the subject property does not lie in a flood zone area or that flood insurance is carried by the borrower. Potentially uninsurable properties include properties that are seriously contaminated with hazardous waste materials or that carry known risks (such as lying directly above a seismic fault) that are deemed too great to insure.

Additionally, known external conditions that, because of their severity, may rise to the level of material facts (such as neighbors who throw loud parties, neighbors with dogs that bark throughout the night, gang activity nearby, etc.) should be disclosed.

Known Alterations or Additions: Many homes have alterations or additions. If these alterations or additions were made without required permits, it is the seller's responsibility to disclose unpermitted alterations or additions. Helpful in selling a home are records that show what alterations or additions have been made, when, by whom, and at what cost.

Zoning and Planning Information: Material facts that must be disclosed to potential purchasers and/or tenants include current and (if known) planned zoning, planned eminent domain, and public utility use of the property.

Boundaries of School/Utility/Taxation Districts, Flight Paths: Sellers, lessors, and their agents must disclose material facts to potential purchasers (or tenants) regarding properties that are within special school or utility taxation districts, or that are affected by nuisances such as airport noise, high-voltage power lines, interstate highways, and cell-phone towers.

Local Taxes and Special Assessments, Other Liens: Sellers, lessors, and their agents must disclose material facts to potential purchasers (or tenants) regarding properties that are within special assessment zones, or that have other liens against the properties.

External Environmental Hazards: External hazards include hazardous waste contaminants from landfills, leaking underground storage tanks, and illegal toxic dumping.

Stigmatized/Psychologically Impacted Property, Megan's Law Issues: A stigmatized property is a property having a condition that certain persons may find materially negative in a way that does not relate to the property's actual physical condition. In states that require sellers and their agents to disclose all material facts about a property to prospective purchasers, for properties whose desirability or value may be detrimentally affected by certain conditions, such conditions should, in general, be disclosed. Some states, however, have exempted certain facts — such as long-ago deaths on the property or the property having been inhabited by a resident who committed suicide or who had AIDS or is HIV-positive — from such disclosures. However, most stigmatized properties should be disclosed as such to prospective purchasers to protect sellers and their agents from lawsuits by disgruntled purchasers.

> **Example:** If in a particular community a house is widely believed to be haunted, what is important with respect to real estate agency disclosure is whether such a belief materially affects the value of the property — not whether such a belief is utter nonsense.

Another category of stigmatized property relates to sex offenders. ***Megan's Law*** is an informal name for various federal and state laws that provide for the registration of sex offenders and for the making available to the public information regarding the location of these offenders. Though federal law does not require that sellers or licensees disclose information of sex offenders in the area, all states have sex-offender registries that can be accessed by the public, and many states require sellers and licensees to disclose the existence of, and how to access, the state's sex-offender registry.

Incorrect "Factual" Statements Versus "Puffing":

(i) Truth in Advertising.

Misrepresentations. Misrepresentations can be either intentional or negligent. However, in real estate law even negligent misrepresentation is often characterized as fraudulent. Normally, to find fraudulent misrepresentation there must be a finding of an intention to deceive; however, even without bad intention and even believing his or her assertions to be true, a real estate agent may be guilty of fraudulent misrepresentation if the assertions are *made in a manner not warranted by the information available to the agent.*

Nondisclosures. As we have seen, a real estate agent has a duty to disclose any known defect in the property or any defect that could have been discovered upon reasonable visual inspection. Civil liability for misrepresentation, as well as disciplinary action by a state licensing agency, can result from an agent's failure to make these required disclosures. Nondisclosure can also result from an affirmative act of hiding defects in the property to prevent the buyer from discovering the defects. Such acts are referred to as ***concealment***, and sometimes as ***negative fraud.***

Puffing. Somewhat overblown "sales talk" or "puffing" can, if taken too far, result in a finding of misrepresentation. While in certain circumstances a statement such as "this property is the best buy in town" likely is acceptable sales talk (until some court finds otherwise), a real estate agent should always maintain keen awareness that if, for any reason, a buyer comes to be unhappy with his or her purchase, such unhappiness is fertile breeding ground for lawsuits against the seller, real estate agents, and anyone else, such as builders, inspectors, or appraisers, who were involved in the transaction.

(ii) Fair Housing Issues in Advertising.

Brokers and salespersons must be particularly careful not to include in advertising for residential properties words, phrases, symbols, or visual aids that might convey either overt or tacit discriminatory *limitations* or *preferences*. What constitutes discriminatory advertising is of particular concern to real estate agents because they are often involved in advertising properties, and are often encouraged by their clients to make certain statements in the advertising, such as that their property is close to certain facilities. If identifying those facilities indicated, for example, a preference for a particular protected group (e.g., "close to Mid-City Korean Recreation Center" or "just two blocks from a popular Jewish deli"), the advertising very likely would be considered impermissibly discriminatory.

The Department of Housing and Urban Development (HUD), which administers the fair housing laws, publishes a list of words, phrases, symbols and visual aids that it considers impermissible in advertising, and also provides an **Equal Housing Opportunity Poster**, which real estate brokers are required to display. The Fair Housing Act also requires that advertisements for the sale, rent, or financing of residential real estate in any print or display advertising (except classified ads) contain the equal opportunity logo.

2. Property Condition

Property Owner's Role Regarding Property Condition:

In many states, the seller of a residential property consisting of 1 to 4 dwelling units is responsible for filling out a **property condition disclosure statement**. On this property disclosure statement, the seller must state the defects in the property that are known, or that upon reasonable inspection should be known, to the seller. This property disclosure statement must be given to the buyer or to the buyer's agent prior to signing a purchase agreement. Failure to state all such defects gives the seller liability to the purchaser.

Pursuant to the federal **Residential Lead-Based Paint Hazard Reduction Act** rule, a seller (or lessor) of a residential dwelling unit built before 1978 must notify a buyer (or tenant) in writing about required disclosures for lead-based paint. The seller must disclose any knowledge he or she has about whether lead-based paint was used in the dwelling unit and must provide the buyer with an EPA pamphlet titled *Protect Your Family From Lead In Your Home*, which describes ways to recognize and reduce lead hazards. The seller must deliver this pamphlet to a prospective buyer before the contract is completed. The seller must also offer a prospective buyer 10 days to inspect for lead-based paint and lead-based paint hazards. The seller is not required to pay for this inspection.

Licensee's Role Regarding Property Condition:

Some states have gone further than to require a seller property disclosure statement by requiring the listing broker to perform a reasonable visual inspection of residential properties consisting of 1 to 4 dwelling units and to disclose defects in the property, both known and discovered through this mandatory inspection, to potential purchasers before a purchase contract is signed.

A licensee may be held responsible for misrepresentations made by sellers if the licensee fails perform due diligence to verify the seller's information.

Home or Construction Warranty Programs:

Home warranty programs are available in most parts of the country both for new homes and for used homes. Builders can obtain insurance for construction defects under a Home Owners Warranty Corporation program.

Existing homes can also be insured to minimize the risks associated with home ownership. These home warranty programs are often purchased by sellers of homes in order to provide an extra incentive to purchase their homes.

A licensee's duty regarding home inspections is to inform clients as to the types of inspections available and the value of having such inspections performed. *A licensee must never recommend a particular inspection company (or other service) in which the licensee has a personal interest without full disclosure to the client.*

The scope of new home (construction) warranties that builders may purchase typically provides that during the first year the builder warrants against structural defects and faulty workmanship and materials. During the second year, the builder warrants against structural defects and defects in wiring and plumbing. Then for an additional number of years, the underwriter ensures against major structural defects, less a deductible of a few hundred dollars.

Homeowners may also purchase, and lenders often require, homeowners insurance, which can be purchased from many different private companies. A basic policy typically covers damage caused by fire, lightning, wind, hail, theft, and vandalism. A broad form homeowners policy typically covers what the basic does plus additional potential causes of damage such as sudden damage to electrical appliances, and damage due to snow and freezing of plumbing or heating/air conditioning systems.

Insurance is also available for tenants (renters policies) that insure against personal liability and against loss of personal belongings due to fire.

Need for Inspection and Obtaining/Verifying Property Condition Information:

One of the fiduciary duties of an agent is to keep the client informed as to all facts that might affect the transaction, including what the agent knows or discovers about the property condition and what potential defects or other problems the agent suspects exist in the property that might affect its value or whether the seller should consider repairing or replacing certain property features before listing the property for sale.

Additionally, even though it may seem that doing so would be a breach of a listing agent's fiduciary duty of loyalty and confidentiality to the seller, many states require an agent to perform *due diligence* to investigate the property to ensure that the property is as represented by the seller and to disclose accurate and complete information regarding the property to potential purchasers. Real estate agents are not expected to be inspection experts, but they are expected to be able to visually inspect properties and to spot "red flag" issues.

Inspections conducted by experts in various fields are often required, both by purchasers and by lenders, as contingencies in purchase contracts. Purchase contracts should specify what remedies should be made, paid by whom, and within what period of time if defects are discovered during the inspection process.

An agent who represents a buyer should recommend that inspections of the buyer's potential new home be conducted by qualified inspectors to:

- evaluate the home's structure, construction, and mechanical systems;
- identify all items that need to be repaired or replaced; and
- estimate the remaining useful life of the plumbing and electrical systems, equipment, structure, and finishes.

Local government inspectors typically inspect new construction before issuing a certificate of occupancy.

Agent Responsibility to Inquire about "Red Flag" Issues:

Licensees should be on the lookout for "red flags" and make inquiry with the owners as to what they know about red-flag issues. It is also important that licensees attempt to verify what sellers tell them before passing such information on to potential customers. Licensees who pass on incorrect information that was given to them by sellers without performing reasonable verification of the information subject themselves to lawsuits from purchasers who, after closing, find that information they were given did not disclose, or, in fact, concealed, material defects. Red-flag issues are conditions that should alert a reasonably attentive person of a potential problem that warrants further investigation. Examples include stains on ceilings or walls, the smell of mold, and warped floors or walls.

Responding to Non-Client Inquiries:

In many states, licensees are responsible for visually inspecting residential properties consisting of 1 to 4 dwelling units, and disclosing to potential purchasers possible defects discovered during this inspection process. Licensees should be on the lookout for "red flags", such as mold smells; stains on, or cracks in, ceilings or walls; warped walls; sloping or cracked floors, and in cracks and foundations, sidewalks, driveways and decks.

Section B: Licensee Advertising

1. Antitrust

Antitrust violations that real estate licensees must avoid is discussed in Chapter 3, Section E, part 4.

2. Do-not-Call List

Prospecting is the process of finding new clients who are interested in selling their properties, and finding customers who are interested in buying the properties. There are many methods of developing new leads, and most of those methods are strictly circumscribed by law.

Phone Calls — the Do-Not-Call Registry. Pursuant to the Telephone Consumer Protection Act (TCPA), the Federal Communications Commission (FCC), together with the Federal Trade Commission (FTC), has established a nationwide Do-Not-Call Registry on which persons may register their phone numbers for free to prevent unwanted phone calls. Once a phone number is on the registry, it will remain there until the person requests that the number be removed or until the person discontinues service of that number.

The Do-Not-Call law applies to nearly all telemarketers and sellers (see exceptions below), including real estate agents who make cold calls, and covers both interstate and intrastate telemarketing calls. Pursuant to the FTC rules, telemarketers are required to search the registry list at least once every 31 days and to remove from their call list all of the phone numbers registered.

Placing a number on the Do-Not-Call Registry does not prevent the following:

- live calls from persons or entities with whom the customer has an established business relationship;

- calls for which the customer has given prior written permission;

- non-commercial calls;

- calls by or on behalf of tax-exempt, non-profit organizations;

- most phone calls to a business made with the intent to solicit business from that business.

Effective October 13, 2013, the FTC imposed additional Do-Not-Call rules, requiring that all sellers and telemarketers must have a consumer's written consent to make prerecorded telephone calls ("robocalls") to residential telephone numbers or auto dialed or prerecorded telemarketing calls or text messages to wireless numbers. This means that business callers must have prior *written* consent before making telemarketing robocalls, even if they have an established business relationship with the consumer. Additionally, robocalls must have an "opt-out" mechanism that allows the receiver of the robocall to opt out of receiving additional calls. This opt-out mechanism must be announced at the beginning of the call and must remain available through the duration of the call.

The FTC has also promulgated regulations implementing the TCPA that are intended to further reduce the number of disturbing calls received by consumers. These regulations include:

- no telemarketing calls before 8 AM or after 9 PM

- a telemarketer must communicate identification of the firm on behalf of which the call is made.

Fines for violation of the Do-Not-Call rules can be up to $16,000 per violation. Additionally, an individual may bring a civil action in state court and receive up to $500 per violation plus actual costs — plus, if the violation was willful or knowing, up to 3 times the damages for each violation.

3. CAN-SPAM Act

CAN-SPAM Act. Despite its name, the *CAN-SPAM Act* does not just cover bulk email; it covers any "commercial email," which is defined as "any electronic mail message the primary purpose of which is the commercial advertisement or promotion of a commercial product or service (including content on an Internet website operated for a commercial purpose)." An email sent to a client or customer concerning an existing transaction or that updates the client or customer about an ongoing transaction is referred to in the law as a *transactional email* and is exempt from the CAN-SPAM rules.

Like the Do-Not-Call and junk-fax laws, each violation of the CAN-SPAM Act is subject to fines up to $16,000. However, unlike the Do-Not-Call and junk-fax laws, recipients have no federal cause of action and most state statutes that deal with spam were preempted by the CAN-SPAM Act. Furthermore, to satisfy the CAN-SPAM Act, a sender need not have prior express approval from, or a prior business relationship with, the recipient in order to send permissible emails to the recipient.

To send a permissible email, the sender must simply satisfy a few requirements. Here is a summary of CAN-SPAM's main requirements, as stated in the FTC's *CAN-SPAM Act: A Compliance Guide for Business*:

1. **Don't use false or misleading header information.** Your "From," "To," "Reply-To," and routing information – including the originating domain name and email address – must be accurate and identify the person or business who initiated the message.

2. **Don't use deceptive subject lines.** The subject line must accurately reflect the content of the message.

3. **Identify the message as an ad.** The law gives you a lot of leeway in how to do this, but you must disclose clearly and conspicuously that your message is an advertisement.

4. **Tell recipients where you're located.** Your message must include your valid physical postal address. This can be your current street address, a post office box you've registered with the U.S. Postal Service, or a private mailbox you've registered with a commercial mail receiving agency established under Postal Service regulations.

5. **Tell recipients how to opt out of receiving future email from you.** Your message must include a clear and conspicuous explanation of how the recipient can opt out of getting email from you in the future. Craft the notice in a way that's easy for an ordinary person to recognize, read, and understand. Creative use of type size, color, and location can improve clarity. Give a return email address or another easy Internet-based way to allow people to communicate their choice to you. You may create a menu to allow a recipient to opt out of certain types of messages, but you must include the option to stop all commercial messages from you. Make sure your spam filter doesn't block these opt-out requests.

6. **Honor opt-out requests promptly.** Any opt-out mechanism you offer must be able to process opt-out requests for at least 30 days after you send your message. You must honor a recipient's opt-out request within 10 business days. You can't charge a fee, require the recipient to give you any personally identifying information beyond an email address, or make the recipient take any step other than sending a reply email or visiting a single page on an Internet website as a condition for honoring an opt-out request. Once people have told you they don't want to receive more messages from you, you can't sell or transfer their email addresses, even in the form of a mailing list. The only exception is that you may transfer the addresses to a company you've hired to help you comply with the CAN-SPAM Act.

7. **Monitor what others are doing on your behalf.** The law makes clear that even if you hire another company to handle your email marketing, you can't contract away your legal responsibility to comply with the law. Both the company whose product is promoted in the message and the company that actually sends the message may be

held legally responsible.

Fax Advertising — the Junk Fax Prevention Act. TCPA and FCC rules also prohibit most unsolicited fax advertisements. Specifically, the *Junk Fax Prevention Act* makes it unlawful to send unsolicited advertisements to any business or residential fax machine without the recipient's prior express permission. However, fax advertisements may be sent to recipients with whom the sender has an established business relationship, as long as the fax number was provided voluntarily by the recipient, such as by a contact form or by posting the fax number in a directory, advertisement, or Internet site. Senders of permissible fax advertisements must notify the recipient that the recipient may opt out of future faxes, and must include a cost-free mechanism, such as a telephone number, fax number, or email address, in which to opt out of future faxes.

As with violations of the Do-Not-Call rules, violations of the rules against sending junk faxes can be up to $16,000 per violation. Additionally, individual recipients of a junk fax may sue in a state court and receive up to $500 per violation plus actual costs — plus, if the violation was willful or knowing, 3 times the damages for each violation.

Internet Advertising. In addition to ensuring that no advertisement is submitted that is deceptive or discriminatory, most states prohibit brokers from running a *blind ad*, which is an advertisement that fails to reveal that the advertiser is an agent, not a principal. In 2014, the National Association of Realtors® (NAR) published their **Model Internet Advertising Rule**, which spelled out Internet marketing rules for licensees and brokerages that advertise properties or brokerage services on the Internet. Among these rules, it is stated that a licensee who authorizes advertising or marketing real property on an Internet site must include on the page of the site on which the licensee's advertisement or information appears the following data:

- the licensee's name;
- the city in which the property being advertised is located;
- the name of the brokerage with which the licensee is affiliated; and
- if the licensee does not hold a real estate license in the jurisdiction in which the property being marketed is located, the name of the regulatory jurisdiction(s) in which the licensee does hold a real estate license.

Electronic Records and Signatures. The National Conference of Commissioners on Uniform State Laws, a nonprofit organization that works for the development of uniformity in state laws, developed the *Uniform Electronic Transaction Act (UETA)*, which provides a legal framework for the use of electronic records and signatures in government or business transactions. UETA provides that electronic records and signatures are as legal as paper and manually signed signatures. As of 2014, 47 states have adopted UETA. Illinois, New York, and Washington have not adopted UETA but have their own laws recognizing electronic signatures.

The *Electronic Signatures in Global and National Commerce Act (E-SIGN)* was enacted by Congress to establish the validity of electronic records and signatures regardless of the medium (e.g., email) in which they are created. E-SIGN governs in the absence of a state law regarding electronic paper and signatures.

4. Fair Housing (e.g., blockbusting, steering)

Protected Classes:

(i) Covered Transactions. Federal fair housing laws prohibit discrimination against members of protected classes in the sale or rental of most residential properties. A *protected class* is any group of people protected from discrimination by federal (or state) law.

(ii) Specific Laws and Their Effects. The Thirteenth Amendment and *Jones v. Mayer*. The *Thirteenth Amendment* to the United States Constitution prohibited slavery in the United States. Using the Thirteenth Amendment as its legal basis, the *Civil Rights Act of 1866* was the first law that protected persons against discrimination in the lease or purchase of real property. *The protections under this Act apply only to race.*

In the 1968 landmark case *Jones v. Mayer*, the United States Supreme Court held that the Civil Rights Act of 1866 *prohibited all racial discrimination, whether private or public, in the sale or rental of either real or personal property.* The important thing to note about *Jones v. Mayer* and the Civil Rights Act of 1866 is that they do not prohibit discrimination only as to certain residential properties (as many later laws do); *they apply to all real property, commercial and residential.*

The Fourteenth Amendment and *Shelley v. Kraemer*. In response to the Civil Rights Act of 1866, many former Confederate states passed laws to limit the rights of former slaves. This led Congress to propose a new amendment to provide protection in the Constitution for rights granted in the 1866 Act. The Fourteenth Amendment prohibited any State from abridging the rights (not just to housing) of any United States citizen.

Following the 1868 enactment of Fourteenth Amendment, courts held that though the Fourteenth Amendment prohibits state and local governments from committing discriminatory acts, it could not be used by courts to prohibit private discriminatory conduct. A notable exception finally came in the 1948 Supreme Court case of *Shelley v. Kraemer*, which held that private racially-based restrictive covenants are invalid under the Fourteenth Amendment. The Court's reasoning was that to enforce such a covenant, the courts would have to be used, and actions of courts are actions of state or federal governments, and hence constitute "state action."

The Civil Rights Act of 1968 and the Federal Fair Housing Act (FFHA). The *Civil Rights Act of 1968* prohibited discrimination in housing based on *race*, *color*, *religion*, or *national origin*. An amendment to this Act in 1974 added prohibition against discrimination based on *sex*, and an amendment in 1988 added prohibition against discrimination based on a person's *disabilities* or *familial status*. Taken together, the Civil Rights Act of 1968 and its subsequent 1974 and 1988 amendments constitute what is called the *Federal Fair Housing Act (FFHA)*, which prohibits discrimination in the sale, rental, and advertising of residential housing.

The FFHA protections for persons with disabilities provides that a blind person may not be prohibited from living with a guide dog in housing projects that prohibit pets. Persons with disabilities must also be allowed to make reasonable modifications to rental units, as long as the modifications are made at the expense of the person with a disability and the person returns the unit to its original state upon termination of occupancy. Additionally, all new residential properties having four or more dwelling units must be constructed to allow access and use by disabled persons.

Equal Credit Opportunity Act (ECOA). Enacted in 1974, the *Equal Credit Opportunity Act (ECOA)* is a federal law that prohibits a lender from discriminating against any applicant for credit on the basis of race, color, religion, national origin, sex, marital status, age (unless a minor), or on the grounds that some of the applicant's income derives from a public assistance program. The law applies to all persons who regularly participate in decisions involving the extending of credit, including retailers, credit card companies, banks and other mortgage lenders.

Under ECOA, an applicant has the right to receive notification from the lender within 30 days as to what action the lender has taken on a loan application. If an adverse action was taken, the lender must send the applicant an ECOA notice about prohibitions against lending discrimination, the name of the federal agency that enforces compliance with ECOA, and the specific reasons for the denial of credit. From its inception in 1974, ECOA has been particularly instrumental in helping women obtain credit on an equal footing with men.

Compliance:

(i) Types of Violations and Enforcement.

FFHA Violations. Real estate salespersons and brokers should be particularly aware that the Federal Fair Housing Act (FFHA) prohibits the following:

- directing people of protected classes away from, or toward, particular areas (a practice called *steering*);

- refusal to loan in particular areas (a practice called *redlining*);

- representing that prices will decline, or crime increase, or other negative effects will occur because of the entrance of minorities into particular areas (a practice called *blockbusting* or *panic selling*);

- discriminatory access to multiple listing services;

- retaliation against, or intimidation of, anyone making a fair-housing complaint; and

- discriminatory advertising, sales, or loan terms.

Equal Credit Opportunity Act Violations. Some of the most important provisions of ECOA are that lenders may not:

- ask if the applicant is divorced or widowed; but may ask if the applicant is married, unmarried (meaning single, divorced, or widowed), or separated;

- ask about birth-control practices, child-bearing capacity or expectations, or whether a woman of child-bearing age will stop working to raise children;

- ask about the applicant's receipt of alimony or child support unless the applicant is first notified that such information need not be given; however, such questions may be asked if the applicant requests that income from such sources be used to qualify for a loan. Lenders may ask whether the applicant has any obligations to pay alimony or child support; or

- discount income based on sex or marital status.

Enforcement of the FFHA. The penalty for a first violation can be up to $50,000; the penalty for each subsequent violation can be up to $100,000. These fines can be supplemented by other civil damages, injunctions, and reasonable attorney's fees and costs.

Enforcement of the Equal Credit Opportunity Act. Failure to comply with the provisions of ECOA can result in punitive damages up to $10,000 for an individual action and up to the lesser of $500,000 or 1% of the creditor's net worth in class actions.

(ii) Exceptions.

The Fair Housing Act does not cover all types of housing. In particular, the Act does not:

- prohibit religious organizations from limiting the sale, rental or occupancy of dwellings to persons of the same religion;

- prohibit a private club, which, incident to its primary purpose, provides lodging for other than a commercial purpose, from limiting the rental or occupancy of such lodging to members;

- limit the applicability of any reasonable local, State or Federal restrictions regarding the maximum number of occupants permitted to occupy a dwelling;

- prohibit conduct against a person because such person has been convicted of the illegal manufacture or distribution of a controlled substance;

- prohibit discrimination in the sale or rental of a single-family house by an owner provided that

    o the owner does not own or have any interest in more than three single family houses at any one time; and

    o the house is sold or rented without the use of a real estate broker, agent or salesperson or the facilities of any person in the business of selling or renting dwellings;

- prohibit discrimination with respect to rooms or units in dwellings containing living quarters occupied or intended to be occupied by no more than four families living independently of each other, if the owner actually maintains and occupies one of such living quarters as his or her residence; or

- prohibit discrimination against children with respect to:

    o properties occupied solely by persons 62 years of age or older; or

    o where at least 80% of the dwelling units are occupied by at least one person who is 55 years of age or older.

CHAPTER 6: PROPERTY MANAGEMENT

Section A: General Principles of Property Management Agreements

In its broadest sense, *property management* is the operation, administration, and maintenance of real estate. Like the role of management in other businesses, the responsibilities of professional property management encompass many functions, including:

- preparing market surveys and advising owners on rental rates;

- advertising for, interviewing, and evicting tenants;

- helping tenants move in and out;

- dealing with tenants and their many diverse complaints related to the premises and to neighbors;

- supervising cleaning, gardening, and landscaping;

- hiring and supervising employees and independent contractors;

- collecting rents, paying expenses and taxes, preparing accounting reports; and

- enforcement of lease provisions, homeowners association rules, and compliance with federal, state, and local laws related to the habitability, maintenance, and occupancy of the properties.

Section B: Basic Provisions/Purpose/Elements of Property Management Agreements

Appointment of the Parties. The Owner and property manager must be identified. Property managers are typically appointed as exclusive agents with the right to rent, lease, operate, and manage certain identified properties. Because a property manager usually acts on behalf of numerous owners, it is important that the broker/manager so inform all of the owners of the properties he or she manages.

Authority and Powers. Typically, a property management agreement grants broad general-agent authority to the property manager to make management decisions regarding the Property without consulting Owner.

Advertising. The property manager will be empowered to display FOR RENT/LEASE and similar signs on the Property and to advertise the availability of the Property for rental or lease. Though not explicitly stated, a property manager, as agent, has the authority to perform those acts that are necessary or normally performed by such agency. All of a property manager's other efforts would be of little value unless the property manager knows how to effectively advertise the property's available space. In the property management context, such advertising activities include placing advertisements in newspapers, maintaining the property website, designing and ordering business cards, billboard advertising, brochures, flyers, and signs for the property. And, of course, when a prospective tenant responds to such advertising, the property manager must possess appropriate person-to-person communication skills and good judgment to secure qualified tenants for vacancies in the property.

117

Rental and Leasing. The property manager will be empowered to sign, renew, modify, or cancel rental and lease agreements for the Property and to collect rents, security deposits, and other appropriate fees and charges. The property management agreement will also limit the rental or lease term that property manager may include in any rental or lease agreement, and provides for some input by the Owner as to the lowest amount of rent acceptable.

Tenancy Termination. The property manager is given broad powers to enforce lease terms, including powers to commence and to prosecute tenant evictions in the Owner's name; to recover possession of the Property; to recover rents and sums due; and, when expedient, to settle tenant law suits and actions.

Repairs; Maintenance. The property manager is empowered to establish and maintain sound repair and maintenance policies.

Contracts and Services. The property manager will be empowered to hire skilled specialists for repair and maintenance of the Property, and may perform any of the manager's duties through attorneys, agents, employees, or independent contractors.

Security Deposits. The property manager is empowered to receive security deposits from tenants and, as instructed by Owner, either give such deposits to Owner or place them in the property manager's trust account.

Reserves. The property manager will be authorized to receive security deposits from tenants and, as instructed by Owner, either give such deposits to Owner or place them in the property manager's trust account.

Disbursements. In property management agreements there is usually a provision regarding the priority of payments. Typically, payments to Owner are made only if there are funds left over after paying the property manager's compensation and all operating expenses and after contributions to the reserve trust account and deposits to the security trust account have been made. Of course, in case of Owner's bankruptcy, these contractually mandated priorities would be preempted by state and bankruptcy law (for example, as to the priority of tenant security deposits).

Owner Representations. Typically, the Owner will represent that unless otherwise specified, the Owner is unaware of

- any recorded Notice of Default affecting the Property (in other words, the commencement of foreclosure proceedings against the Property);
- any delinquency of loans secured by or affecting the Property;
- any bankruptcy, insolvency, or similar proceeding affecting the Property;
- any litigation or government action or other pending or threatened action that may affect the Property or Owner's ability to transfer it; and
- any current, pending, or proposed special assessments affecting the Property.

Furthermore, owner agrees to promptly notify Broker in writing if Owner becomes aware of any of the above items during the term of the agreement.

Compensation. The property management agreement will list the numerous activities for which the property manager will receive compensation. Such compensation is usually stated as a flat fee, a percentage of the property's gross income, or commissions and/or bonuses on new rentals.

Section C: Types of Contracts

Rental and Lease Contracts. The property manager will be empowered to sign, renew, modify, or cancel rental and lease agreements for the Property and to collect rents, security deposits, and other appropriate fees and charges.

Repair and Maintenance Contracts. The property manager will be empowered to establish and maintain sound repair and maintenance policies. Typically, the property manager will not need to get prior Owner approval

- for monthly or recurring operating charges and expenses; or

- for emergency expenses needed (1) to protect the Property or other properties from damage, (2) prevent injury to persons, (3) avoid suspension of necessary services to the Property, (4) avoid penalties or fines; and (5) avoid suspension of services to tenants required by law.

Section D: Duties and Obligations of the Parties

Property Manager Duties and Obligations. A property manager's duties and obligations are discussed in Sections A and C above, and in Sections E-G below.

Owner Duties and Obligations.

In a property management agreement, the owner also has responsibilities — most importantly, (1) to provide the property manager with the records and documents that the manager will need to carry out his or her management duties, (2) to maintain the building in habitable condition, and (3) to ensure that the Property is properly insured and in compliance with all applicable laws, such as zoning and building codes. Of course, the owner and property manager are expected to work together to ensure that most of these owner responsibilities, such as maintaining the property in habitable condition, are in fact fulfilled.

The Owner must provide the property manager with all documents, records, and disclosures required by law to manage and operate the Property, and to immediately notify the property manager of any changes in such documentation, records, or disclosures that Owner becomes aware of.

A property management agreement will have a provision that is often referred to as the *handover process*. A property manager should always approach a potential new client with a healthy degree of skepticism. Understandably, owners often will try to present their properties in the best light — even properties that have been poorly kept up and less-than-well managed. Therefore, it is important that a property manager create a checklist of required information relevant to the property in question.

The following is a list of suggested questions that should be asked about nearly every property; however, each property is unique, having its own problems and potentials, so a broker considering managing the property should create a detailed list of questions, the answers to which will give the property manager a good idea as to what he or she may be getting involved with:

- owner details and contact information;
- tenant and occupant details and contact information;
- tenant and occupant mix, employment, and income;
- details of leases;
- arrears;
- property business plan;
- property layout and building plans;
- property income and expenditures;
- habitability, health, and safety concerns;
- contractor and employee details and contact information;
- past and current maintenance issues;
- reserve funds and potential need to use those funds;
- insurance policies that affect the property or the owner's interest in the property;
- legal documents related to the property.

Section E: Market Analysis and Tenant Acquisition

Market Analysis. A property manager typically is responsible for establishing rental or lease schedules (impliedly, to bring in the highest yield consistent with the owner's expressed wishes). To create optimal rental or lease schedules, the property manager must survey comparable buildings in the area to determine proper rental levels based on the scarcity and comparability of rental rates in the neighborhood. The property manager must also become thoroughly acquainted with the Property so that he or she can objectively assess the Property's assets in relation to the competitive properties surveyed.

To establish optimal rental or lease schedules that will bring in the maximum income obtainable for the owner (consistent with good economics), the property manager should analyze the following characteristics of the neighborhood:

- the character and amenities of competing properties;
- the family size, typical age, and personal income range of prospective tenants;
- the availability of transportation, shopping malls, churches, schools, parks and other recreational facilities;
- the availability of employment and the growth or decline of local industries;
- trends in population growth or decline and the number of occupants per rental unit
- vacancy rates and trends in construction of new residential units intended for rent or lease.

Tenant Acquisition. One of the most important functions of residential property management is keeping the vacancy rates low. To do this, the property manager must be knowledgeable about effectively marketing the property.

Advertising, though necessary, can be quite expensive, so care must be taken to test different advertising media and to write accurate, convincing copy that includes facts potential renters want to know about before going to the effort of responding — facts such as the dwelling's number of rooms, bedrooms, and bathrooms; the square footage; the age and architecture of the property; the views; the property's parking and amenities; the rental and security deposit amounts; and the desirability of the location, including its proximity to schools, shopping centers, transportation, entertainment, and recreational facilities.

There are numerous methods of effectively marketing residential properties:

- newspaper ads;
- signs;
- billboards;
- public transit ads;
- radio ads;
- direct mail;
- rental magazines;
- craigslist;
- online advertising services
- telephone directory ads; and
- referrals.

Regardless of the types of advertisements that the property manager chooses to utilize, there are a few basic pieces of information about the Property that are important to present, given space and price limitations. Prospective tenants will typically scan through a number of ads, eliminating those they deem not worth calling, so advertisements should briefly provide the information that most prospects will want to know before deciding to contact the property manager's rental agent. Such information for rental properties includes:

- location and address of the Property;
- number of bedrooms and bathrooms;
- monthly rent and security deposit;
- utilities;
- amenities; and
- whether the property is furnished or unfurnished

Advertising Laws. When residential property managers prospect for new management business and when they advertise to fill vacancies in managed properties, it is important to keep in mind the various laws — both federal and state — that regulate advertising and promotions regarding residential properties.

The Civil Rights Act of 1968 prohibited discrimination in housing based on race, color, religion, or national origin. An amendment to this Act in 1974 added prohibition against discrimination based on sex, and an amendment in 1988 added prohibition against discrimination based on a person's disabilities or familial status. Taken together, the Civil Rights Act of 1968 and its subsequent 1974 and 1988 amendments constitute what is called the Fair Housing Act.

Real estate salespersons and brokers should be particularly aware that the Civil Rights Act of 1968 and its 1974 and 1988 amendments prohibit the following:

- directing people of protected classes away from, or toward, particular areas (a practice called *steering*);

- refusal to loan in particular areas (a practice called *redlining*);

- representing that prices will decline, or crime increase, or other negative effects will occur because of the entrance of minorities into particular areas (a practice called *blockbusting* or *panic selling*);

- discriminatory advertising, sales, or loan terms;

- discriminatory access to multiple listing services; and

- retaliation against, or intimidation of, anyone making a fair-housing complaint.

It is especially important for property managers to take care not to include in advertising for residential properties words, phrases, symbols, or visual aids that might convey either overt or tacit discriminatory *limitations* or *preferences*. What constitutes discriminatory advertising is of particular concern to residential property managers because they are often involved in advertising properties, and are sometimes encouraged by their clients to make certain statements in the advertising, such as that their property is close to certain facilities. If identifying those facilities indicates, for example, a preference for a particular protected group (e.g., "close to Mid-City Korean Recreation Center" or "just two blocks from a popular Jewish deli"), the advertising very likely would be considered impermissibly discriminatory.

Other words, phrases, symbols, and visual aids that residential property managers should take care never to allow into any of their advertising include:

- words descriptive of the property, the landlord, or current tenants, such as Hispanic residence or Jewish home;

- words indicative of race, color, religion, sex, handicap, familial status, or national origin;

- symbols or logotypes that imply or suggest race, color, religion, sex, handicap, familial status, or national origin;

- directions to the property for rent (whether by written instructions or by use of maps) that may tend to imply a discriminatory preference, limitation, or exclusion, such as references to a synagogue, congregation, or parish, or to existing areas known for its exclusion of, or preference for, particular ethnic or religious groups; or

- descriptions of the location of the property that refer to names of facilities that cater to particular racial, national origin, or religious groups, such as country club or private school designations.

Properties in areas with a high concentration of immigrants might be effectively advertised in foreign language newspapers. *Care must be taken, however, to avoid illegal steering* by also utilizing a suitable mix of advertising channels intended to appeal to a broad range of religious, ethnic, and national origin groups.

In addition to ensuring that no advertisement is submitted that is deceptive or discriminatory, a property manager must be careful not run a **blind ad**, which is an advertisement that fails to reveal that the advertiser is an agent, not a principal.

Section F: Accounts and Disbursement

Trust Fund Accounts for Income Property: The maintenance of proper trust fund accounting is a necessary fiduciary duty of a property manager. A property manager must therefore keep accurate records of all trust funds in accordance with the laws and regulations regarding trust funds. (See Chapter 4, Section E, part 9).

The size of the property management operations will influence the number of bookkeeping records required — a large operation with many clients and office assistance almost certainly will require the bonding of unlicensed persons who can legally handle clients' funds under the supervision of the property management broker. In such a case, an outside accountant should be retained to periodically audit the management accounting records.

Property managers typically maintain three different trust accounts:

- an **operating account** (to handle the generally recurring monthly operating expenses;

- a **reserve fund account** (to handle reserves to pay for items that do not recur on a monthly basis, such as elevator or roof repair or replacement, property taxes, and insurance premiums. By contributing an appropriate amount to such a reserve account on a monthly basis, the monthly financial report given to the owner will give the owner a more accurate picture of the property's ongoing financial condition); and

- a **security deposit account** (to handle the security deposits the property manager is authorized to collect. Having a separate security trust account is recommended because local and state laws relating to security deposits differ from laws relating to other trust funds — for example, local laws may require that tenants receive interest on their security deposits, and state law may give the claim of a tenant priority over the claim of any other creditor of the landlord/owner).

Section G: Property Maintenance and Improvements

Property managers must create and maintain sound policies to routinely inspect the Property and to correct any repair or maintenance problems as soon as they are discovered. Daily, weekly, and monthly checklists should be created and routinely followed by the manager or an employee designated by the manager. Ongoing preventive maintenance is less expensive than delay, which allows such problems to worsen and become more expensive to remedy.

Of course most things, including maintenance, can be overdone; consequently, a property manager should be careful not to use all of the Property's income on maintenance, or such property manager may soon be looking for another job. Maintaining a balance between sound maintenance and satisfying the owner's reasonable expectation of profit can best be achieved by meticulous supervision of all hiring and purchasing operations.

State laws impose strict duties on the owners and property managers of a *residential* building to keep the dwelling in a habitable condition. A breach by a landlord of its duty to maintain the dwelling in a habitable condition, or of its duty to provide tenants with quiet enjoyment of the premises, is called **constructive eviction**.

State laws typically enumerate criteria of habitability, which may include such items as:

- providing effective waterproofing and weather protection of the roof and exterior walls, including unbroken windows and doors;
- installing and maintaining plumbing and gas facilities that conform to applicable law;
- providing hot and cold running water furnished to appropriate fixtures and connected to a sewage disposal system approved under applicable law;
- providing and maintaining heating facilities that conform to applicable law;
- providing and maintaining electrical lighting that conforms to applicable law;
- providing that the building, grounds, appurtenances, and all areas under the control of the landlord be kept clean, sanitary, and free from all accumulations of debris, filth, rubbish, garbage, rodents, and vermin;
- providing and maintaining an adequate number of appropriate receptacles for garbage and rubbish; and
- providing and maintaining floors, stairways, and railings in good repair.

In addition to the above statutory duties of habitability for residential buildings, in many states there is a common-law **implied warranty of habitability** to meet bare living requirements, and that if the landlord breaches this implied warranty the tenant will remain liable for the reasonable rental value of the property in its existing condition as long as the tenant remains in possession of the premises.

For a non-residential lease, the landlord has no legal duty to make repairs or to provide the premises in a condition suitable for the tenant's intended purpose; except that (1) the landlord must maintain and repair those parts of the premises for which the landlord has contractually assumed such obligation pursuant to the terms of the lease, and (2) the landlord must ensure that building codes and other government ordinances are satisfied if the tenant has not assumed those obligations in the lease.

Section H: Evictions

Tenants need landlords/property managers, and landlords/property managers need tenants — they have a natural, mutual attraction for each other — and if they would simply make an effort to understand and respect each other's legitimate rights and interests in the property they both share rights and interests in, unlawful detainer actions (evictions) would, in most cases, be avoided.

If the tenant breaches the lease, the landlord may sue for damages. However, because of the severity of the remedy of termination, courts are unlikely to allow the landlord to terminate the lease for cause unless the breach is material and substantial. Such material and substantial breaches include failure to pay rent, material damage to the property, interference with other tenants' right to quiet enjoyment, breach of a covenant not to assign or sublease the premises, and illegal use of the premises.

Eviction. The word "evict" comes to us from Latin, where it meant to vanquish or to win a point. Today, in English, the word means to win through legal process a court judgment ordering a sheriff to remove a tenant or other occupiers of property from the property.

Eviction of a tenant is a three-step process, involving:

> 1. termination of the lease;

> 2. filing, serving, and succeeding in an unlawful detainer action; and

> 3. if the tenant has not already vacated, physical removal of the tenant by the sheriff.

Termination. A breach of a lease by a tenant, even nonpayment of rent, does not terminate the lease — the tenancy continues until the landlord gives proper notice, which typically is a 3-day, 30-day, 60-day, or 90-day notice, depending on the reason for termination and the type of tenancy involved.

Both tenants and landlords should be aware that because the law of most states (1) frowns on the forfeiture of leases, and (2) provides landlords with expedited eviction procedures, if the landlord makes even a small mistake in drafting or serving the required notice, the court may deny the eviction, thereby returning the landlord to step one: the drafting and serving of a new termination notice.

Illegal Retaliatory Eviction. A typical affirmative defense that a tenant might state in a written answer to an unlawful detainer complaint is that the landlord filed the eviction action in retaliation for the tenant's having exercised one of the tenant's rights, such as complaining to a governmental agency about the habitability of the premises.

Illegal Self-Help Evictions. It is illegal for a landlord to evict a tenant by any means other than by way of the unlawful detainer process as prescribed by state law. Even if the tenant is behind on rent, the landlord may not:

- physically remove the tenant (which may result in a civil action of forcible detainer, and criminal charges of assault, battery, and kidnapping);

- changing the locks or otherwise preventing the tenant from occupying the premises;

- removing any of the tenant's personal property;

- cutting off the utilities; or

- removing any outside doors or windows.

CHAPTER 7: REAL ESTATE CALCULATIONS

Section A: Compensation, Commission, and Fees

Because nearly every real estate agent expects to receive commissions (many, hopefully!), it is not unlikely that a question or two relating to commissions might appear on an exam.

Example: *Jessica is a real estate salesperson who found a buyer for a home that sold for $800,000. Jessica's employing broker received a 5% commission for the sale. The agreement between the broker and Jessica provides that she receive 40% of the broker's commission on every sale she procures. What is Jessica's commission on this transaction?*

Answer: Here the solution is to first find the broker's commission:

5% of $800,000 = .05 × $800,000 = $40,000. Jessica is to receive 40% of $40,000 = .40 × $40,000 = $16,000.

Another way to think about such a problem is to note that Jessica receives 40% of 5% = .40 × .05 = .02 = 2% of the sales price. Using this 2% figure, we find that 2% of $800,000 = .02 × $800,000 = $16,000.

Example: *Bob is a salesperson who works for broker Janet. Bob's agreement with Janet is that he gets a commission of 40% of whatever commission Janet receives on sales made by Bob. Bob procures a sale of a house that was listed by broker Susan, who had a cooperating agent agreement with Janet to split the commission on the sale 50-50. Susan's listing agreement with the owner called for a 6% commission. Bob's commission on the sale was $6,000. How much did the house sell for?*

Answer: Because they tend to be long-winded, these types of problems *appear* to involve much more thought than they actually do — they simply need to be approached methodically, step-by-simple-step, until the answer falls out:

The problem tells us that:

$6,000 = 40% of 50% of 6% of Sales Price

$$= (.4 × .5 × .06) × \text{Sales Price}$$

$$= .012 × \text{Sales Price (i.e., 1.2% of Sales Price)}$$

Therefore, dividing each side of the equation by .012, we get

$500,000 = Sales Price.

Section B: Valuation/Market Sale Price and Yields

Competitive/Comparative Market Analyses (CMA):

We discussed in Chapter 4, Section C, part 3, some of the differences between a comparative market analysis (also referred to as a competitive market analysis) (CMA) and the sales comparison approach to appraisal. However, both the sales comparison approach and a CMA compare in the same manner recent sales of similar local properties to arrive at an estimated market value of a subject property. A detailed example of the sales comparison approach can be found in Chapter 4, Section D, part 1.

The most important thing to keep in mind in a sales comparison appraisal or in a CMA problem is that it is *the values of items of the comparable properties, not the value of items of the subject property, that are adjusted* for differences between the comparables and the subject property. The second most important thing to keep in mind is that if a comparable property has a *superior* feature (such as a better pool) the value of the comparable is adjusted *down* in the amount of the difference between the value of the comparable pool and the value of the subject property pool. On the other hand, had the value of the comparable pool been *less* than the value of the subject pool, the value of the comparable property would have been adjusted *up* accordingly.

Example: *The subject property and a comparable are tract homes that share a common wall. The two houses appear almost exactly the same except that the comparable has an inferior view estimated to be worth $3,000 less than the subject view, and the comparable has superior landscaping estimated to be worth $4,500 more than the subject landscaping. What adjustments should be made?*

Answer: The comparable has a view and landscaping combined value of $1,500 more than the subject view and landscaping value. Therefore, the comparable value should be adjusted down by $1,500.

Net Operating Income:

Net operating income (NOI) is determined as follows:

a) estimate the potential annual gross income the property;

b) deduct from the gross income an annual allowance for vacancies and uncollectible rents to arrive at the ***effective gross income***; and

c) deduct from the effective gross income the estimate of annual operating expenses, including fixed expenses (such as hazard insurance and real estate taxes), maintenance, and reserves for replacements of building components.

Not all expenses are deducted from effective gross income to obtain net operating income. Examples of such expenses include mortgage payments and taxes on income.

Example: *What is the value of a property based on the following information?*

Estimated potential annual gross income: $95,000

Vacancies and uncollectible rents: 7%

Annual maintenance expenses and utilities: $10,000

Annual property taxes: $9,500

Annual insurances: $1,500

Capitalization rate: 9.5%

Answer: $95,000 × .07 = $6,650 (vacancy and uncollectible rents losses)

$95,000 - $6,650 = $88,350 (effective gross income)

$88,350 - $21,000 (operating expenses) = $67,350 (NOI)

$67,350 ÷ .095 = $708,947 (rounded).

Depreciation:

Although many different ways to calculate depreciation are allowed by law (depending on what law one has to satisfy), the only method of depreciation that appears to be tested on real estate license exams is ***straight-line depreciation***, which assumes that the property depreciates by an *equal amount* each year.

Depreciation is based on what is considered the ***useful life*** (also referred to as the ***economic life***) of the property and on the estimated ***residual value*** (also referred to as ***salvage value*** or ***scrap value***) of the property at the end of the property's useful life. Some property, such as computers, have a much shorter useful life than do buildings, so it is always important when considering depreciation to know what the useful life of the item being depreciated is. Straight-line depreciation is defined as:

Annual Depreciation = (Cost of Property - Residual Value) ÷ (useful life in years).

Thus, if the property has a 5-year useful life and no residual value, the rate of (straight-line) depreciation is 100% ÷ 5 years = 20% per year.

Example: *Evan purchases a building for $3,000,000 that has a useful life of 30 years and salvage value of $0. After 10 years, what is the value of the building, if by "value" we mean the original cost less accumulated straight-line depreciation?*

Answer: Here the depreciation rate is: 100% ÷ 30 years = 3⅓ % per year.

3⅓ % per year × 10 years = 33⅓ % depreciation.

33⅓ % of the initial value = 33⅓ % × $3 million = $1 million.

Therefore, value = cost - depreciation = $2,000,000.

Example: If in the above example the land the building was on was worth $750,000, and the question asked for the value of the property after 10 years, the answer would be $2,750,000.

Section C: Net to Seller, Cost to Buyer (credits & debits)

As a general rule, at the close of escrow in a real estate transaction certain allocations of expenses incurred in the ordinary course of property ownership must be made. For example, if the escrow closes midyear or midmonth, the seller may have prepaid taxes, insurance, or association dues, in which case credit to the seller's account should be made. Conversely, if the seller is behind on paying taxes or insurance, etc., the seller's account should be debited. Such an adjustment of expenses that either have been paid or are in arrears in proportion to actual time of ownership as of the closing or other agreed-upon date is called ***proration***. (See Section D immediately below). Proration, like ordinary interest, is generally calculated according to the 30/360 day count convention (statutory year).

To compute proration, follow these steps:

1. determine which, if any, expenses are to be prorated;

2. determine to whom the expenses should be credited or debited;
3. determine how many days the expenses are to be prorated;
4. calculate the per day proration amount; and
5. multiply the number of days by the per day proration amount.

Example: *Susan purchased a condo for $200,000 that had been rented from Bob at $1,500 a month. Escrow closed on September 16. How should the $200,000 selling price be adjusted at close of escrow if the day of closing belongs to the buyer?*

Answer: Rent is normally collected *in advance* on the first day of the month, so unless stated otherwise one should make this assumption in proration of rent problems. Under this assumption, Bob received $1,500 on or about September 1, but only deserved to keep half of the month's rent because Susan acquired ownership of the condo on September 16. Therefore, Susan should be credited $750 at the close of escrow.

Example: Bob sold his condo to Sandra, closing date October 16. Bob had prepaid his monthly homeowner's fee of $465 on the first of the month. How much of the homeowner's fee must the buyer reimburse Bob for if a calendar year is used for the calculation and the closing day belongs to the buyer?

Answer: The number of days the buyer must reimburse Bob for is 31-15 = 16. The daily rate of the homeowner's fee for October was $465 ÷ 31 = $15. Therefore the buyer must reimburse Bob in an amount of $15 × 16 = $240.

Section D: Tax and Other Prorations

When calculating proration problems, it is important to know what *day count convention* to use. An exact calculation would take into account the precise number of days: 30 days for some months, 31 or 28 or 29 for other months; 365 days for some years, 366 for leap years. In the days before computers, such calculations would have been quite burdensome, so the *30/360 day count convention* was adopted to simplify certain calculations. When using the 30/360 day count convention, each month is considered to have 30 days, and each year is considered to have 360 days. A year consisting of 360 days with 12 months of 30 days each is often referred to as a *statutory year*, or a *banker's year*. The 30/360 day count convention for calculating *proration, interest, insurance premiums*, and similar expenses is standard in the real estate market. However, in some areas, rules for calculating proration, interest, etc., are based on the actual number of days in a month or year.

Proration questions that appear on your real estate exam will state whether calculations should be based on 360 or 365 days a year, and whether the day of closing belongs to the seller or to the buyer.

Property taxes are assessed on an *ad valorem* (according to value) basis. The value used is not necessarily the fair market value; rather, it is the assessed value. To find the annual property tax, take the assessed value, subtract any applicable exemption (such as a homestead exemption), and multiply by the annual tax rate.

Example: *A home has a fair market value of $450,000, a homestead exemption of $75,000, an assessed value of $368,000, and a county property tax of 1.2%. What is the annual county property tax on this home?*

Answer: ($368,000 - $75,000) × .012 = $3,516.

Example: *In the above example, what is the amount of tax savings due to the homestead exemption?*

Answer: $75,000 × .012 = $900.

Example: Janet sells her condo to Martha for $200,000, closing date May 16. If property taxes on the condo are $1,800 for each six-months, payable in arrears on July 1 and January 1 of each year, and if proration is calculated on the basis of a banker's year (statutory year), what is the proration amount at closing and is who credited/debited if the day of closing belongs to the buyer?

Answer: Using the banker's year of 30 days per month, at the closing Janet is in arrears in her payment of taxes by 15 days in May and 4 × 30 = 120 days for January through April, total 135 days. Because there are 180 days in six months of a banker's year, the per day tax rate on the $1,800 tax bill is $10. Therefore, 135 days × $10 per day = $1,350, which should be debited to Janet and credited to the Martha.

Transfer Tax. Many states tax the transfer of real estate. These taxes are variously referred to as transfer taxes, conveyance taxes, or stamp taxes and are usually imposed either (1) on the total amount of the transfer price (usually less the amount of a loan or other liens the seller had on the property that the buyer assumes responsibility for paying), or (2) imposed on the amount of either assumed mortgages or newly created mortgages.

Example: *A residential property was purchased for $450,000. The state documentary transfer fee is $.55 for each $500 or fraction thereof. The property was purchased with $400,000 cash and an assumption of the $50,000 seller's mortgage. Assumed mortgages are exempt from the transfer fee in this state. What is the documentary transfer fee?*

Answer: $400,000 = $500 × 800.

800 × $0.55 = $440.

Section E: Amortization

Although interest and principal payments for loans are now calculated on financial calculators or on calculation software freely available on the Internet, we will look briefly at a simplified amortization table to get a feel for how such a chart was used (in the old days) to calculate the monthly payments for fixed-rate loans at various interest rates. (See Figure 10).

The table displays in the left column the interest rate, and in columns to the right, the term in years of a fixed-rate, fully amortized loan. To find the monthly payment *per $1,000* principal borrowed, simply find the intersection of the rate and term of the loan.

Fig. 10

Monthly Payment Per $1,000 on Fixed-Rate, Fully Amortized Loans				
Rate	10-year term	15-year term	30-year term	40-year term
4%	10.125	7.397	4.775	4.180
5%	10.607	7.908	5.369	4.822
6%	11.102	8.439	5.996	5.503
7%	11.611	8.989	6.653	6.215
8%	12.133	9.557	7.338	6.954

Example: *Susan makes payments of $936 per month, including 6% interest on a fixed-rate, fully amortized 30-year loan. What was the initial amount of her loan?*

Answer: Finding where 6% and a 30-year term intersect in the table, we obtain the number 5.996 which is the dollar amount per month per $1,000 of the initial loan.

$5.996/$1,000 = $936/loan amount. Therefore,

loan amount = ($936 ÷ $5.996) × $1,000 = $156,104.

Section F: Points

In finance, a point is equal to 1% of the loan amount. The term is used by lenders to measure charges and other costs such as origination fees and private mortgage insurance premiums. If 1.25 points are charged on a $150,000 loan, the lender would collect 1.25% of $150,000, or $1,875.

Example: *Suppose that Sally is purchasing a house for $250,000 with 20% down. The lender requires 2.5 discount points. How much will Sally pay the lender for the discount points?*

Answer: The loan amount is $250,000 - $50,000 (the down payment) = $200,000.

$200,000 × .025 = $5,000

Section G: Prepayment Penalties

A prepayment penalty is a fee charged to a borrower for paying off a loan faster than scheduled payments call for. The penalty is usually calculated as a percentage of a certain number of months of interest on the loan. Therefore, if the borrower has a $200,000 loan with interest at the rate of 4%, and the prepayment penalty is 80% of six months interest, the prepayment payment would be 80% × 4%/year × ½ year × $200,000 = $3,200.

Section H: Loan-to-Value Ratios

The *loan-to-value ratio (LTV)* is an important risk factor lenders use to assess the viability of a proposed loan. LTV is defined as the amount of a first mortgage divided by the *lesser* of (1) the appraised value of the property or (2) the purchase price of the property. As a general rule, a high LTV (usually seen as over 80%) will either cause:

- the loan to be denied;

- the lender to increase the cost of the loan to the borrower; or

- the lender to require that the borrower pay for private mortgage insurance.

Example: For a property with an appraised value of $100,000, a sales price of $110,000, and a loan of $90,000, the LTV would be $90,000/$100,000 = 90%.

Example: *If a loan has an LTV of 80%, an appraised value of $120,000, and the sales price of $110,000, what is the amount of the loan?*

Answer: LTV = .8 = loan amount/$110,000.

Therefore, loan amount equals $110,000 × .8 = $88,000.

Equity:

Equity is the difference between the current market value of a property and the total indebtedness against the property. If each mortgage payment pays all of the current interest plus some part of the outstanding principal, then the equity increases with each mortgage payment in the amount of the outstanding principal reduction due to the mortgage payment.

Example: Suppose that you have a home with a fair market value $300,000, a first mortgage with outstanding principal of $200,000, and a home equity loan with outstanding principal of $27,000. The equity in your home would be ($300,000 - $200,000) - $27,000 = $73,000.

Home equity loans and home equity lines of credit (HELOC) are loans and lines of credit based on the equity of your home. Typically, these kinds of loans give a loan (or credit line) up to 80% of the appraised value of your home, minus total outstanding indebtedness against the home.

Example: *Joe's home is appraised at $200,000. The first mortgage against his home has an outstanding balance of $100,000. Joe has just arranged to obtain an 80% home equity line of credit of the type described above. What is the amount of his line of credit?*

Answer: ($200,000 × .8) - $100,000 = $60,000.

Note that the answer is NOT ($200,000 - $100,000) × .8 = $80,000.

Down Payment/Amount to Be Financed:

A down payment is the amount of money that a lender requires a purchaser to pay toward the purchase price. Note that a down payment is what a lender requires; an earnest money deposit is what a seller requires. The two are different, though an earnest money deposit is often applied toward the down payment.

Example: Andrew is purchasing a home with a purchase price of $300,000 and an appraised value of $290,000. If the lender is willing to loan 80% of the lesser of the purchase price and the appraised value, how much will be Andrew's down payment?

Answer: Loan amount = $290,000 × .8 = $232,000.

Down payment = purchase price - loan amount = $300,000 - $232,000 = $68,000.

Mortgage Calculations:

Installment loans require periodic payments that include some repayment of principal as well as interest. Installment loans are the most common type of loan used to finance real estate, and the most frequently used installment loan is the *level payment loan* — a loan under which all periodic installment payments are equal, though the amount allocated to principal and interest may vary over the term of the loan. A loan wherein the payments are sufficient to pay off the entire loan by the end of the loan term is referred to as a *fully amortized loan*.

Example: *José purchased a home for $195,130 with a 6% fixed-rate, fully amortized 30-year loan in the principal amount of $156,104. He makes payments of $936 per month. What is the amount of unpaid principal on this loan after the first month's payment?*

Answer: $156,104 × .06 ÷ 12 = $780.52 (first month's interest)

$936 - $780.52 = $155.48 (first month's principal payment)

$156,104 - $155.48 = $155,948.52 (principal balance after first month's payment).

Section I: Measurement (e.g., square footage, acreage, volume)

When calculating the area of something (usually expressed in square feet), remember that the area of a rectangle is base × height and the area of a triangle is ½ × base × height.

Example: *Kevin is going to purchase the lot shown in Figure 11 below and build on it a house and garage, also shown in Figure 10. He has been quoted the following: $150 per square foot for the house; $40 per square foot for the garage; $10 per square foot for the land. What is the total amount that Kevin will pay for this lot, house, and garage?*

Answer: First we calculate the square footage of each item:

house area = 60' × 30' = 1,800 ft.²

garage area = 25' × 18' = 450 ft.²

lot area = ½ × 100' × 150' = 7,500 ft.²

cost of house = 1800 ft.² × $150 per ft.² = $270,000

cost of garage = 450 ft.² × $40 per ft.² = $18,000

cost of the lot = 7500 ft.² × $10 per ft.² = $75,000

Total = $363,000

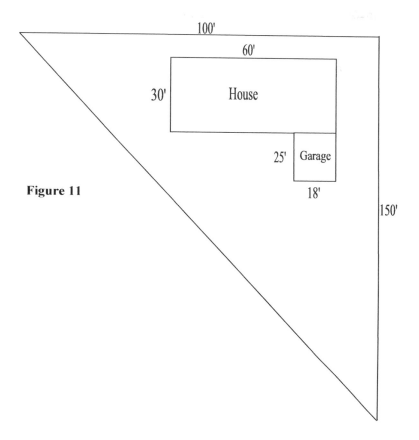

Figure 11

Example: The SW¼ of the SW¼ of the NW¼ of section 10 of Baker Township contains how many square feet?

Answer: A section of a township contains 640 acres. Therefore, ¼ × ¼ × ¼ × 640 acres = 10 acres. Because there are 43,560 square feet per acre, we get 435,600 square feet.

Section J: Property Management/Investment (e.g., rate of return)

Capitalization Rate and Return on Investment. The *capitalization rate* (also referred to as the *cap rate*) is the rate that an appraiser estimates is the yield rate expected by investors from comparable properties in current market conditions. To estimate the capitalization rate of a certain property, an appraiser will collect data on the market value of comparable properties, on the vacancies and uncollectible rents of these comparable properties, and on the operating expenses of these comparable properties. Then, because value = net income ÷ capitalization rate, the capitalization rate can be calculated for these comparable properties as net income ÷ market value.

Example: If the net annual income of a property is $20,000 and the capitalization rate is 8.5% per year, then the income approach valuation of the property would be $20,000 ÷ 8.5% = $235,294 (rounded).

The above example might also take the following form: if an investor purchased a property for $235,294 and derives an annual net income from the property of $20,000, what is the property's capitalization rate? Answer: $20,000 ÷ $235,294 = 8.5%.

A finance concept closely related to the capitalization rate is ***return on investment (ROI)***, which is the investor's cash flow (net income minus financing charges) divided by the investor's *actual cash investment* (as distinct from the purchase price). *Note that the capitalization rate and the ROI would be the same if the investor had paid all cash for the property because in such a case there would be no finance charges and the initial investment would be equal to the sale price.*

Gross rent and gross income multipliers (GRM, GIM). As we have seen, the income approach uses capitalization of *net* operating income to arrive at the valuation of a property. However, some investors, especially of single-family homes, use a simpler method of determining value: capitalization of *gross* income. If only gross rents are capitalized, this approach to value is called the ***gross rent multiplier (GRM)*** approach; if additional income is involved (such as from parking fees), the method is called the ***gross income multiplier (GIM)*** approach.

Example: *Using the gross rent multiplier approach, suppose the sales price of a condo is $1,400,000 and the monthly rent is $5,000. What is the monthly gross rent multiplier of this condo?*

Answer: In this case the sales price is $1,400,000 ÷ $5,000 = 280 times the monthly rental; i.e., the monthly gross rent multiplier is 280.

Example: Suppose now that other comparable homes in the area have a monthly gross rent multiplier similar to the home in the prior example. Further, suppose that a comparable home in the area with a fair market value of $900,000 is to be rented. Using the gross rent multiplier approach, what would be the monthly rent for this subject property.

Answer: By dividing the value ($900,000) by the monthly gross rent multiplier (280), we calculate a rent of $3,214 per month.

Interest Rates:

Interest is the "rent" we pay to possess, use, and enjoy someone else's money. The yearly rent for each dollar we use (borrow) is called the interest rate — if we pay 8¢ each year for each dollar, the interest rate is 8% per year.

Interest problems generally involve four simple concepts:

1. *Interest Rate* (which, to avoid wordiness, we will call Rate);

2. *Principal* (the amount of money borrowed);

3. *Time* (the number of years or fraction of years the principal is borrowed);

4. *Interest Due and Owing* (which we will call Interest).

Because the interest due and owing (Interest) is equal to the interest rate (Rate) times the amount of money borrowed (Principal) times the amount of time the money is borrowed (Time),

Interest = Rate × Principal × Time

The above formula is known as *simple interest*, which considers interest to be generated only on the principal invested. A more rapid method of generating interest earnings is referred to as compounding. **Compound interest** is generated when accumulated interest is reinvested to generate interest earnings from previous interest earnings. Though the amount of interest generated can be revved up by compounding yearly, semiannually, quarterly, daily, or even continuously, real estate exams stick with simple interest, as do most real estate loans on which interest is paid monthly. Interest calculated by the 30/360 day count convention is referred to as **ordinary interest**.

Example: *If $6,000 is loaned for one 30-day month on the basis of simple interest, and the total amount of principal and interest due at the end of that month is $6,017.5, what annual rate of interest was charged?*

Answer: $17.50 (interest) = $6,000 (principal) × (annual interest rate/12).

Therefore, annual interest rate = ($17.50 ÷ $6,000) × 12 = 3.5%

Interest Amounts:

Example: *What is the interest on a $400,000 loan for 1 year, 2 months, and 10 days at 6% interest (using a statutory year)?*

Answer: The time elapsed is 360 days + 60 days +10 days = 430 days.

430 ÷ 360 = 1.19444 years. Therefore, applying our formula

Interest = Rate × Principal × Time, we get

Interest = .06 × $400,000 × 1.19444 = $28,666.56.

Example: *Jessica borrows $12,000 from her friend Susan. The terms of the loan are that principal will be paid back in equal monthly installments over a five-year period along with the interest that was generated at the annual rate of 6% during the month on the outstanding balance of principal owing. What is Jessica's payment to Susan at the end of the second month?*

Answer: To answer this question, we first have to answer another question; namely, how much principal does Jessica pay Susan at the end of the first month? This is due to the fact that Jessica's first month payment will reduce the principal amount on which the second month payment must be calculated.

Because there are 60 months in 5 years, the amount of Jessica's monthly payment attributable to principal is $12,000 ÷ 60 = $200. Therefore, the amount of principal owed after the first-month payment is made is $12,000 - $200 = $11,800. Consequently, the second month payment will be $200 + the interest due on $11,800 *for one month*. Because the interest rate is 6% annually, the monthly rate is 1/2%. Thus, the second-month payment is $200 + 1/2% of $11,800 = $259.

EXAM TEST-TAKING TIPS

- The AMP exam potentially covers a vast amount of real estate knowledge; therefore, taking practice exams — and studying the answers that you get wrong — during the weeks immediately prior to exam day can be highly beneficial.

- You will be graded on the number of correct answers you give. You will not be penalized for giving incorrect answers. Therefore, it is important to answer all of the questions, even if you are not sure of the correct answer. Often, of the four possible answers presented, at least two answers are clearly wrong. Of the remaining two, both might appear correct, in which case you should choose the answer that you feel is the better one. If you cannot decide which one is the better, take your best guess — you'll probably have about a 50-50 chance of being correct.

- Take the time to read each question carefully. It is altogether too easy to interpret a question in a way that you expect the question to read, rather than as it is actually stated. This is especially true for questions that are stated in the negative ("it is not true that…" or "which of the following is false"). Other keywords that can significantly alter the meaning of a question are "except," "but," "if," and "generally."

- Do not rush to choose an answer just because you are relatively certain that it is true. This is because there may be two or more answers given that correctly answer the question, in which case such answers as "both a and b" or "all of the above" may be the best, and correct, answer.

- If math is your most problematic and anxiety producing area, consider saving the math questions to the end and coming back to them when you have completed the rest of the exam. This will prevent you from becoming frustrated and discouraged through most of the exam and will likely give you more time to figure out the correct answers to the math questions.

- You should try to estimate the correct answer to math questions before you begin your calculations. If you find that your estimate is far different from the result of your calculation, carefully go back and check your calculation. Also, be aware that the possible answers presented for math questions usually contain answers that examinees can arrive at by making some common error, such as by calculating based on the number of years rather than on the number of months. Therefore, just because the result of your calculation exactly matches one of the possible answers does not mean that your result is correct.

- Additionally, math real estate questions often use "none of the above" as the fourth possible answer. This means that if you do not get an answer that matches one of the first three possible answers, either your calculation was incorrect or the correct exam answer is "none of the above."

Exam Test-Taking Tips

- Because the extensive glossary included in this book includes terms often found on AMP real estate exams, it is recommended that you review these important key real estate terms at least once each week prior to taking the official AMP exam.

- Finally, if you complete the exam early, as many examinees do, take the remaining time to read over as many of the questions as you can to be sure that you did not make the all-too-common mistake of misreading certain questions the first time around. As you take the following practice exam, you will probably find that you make several "foolish" errors — errors that result not from your lack of knowledge, but from your failure to carefully read certain questions that can at times appear to be a bit tricky. Don't let such "foolish" errors spoil the result of your official exam.

Good luck! And may you have a long and rewarding career as a real estate licensee.

PRACTICE AMP NATIONAL REAL ESTATE EXAM

1. In many states, the seller of a residential property consisting of 1 to 4 dwelling units is responsible for filling out a

   a. sales comparison statement

   b. self-contained report statement

   c. property condition disclosure statement

   d. land condition statement

2. John sees a listing for 32 Oak Avenue published by the seller's agent on the Internet that states the price is $199,000 and that "all cash will take this beauty." John writes to the listing agent the following: "I accept your offer of $199,000, all cash, for 32 Oak Avenue."

   a. The seller has given John a counteroffer.

   b. John has accepted the offer, thereby forming an enforceable contract to purchase the house.

   c. The seller must accept John's offer or issue a counteroffer.

   d. The seller need not accept John's offer or issue a counter offer.

3. The lease that Sherry has for her townhouse contains a provision that gives her the right to purchase the townhouse if the landlord puts the property up for sale and she matches the price and other terms offered by any other potential buyer. Sherry probably has

   a. a right of first refusal

   b. an option to purchase

   c. a lease-purchase agreement

   d. a lease-option agreement

4. A signed will giving his farm to his friend Susan, and a deed granting his farm to his daughter Emily, were discovered in Frank's safe after he died. If the deed was signed before the will, who will probably acquire the farm?

   a. Susan.

   b. Emily because the deed was signed before the will.

   c. Emily because a deed signed during the grantor's life has priority over a will.

   d. Emily because blood relatives have priority over friends.

5. Which of the following items related to a homeowner's personal residence are deductible from federal income tax?

   a. private mortgage insurance

b. repairs on the residence

c. property taxes paid on the residence

d. maintenance and other operating expenses of owning a principal place of residence

6. John and Susan decide to lease their single-family home for the months of June and July while they vacation in Alaska. They authorize ABC Realty to handle the rental, specifying that they want the rental to go only to another African-American couple because they do not want to upset their neighbors. Pursuant to the Federal Fair Housing Act, John and Susan's instruction to ABC Realty is

a. legal because minorities can give preference to members of the same minority in rentals

b. legal because owner-occupied, single-family homes are exempt under the FFHA

c. legal because John and Susan were just looking out for the sensibilities of their neighbors

d. illegal

7. Susan is a land developer, and Emily is a broker whom Susan approaches to handle the sale of one of Susan's newly developed lots. Emily agrees to handle the sale, but only on condition that Susan agrees to hire Emily to sell Susan's remaining lots. This is an example of

a. a tying arrangement

b. market allocation

c. price-fixing

d. group boycott

8. Evan purchased a rectangular lot measuring 125' deep by 160' along the street. Zoning regulations require a 15' setback from the street and a 10' setback along all other sides. What are the buildable dimensions of Evan's lot?

a. 115' × 145'

b. 110' × 140'

c. 100' × 140'

d. 115' × 145'

9. Sally dismantled her pergola, stacking the lumber in a corner of her backyard. The lumber became personal property through an act of

a. annexation

b. heterogeneity

c. severance

d. fixity

10. To exercise eminent domain, an appropriate governmental body must satisfy certain requirements, including that

    a. the governmental body demonstrate that the taking will result in an increase in the property's fair market value

    b. the governmental body must pay at least 110% of the property's assessed value

    c. the governmental body must demonstrate that the property was not used in conformance with existing zoning laws

    d. the property must be necessary for the public purpose for which it is supposedly being taken

11. Which of the following is not an aspect of the definition of the market value of a property?

    a. the seller is not under undue pressure to sell

    b. the buyer and seller are not related

    c. the buyer and seller are operating in a competitive and open market

    d. the buyer and seller must agree on the market value before signing a purchase agreement

12. Private mortgage insurance (PMI)

    a. is insurance that lenders often require for loans with an LTV more than 75%

    b. covers the top amount of a loan in case of default

    c. insures the borrower

    d. insures the trustee

13. In states that permit the practice, a _____ owes fiduciary duties to a specified principal, but other agents in the brokerage may represent other parties to the same transaction that the specified principal is a party to without creating a dual agency situation.

    a. dual agent

    b. designated agent

    c. subagent

    d. single agent

14. There is a rule of equity known as _____ that holds that one who causes another to rely on his or her words or actions shall be prohibited from later taking a contrary position detrimental to the person who so relied.

    a. estoppel

    b. ratification

    c. express agreement

d. the equal dignities rule

15. If I promise to pay you $20 if you mow my lawn on Tuesday, and you shrug your shoulders and say, "I'll see if I have the time," then unless I withdraw my offer in the meanwhile and you go ahead and mow my lawn on Tuesday

    a. I will owe you $20.

    b. I will not owe you $20 because you did not expressly accept my offer.

    c. I will not owe you $20 because there was never a "meeting of the minds."

    d. I will not owe you $20 because of the parol evidence rule.

16. A chain of title is

    a. a complete chronological history of all documents affecting the title to a property

    b. a statement by the title insurance company of the condition of the title and of the terms and conditions upon which it is willing to issue a policy

    c. a duplicate of county title records maintained at title insurance companies for use in title searches

    d. a court proceeding intended to establish the true ownership of a property

17. Examples of trust funds include

    a. advance fees paid by a seller to an agent to cover expected outlays of the agent

    b. a broker's real estate commissions

    c. security deposits from a broker's own real estate

    d. rent from a broker's own real estate

18. John's lender gave him an $88,000 loan based on a loan-to-value ratio (LTV) of 80% of the lesser of the appraised value of the property, which was $120,000, or the sales price. What was the sales price of John's property?

    a. $110,000

    b. $120,000

    c. $100,000

    d. none of the above

19. Joe permits his friend Bob to park Bob's motorcycle in Joe's garage, but Joe does not want to say or write anything about making this arrangement permanent because Joe is not sure how long he will be able to put up with the coming-and-going noise. Joe should give Bob what?

    a. a month-to-month lease

    b. a license

    c. an easement

d. a riparian right

20. As a general rule, zoning that merely reduces the value of a property does not give the owner the right of _____ as long as the property still has viable economic use.

   a. inverse condemnation

   b. escheat

   c. injunction

   d. special assessment

21. When using the sales comparison approach to appraisal,

   a. if a feature of a comparable is inferior to the same type of feature in the subject property, then the difference in value of features is added to the comparable property

   b. if a feature of a comparable is inferior to the same type of feature in the subject property, then the difference in value of features is subtracted from the comparable property

   c. similar properties that were sold through short sales are used

   d. similar properties that were sold at foreclosure sale are used

22. Helen owns a home in which she has a large amount of equity. She wishes to acquire a loan to help with monthly expenses over the rest of her life. What type of mortgage may be best suited for Helen's needs?

   a. a fully amortized mortgage

   b. a level payment mortgage

   c. a reverse mortgage

   d. a conforming mortgage

23. Most states require that the buyer's agent disclose the agency relationship to the buyer

   a. before close of escrow

   b. before the buyer signs the purchase agreement

   c. as soon as all contingencies have been met

   d. before the seller signs the listing agreement

24. Which of the following statements is false?

   a. All real estate agency compensation is subject to negotiation.

   b. If an agent representing a buyer receives compensation indirectly from the seller, the agent is a dual agent.

c. By accepting or retaining the benefit of an act made by an unauthorized agent or by an agent who has exceeded his or her authority, a principal can create an agency by ratification.

d. An agent does not necessarily represent the person paying the commission.

25. John goes into Joe's Eats and orders a hamburger, fries, and a beer. The surly waiter just grunts, and walks toward the kitchen. Before the order is served, John and Joe's Eats have

   a. no contract

   b. an implied, executed contract

   c. an express, executed contract

   d. an implied, executory contract

26. Emily entered into a written contract to sell her condo to John, but John breached the contract and refused to go through with the sale. If Emily wants a court to order John to complete the sale, she should

   a. seek rescission of the contract

   b. seek liquidated damages

   c. seek specific performance

   d. seek compensatory damages

27. Emily sells her house, giving a deed that warrants that she owns the property, has the right to convey it, and that the property was not encumbered during the period of time that she owned the house. Emily gave what type of deed?

   a. quitclaim deed

   b. grant deed

   c. special warranty deed

   d. general warranty deed

28. A broker with a net listing on a condo finds a buyer who pays $300,000 for the condo. The condo had a loan balance of $100,000; the closing costs were $5,000; the seller's specified net was $200,000; and there were no other claims against the property or cost of sale. How much commission would the broker receive from this transaction?

   a. $20,000

   b. $15,000

   c. $5,000

   d. $0

29. The subject property and a comparable are homes that appear almost exactly the same except that the comparable as an inferior pool estimated to be worth $2,000 less than the

subject pool, and the comparable has superior landscaping estimated to be worth $1,500 more than the subject landscaping. What adjustments should be made?

   a. adjust the subject property value up by $500

   b. adjust the subject property value down by $500

   c. adjust the comparable property value up by $500

   d. adjust the comparable property value down by $500

30. A point of beginning is a necessary feature of the

   a. U.S. government survey system

   b. metes and bounds system

   c. rectangular survey system

   d. recorded plat system

31. Which of the following is not an example of police power?

   a. Zoning codes

   b. Eminent domain

   c. Building codes

   d. Subdivision regulations

32. The replacement cost approach is likely to be the appraisal approach of choice if

   a. the property is an old house

   b. zoning laws have recently increased the market value of the property

   c. a recent increase in crime in the area has had a significant detrimental effect on the value of the property

   d. there are few if any comparables in the area and the income approach is inappropriate

33. Which of the following statements is false?

   a. A seller carry back loan is a loan or credit given by a seller of real property to the purchaser of that property.

   b. Under a land installment contract, the seller does not convey legal title to the buyer until all installments are paid.

   c. The buyer under a land installment contract is referred to as the vendee.

   d. Upon the closing of a land installment contract, the seller conveys legal title to the buyer.

34. A property management agreement is usually

   a. created by ratification

b. a verbal agreement between a property owner who has property to manager and a property manager

c. created by estoppel

d. a written agreement between a property owner who has property to manage and a property manager

35. Randy owns a shoe store in a shopping mall. His lease calls for a base rent amount plus 1% of the gross receipts of his store. What type of lease does Randy have?

a. net lease

b. graduated lease

c. percentage lease

d. ground lease

36. Ronald enters into a contract to sell his condo to Bob. The purchase agreement contains a clause that specifically states what each party must pay in damages in case of a breach. This clause is called a

a. liquidated damages clause

b. specific performance clause

c. severability clause

d. ironclad merger clause

37. Recording a deed to real property with the county recorder provides

a. actual notice to subsequent purchasers or encumbrancers.

b. constructive notice to subsequent purchasers or encumbrancers.

c. acknowledgment to subsequent purchasers or encumbrancers.

d. responsibility to subsequent purchasers or encumbrancers.

38. During an open house, the listing agent tells a prospective customer: "In my opinion, you won't find a house with a more tranquil, resort-like feel anywhere else in the city." This agent's statement most likely would be considered

a. negligent misrepresentation

b. negative fraud

c. puffing

d. intentional misrepresentation

39. Which of the following statements is false?

a. A broker is responsible for training and supervising his or her salespersons.

b. A protection clause is a concept developed by the courts to determine the proportioning of commissions among agents involved in a real estate transaction.

c. most states have adopted the Uniform Electronic Transaction Act.

d. an independent contractor is a person who performs work for someone, but does so independently in a private trade, business, or profession, with little or no supervision from the person for whom the work is performed.

40. To obtain a lower interest rate for the purchase of a $300,000 condo, Joyce has arranged to pay the lender 1.5 points for a loan in the amount of 80% of the purchase price. How much will Joyce have to pay for these discount points?

a. $4,500

b. $3,000

c. $2,400

d. none of the above

41. States where water is scarce typically adopt water rights based on

a. prior appropriation theory

b. riparian rights

c. littoral rights

d. the doctrine of capture

42. When two or more parcels are assembled together to make a larger parcel, the value added resulting from this assemblage is called

a. plottage value

b. progression value

c. utility value

d. integration value

43. In an adjustable-rate mortgage, the margin generally is

a. a predetermined number of percentage points

b. a benchmark rate of interest that is adjusted periodically

c. subtracted from the index to obtain the fully indexed rate

d. an initial rate often referred to as a teaser rate

44. If a broker is a co-owner of a property and the other owners authorize the broker to represent the property for sale,

a. the broker's agency is coupled with an interest

b. the seller may terminate the listing because agency is a personal relationship based on trust and confidence

c. the seller may terminate the agency because of the conflict of interest

d. the broker is what is referred to as a designated agent

45. Categories of stigmatized properties include

a. properties that were once used as brothels

b. properties located in floodplains

c. properties with defective heaters

d. properties with leaky roofs

46. After Olivia received an offer of $375,000 for her house from Bob, she counteroffered at $395,000. Before Bob accepted the counteroffer, Olivia received an offer from John for $399,000. Olivia can accept John's offer if

a. she notifies Bob of the better offer and gives him a chance to match John's offer

b. John's offer satisfies every term of her offer to Bob

c. she withdraws her counteroffer to Bob before his acceptance is delivered to her

d. she waits to hear from Bob

47. Evaluate the following two statements: (1) the parol evidence rule is a law that requires particular types of lawsuits to be brought within a specified time after the occurrence of the event giving rise to the lawsuit; (2) in a court action for specific performance, the amount of consideration is important.

a. Both statements are correct.

b. The first statement is correct and the second statement is false.

c. The first statement is false and the second statement is true.

d. Both statements are false.

48. The type of nondisclosure known as concealment refers to

a. the act of expressing a positive opinion about something to induce someone to become a party to a contract

b. the act of preventing disclosure of something

c. the unauthorized misappropriation and use of another's funds or other property

d. an event that may, but is not certain to, happen, the occurrence upon which the happening of another event is dependent

49. Margaret is purchasing a home with a purchase price of $280,000 and an appraised value of $275,000. If the lender is willing to loan 80% of the lesser of the purchase price and the appraised value, how much will be Margaret's down payment?

a. $60,000

b. $56,000

c. $55,000

d. none of the above

50. In a particular township, which section is just south of section 2?

    a. 9

    b. 10

    c. 11

    d. 12

51. A house has recently been built. The building inspector has discovered that the height of the house is 1½ feet greater than allowed by applicable zoning regulations. The owner of the house should apply for

    a. variance

    b. conditional use

    c. spot zoning

    d. nonconforming use

52. David added a pool and an elevator to his two-story house. The resulting value of David's house increased by an amount less than the combined cost of the pool and elevator. This is an example of the principle of

    a. anticipation

    b. contribution

    c. assemblage

    d. progression

53. Which of the following statements is false?

    a. A universal agent is an agent given power of attorney to act on behalf of a principal for an unlimited range of legal matters.

    b. A dual agent is a real estate broker who represents both the buyer and the seller in a real estate transaction.

    c. An ostensible agent is an agent authorized by a real estate broker to represent a specific principal to the exclusion of all other agents in the brokerage.

    d. A subagent is an agent of an agent.

54. A broker has the least protection with

a. a multiple listing

b. an open listing

c. an exclusive agency listing

d. an exclusive right to sell listing

55. George offers to buy Emily's condo for $150,000. Emily replies that she needs at least $175,000. George replies that he is no longer interested because he has found a more suitable property. Emily, desperate to move, emails back that she will accept the $150,000. George replies that now he will only pay $130,000. George and Emily have

a. a contract to purchase the condo for $150,000

b. a contract to purchase the contract for $130,000

c. a contract to purchase the condo for $175,000

d. no contract

56. Under _____, the lender merely gives the debtor proper notice and prepares the proper papers; a court sets a period of time for the debtor to redeem the property by paying all past-due payments; and if the debtor fails to so redeem the property, title passes to the lender and the debtor loses all rights and interests (including equity) in the property.

a. nonjudicial foreclosure

b. judicial foreclosure

c. strict foreclosure

d. one-action foreclosure

57. John is a widower who lives in a rather large home the couple purchased 40 years ago. Wanting some company in his old age, and a little extra income, John decides to rent the maid's room. While interviewing prospective renters, John makes it known that he only wants to rent to a white Christian woman over the age of 50.

a. John is doing nothing illegal because his is an owner-occupied, single-family home, which is exempt from Federal Fair Housing Act rules.

b. John is violating Federal Fair Housing Act rules that protect against religious discrimination in housing.

c. John is violating Federal Fair Housing Act rules that protect against sex and age discrimination in housing.

d. John is violating the Civil Rights Act of 1866.

58. A home has a fair market value of $550,000, a homestead exemption of $100,000, an assessed value of $468,000, and a county property tax of 1.2%. What is the annual county property tax on this home?

a. $5,400

b. $5,616

c. $4,320

d. none of the above

59. A mechanics lien is a _____; a judgment lien is a _____.

a. voluntary lien, involuntary lien

b. specific lien, general lien

c. general lien, specific lien

d. involuntary lien, voluntary lien

60. The SW¼ of the SW¼ of the NW¼ of Section 10 of Baker Township contains how many acres?

a. 80

b. 40

c. 160

d. 10

61. What federal law was designed to ensure that the parties responsible for polluting a site would be held responsible for its cleanup?

a. Coastal Zone Management Act

b. Clean Water Act

c. Comprehensive Environmental Response, Compensation, and Liability Act

d. Brownfields Revitalization Act

62. The income approach to appraisal estimates the value of an income-producing property through which of the following three-step process?

a. determine the gross annual income, determine the appropriate depreciation rate, divide the net income by the capitalization rate

b. determine the net annual income, determine the appropriate capitalization rate, divide the net income by the capitalization rate

c. determine the net annual income, determine the appropriate depreciation rate, divide the gross income by the capitalization rate

d. determine the gross annual income, determine the appropriate capitalization rate, divide the gross income by the capitalization rate

63. One of the disadvantages of an FHA-insured loan is

a. relatively high LTVs

b. down payments can be gifted by a relative

c. upfront mortgage insurance premiums (upfront MIP) and annual MIP premiums

d. the loans cannot have a prepayment penalty

64. Broker Greg knows that Susan lost her job 3 months ago and is desperate to sell her house and move into a rented apartment. If he discloses Susan's plight to Julie, Greg would not be violating real estate law.

a. Greg likely is a dual agent.

b. Greg likely is the listing agent for the house.

c. Greg likely is a buyer's agent.

d. Greg likely is Susan's attorney in fact.

65. An informal name for various federal and state laws that provide for the registration of sex offenders is

a. Stigmatized Property Disclosure Law

b. Sex Registration Law

c. Megan's Law

d. Mitchell's Law

66. Which of the following statements regarding the Residential Lead-Based Paint Hazard Reduction Act is false?

a. A seller (or lessor) of a residential dwelling unit built before 1978 must notify a buyer (or tenant) in writing about required disclosures for lead-based paint.

b. A lead-based paint hazard pamphlet must be given to prospective purchasers but not to tenants.

c. A seller must disclose knowledge that the seller has about whether lead-based paint was used in the dwelling.

d. A seller must offer a prospective buyer 10 days to inspect for lead-based paint and lead-based paint hazards.

67. The escrow instructions for Larry's purchase of a condo from Emily state that Larry is assuming Emily's $85,000 mortgage. The escrow holder will make what adjustment(s) at closing?

a. credit Emily $85,000, debit Larry $85,000

b. debit Emily $85,000, credit Larry $85,000

c. no adjustment to either Emily or Larry

d. credit Emily $85,000, no adjustment to Larry

68. Placing a number on the Do-Not-Call Registry prohibits

a. live calls from persons or entities with whom the customer has an established business relationship

b. Commercial calls from persons with whom the receivers of the calls have no established business relationship

c. calls for which the customer has given prior written permission

d. calls by or on behalf of tax-exempt, non-profit organizations

69. Stephen makes payments of $1,275 per month, including 4% interest on a fixed-rate, fully amortized 15-year loan. What was the initial amount of his loan?

Monthly Payment Per $1,000 on Fixed-Rate, Fully Amortized Loans				
Rate	10-year term	15-year term	30-year term	40-year term
4%	10.125	7.397	4.775	4.180
5%	10.607	7.908	5.369	4.822
6%	11.102	8.439	5.996	5.503
7%	11.611	8.989	6.653	6.215
8%	12.133	9.557	7.338	6.954

a. $305,024

b. $267,016

c. $172,367

d. none of the above

70. Which of the following does *not* represent an exception to "first to record, first in right"?

a. real estate taxes

b. judgment liens

c. subordination agreements

d. special assessments

71. Under the Residential Lead-Based Paint Hazard Reduction Act a seller of a residential dwelling unit built before 1978 does not need to

a. notify a buyer in writing about disclosures for lead-based paint

b. pay for a lead-based paint inspection prior to close of escrow

c. disclose any knowledge the seller has about whether lead-based paint was used in the dwelling unit

d. provide the buyer with a pamphlet titled *Protect Your Family From Lead in Your Home*

72. The process of ascertaining value by comparing and evaluating values obtained from different valuation approaches is called

a. averaging the valuations

b. adjustment

c. reconciliation

d. value correction

73. Which of the following statements is false about the VA-guaranteed loan program?

   a. The VA does not make loans.

   b. Approved lenders make the VA-guaranteed loans.

   c. Persons who served only in the National Guard are not eligible.

   d. The VA guarantee works much like PMI.

74. Which of the following statements is true?

   a. Typically, real estate law requires that a licensee who is acting *solely* as a principal in a real estate transaction must reveal his or her status as a licensee.

   b. A conflict of interest can only exist if there is actual undue influence.

   c. Conversion is the act of improperly segregating the funds belonging to the agent from the funds received and held on behalf of another.

   d. Real estate law typically does not require that a licensee who is acting *solely* as a principal in a real estate transaction must reveal his or her status as a licensee.

75. A seller of a single-family home tells the listing agent that she is moving because of gang activity nearby. The agent should

   a. contact the police

   b. keep the seller's information confidential because the agent's fiduciary duty to the seller includes loyalty and confidentiality

   c. disclose this fact to potential purchasers

   d. only schedule showings after sunset

76. A lease of a single-family home is

   a. a contract and a conveyance

   b. a contract but not a conveyance

   c. a conveyance but not a contract

   d. neither a contract nor a conveyance

77. Related to the sale of real estate, which of the following is not required on form 1099-S?

   a. seller's name

   b. seller's Social Security number

   c. market value appraisal of the property transferred

d. gross sale proceeds of the transfer

78. Even though a broker may not be personally at fault, the broker

a. can be held responsible for all of the conduct of his or her employees or agents

b. can be held responsible for any negligent act of his or her employees or agents

c. can be held responsible for any tortious conduct of his or her employees or agents

d. can be held responsible for the negligent conduct of employees or agents who act within the scope of their employment or agency

79. Kathy is a salesperson who receives 45% of the total commission received by her broker from the sale of a house Kathy listed. What is the broker's net share of the commission if the house sold for $845,000, the commission rate was 6%, and a cooperating broker received half of the commission?

a. $11,407.50

b. $13,942.50

c. $27,885.00

d. none of the above

80. A cable company is planning to extend new fiber optic cable across Sally's backyard. The cable company should apply for

a. an easement in gross

b. a license

c. an easement appurtenant

d. an encroachment variance

81. Arnold sells Bob a parcel of land "on condition" that the land never be used to sell alcoholic beverages. Two years later, Bob builds a retail building on the site, obtains a license to sell alcoholic beverages, and subsequently begins selling wine and beer at the site. Who may bring an action for forfeiture of title against Bob?

a. Arnold

b. the zoning commission

c. the state alcoholic beverages board

d. the county Board of Supervisors

82. Which of the following statements is true?

a. a CMA never considers properties that have not sold

b. a CMA takes into consideration square footage of comparable properties

c. a CMA can only be prepared by a licensed appraiser

d. a CMA is typically not used to help set the list price for a property

83. A developer has a mortgage loan that secures three different parcels of land. This developer has what kind of mortgage?

    a. an assumption mortgage

    b. a subordination mortgage

    c. a level payment mortgage

    d. a blanket mortgage

84. Which of the following statements is true?

    a. In dual agency, conflicts of loyalty and confidentiality cannot arise.

    b. Conversion is the act of placing funds belonging to clients or customers into accounts also holding the agent's funds.

    c. If the seller wants to know whether the buyer is willing to pay a higher price, the listing agent who is a dual agent must not disclose a price concession from the buyer without the buyer's consent.

    d. Conversion is the act of placing funds belonging to clients or customers into accounts also holding the agent's funds.

85. Many states have a _____, under which a choice of either a judicial or nonjudicial foreclosure must be made

    a. judicial foreclosure rule

    b. nonjudicial foreclosure rule

    c. one-action rule

    d. limited choice rule

86. A desert city passes a zoning ordinance that prohibits swimming pools containing more than a certain number of cubic meters of water. Susan's pool is considerably larger than the new zoning ordinance allows, but she is told by the zoning board that she may keep her pool. This is an example of

    a. nonconforming use

    b. spot zoning

    c. conditional use

    d. inclusionary zoning

87. Which of the following is not a triggering term?

    a. amount of down payment

    b. annual percentage rate

    c. amount of any payment

d. number of payments to be made

88. George knowingly misrepresented the size of his house when he sold it to Susan. The purchase contract between them is

a. valid and enforceable because escrow closed

b. void from its inception

c. voidable by either George or Susan

d. voidable by Susan

89. Which of the following statements is false?

a. A lease-option provides that the lessee has the right to purchase the property at the specified price and terms any time prior to a specified date, but has no obligation to do so.

b. A graduated lease is similar to a gross lease except that it provides for periodic increases in the rent, often based on the Consumer Price Index.

c. In an option contract, the optionee grants to the optionor the right to purchase property for a specific sum at any time during the option term without creating an obligation by the optionee to do so.

d. Under a gross lease, the tenant pays a fixed rental amount, and the landlord pays all of the operating expenses for the premises.

90. One of the implied warranties in a grant deed is that the grantor will convey all after-acquired title. This warranty means that

a. the grantor has not transferred title to anyone else

b. all interests in the property acquired by the grantor subsequent to the conveyance of the deed automatically pass to the grantee

c. the property at the time of execution is free from any encumbrances made by the grantor, except for those disclosed

d. the grantor owned the property and has the right to sell it

91. A residential property was purchased for $375,500. The state documentary transfer fee is $.75 for each $500 or fraction thereof. The property was purchased with $300,500 cash and an assumption of the $75,000 seller's mortgage. Assumed mortgages are exempt from the transfer fee in this state. What was the documentary transfer fee?

a. $562.50

b. $112.50

c. $450.75

d. $450.00

92. Which of the following statements is false?

a. The largest real estate trade association in the United States is the National Association of Real Estate Brokers.

b. Most states have adopted the Uniform Electronic Transaction Act.

c. The Electronic Signatures in Global and National Commerce Act was enacted by Congress to establish the validity of electronic records and signatures regardless of the medium (e.g., email) in which they are created.

d. An email sent to a client or customer concerning an existing transaction or that updates the client or customer about an ongoing transaction is referred to in the law as a transactional email and is exempt from the CAN-SPAM rules.

93. Under a deed of trust, who typically holds the promissory note?

    a. the trustee

    b. the beneficiary

    c. the trustor

    d. the borrower

94. The monthly gross income multiplier is calculated by

    a. dividing the sales price of the property by the monthly net rental income

    b. dividing the sales price of the property by the monthly gross rental income

    c. dividing the sales price of the property by the monthly net income

    d. dividing the sales price of the property by the monthly gross income

95. John, a known hermit, died without leaving a will. No heirs could be found. Eventually, a court ruled that title to John's home be transferred to the state. This is an example of

    a. eminent domain

    b. escheat

    c. progressive taxation

    d. condemnation

96. Susan granted her sister, Mary, an estate for the life of her brother, John. If Mary dies before John, the estate

    a. vests in John for his life

    b. reverts to Susan

    c. vests in whoever is entitled to Mary's interest in the estate for the life of John

    d. ceases to exist

97. Bob sold his condo to Sandra, closing date October 16. Bob had prepaid his monthly homeowner's fee of $465 on the first of the month. How much of the homeowner's fee must

the buyer reimburse Bob for if a calendar year is used for the calculation and the closing day belongs to the buyer?

    a. $232.50

    b. $240

    c. $225

    d. none of the above

98. Amanda is involved in the sale of a condo, is not an agent for either the buyer or the seller, but owes both the buyer and the seller the obligation to act fairly, honestly, and competently toward them. Amanda likely is a

    a. dual agent

    b. seller's agent

    c. transactional broker

    d. designated agent

99. A developer has a mortgage from XYZ Bank that states that construction liens recorded against the secured property later than XYZ's lien will take priority over XYZ's lien. The XYZ mortgage contains a

    a. prepayment penalty clause

    b. partial release clause

    c. subordination clause

    d. subrogation clause

100. Emily and Olivia, though close friends, are competing brokers in the same small town. They agree that it would be in their mutual best interests, and in the interests of their clients, if Emily handled all of the town's "luxury listings" (list price over $200,000) and Olivia handled all of the other listings. This is an example of

    a. an impermissible tying arrangement

    b. price-fixing

    c. illegal market allocation

    d. a legal agreement because both brokers decided that they could better serve their clients through this kind of specialization

Answers

1.   c. In many states, the seller of a residential property consisting of 1 to 4 dwelling units is responsible for filling out a property condition disclosure statement.

2.   d. An MLS listing, or an advertisement for a listed property, is not an offer that can be accepted — it is merely a public notification that a certain property is available for which an offer is being solicited.

3.   a. A right of first refusal is the right to be given the first chance to purchase a property at the same price, terms, and conditions as is offered to third parties if and when the property is put up for sale.

4.   a. Emily could acquire the property only if she could prove that the deed had been legally delivered to her during her father's life. The fact that the deed was found in his safe after his death creates a (rebuttable) presumption of nondelivery.

5.   c. Property taxes paid on the residence are deductible.

6.   d. There is nothing in the FFHA that says that a member of a minority may discriminate based on race. Answer b is incorrect because the owner-occupied, single-family home exemption does not apply if the sale or rental is handled by a real estate licensee.

7.   a. In real estate agency, a typical case of an *impermissible* tying arrangement occurs when the sale of a property is conditioned upon the agent's obtaining the listing for future sales.

8.   c. The zoning regulations require that the depth of the lot (125') be reduced by 15' + 10' = 25' and that the length of the lot (160') be reduced by 10' + 10' = 20'. Therefore, the dimensions of the buildable area of the lot are 100' × 140'.

9.   c. Severance is the act of detaching an item from real property that changes the item to personal property.

10.   d. To exercise eminent domain, an appropriate governmental body must satisfy certain requirements, including that the property must be necessary for the public purpose for which it is supposedly being taken.

11.   d. The buyer and seller must agree on a selling price, but not on the market value.

12.   b. PMI *insurers the lender*, not the borrower, and covers the top amount of the loan in case of default.

13.   b. In states that permit the practice, a designated agent owes fiduciary duties to a specified principal, but other agents in the brokerage may represent other parties to the same transaction that the specified principal is a party to without creating a dual agency situation.

14.   a. There is a rule of equity known as estoppel that holds that one who causes another to rely on his or her words or actions shall be prohibited from later taking a contrary position detrimental to the person who so relied.

15.   a. Your act of mowing my lawn constituted both your acceptance of my offer and your full performance.

16.   a. A chain of title is a complete chronological history of all documents affecting the title to a property.

17.   a. Examples of *non*-trust funds include a broker's real estate commissions, rent and security deposits from a broker's own real estate, and any other funds personally owned by a broker.

18.   a. $88,000 = 80% × (the lesser of $120,000 or the sales price). Therefore, $88,000 ÷ .8 = $110,000 = (the lesser of $120,000 or the sales price), so the sales price was $110,000.

19.   b. Joe should give Bob a license because, unless otherwise agreed, a license can be revoked at any time.

20.   a. Zoning that merely reduces the value of a property does not give the owner the right of inverse condemnation as long as the property still has viable economic use.

21.   a. If a feature of a comparable is inferior to the same type of feature in the subject property, then the difference in value of features is added to the comparable property.

22.   c. A reverse mortgage is loan for homeowners 62 years of age or older who have a large amount of equity in their homes, usually designed to provide such homeowners with monthly payments, often over the lifetime of the last surviving homeowner who either moves out of the house or dies.

23.   b. Most states require that the buyer's agent disclose the agency relationship to the buyer before the buyer signs the purchase agreement.

24.   b. The source of compensation does not determine agency representation. For example, an agent may represent only the buyer, but receive his or her entire commission as a commission split with the listing broker, in which case 100% of the buyer's agent commission would come (indirectly) from the seller.

25.   d. The contract is executory because it has not been fully performed (the food has not yet been served, and John has not paid). The contract is implied because no promises have been expressed. The enforceable implication is that if John is served, he will pay the price listed on the menu.

26.   c. Emily is requesting the court to order John to complete the sale; she is not requesting monetary damages. Therefore, she should seek specific performance.

27.   c. In a special warranty deed, the grantors warrant that they own the property and have the right to convey it, and that the property was not encumbered during the period of their ownership.

28.   d. In this transaction, the seller got less than the net amount that the seller specified in the listing. Because the broker owed a fiduciary duty to the seller, the broker had to present all offers to the seller, even offers that might result in the broker receiving no compensation whatsoever.

29.   c. The comparable has a pool and landscaping combined value of $500 less than the subject pool and landscaping value. Therefore, the comparable value should be adjusted up by $500.

30.   b. The metes and bounds system starts at a point of beginning, then works around the parcel, and finally ends at the beginning point.

31.   b. One should be careful to distinguish eminent domain, for which just compensation must be made, from police power, which is the power of a government to impose restrictions on private rights, including property rights, for the sake of public welfare, health, order, and security, for which no compensation need be made. Examples of the use of police power in

regard to real property include the creation and enforcement of zoning codes, building codes, subdivision regulations, and property setbacks.

32.　　d. The cost approach is likely to be the approach of choice if (1) there are few if any comparables in the area (thus eliminating the sales-comparison approach) and the income approach is inappropriate, or (2) the improvements are quite new so that data on precise current costs can be gathered.

33.　　d. Upon the closing of a land installment contract, the buyer takes immediate possession of the property, but the seller does not convey legal title to the buyer until all installments are paid.

34.　　d. A property management agreement is usually a written agreement between a property owner who has property to manage and a property manager.

35.　　c. Under a percentage lease, which is often used in shopping centers, the tenant typically pays a base rent amount plus a percentage of the gross receipts of the tenant's business.

36.　　a. A liquidated damages clause provides that that a certain sum of money will serve as the exact amount of damages that will be paid upon a breach of the contract.

37.　　b. Recording provides access to information regarding ownership of the property and imparts constructive notice to subsequent purchasers or encumbrancers.

38.　　c. Couched as an opinion and absent an intent to deceive, this statement would most likely be viewed as puffing — mere sales talk.

39.　　b. A protection clause (also referred to as a safety clause) provides that the broker will earn the full commission under certain circumstances for a sale made after the termination of the agency.

40.　　d. Loan amount = 80% of $300,000 = $240,000.
The cost of 1.5 points on a $240,000 loan is .015 × $240,000 = $3,600.

41.　　a. States where water is scarce typically adopt water rights based on prior appropriation theory.

42.　　a. When two or more parcels are assembled together to make a larger parcel, the value added resulting from this assemblage is called plottage value.

43.　　a. In an adjustable-rate mortgage, the margin generally is a predetermined number of percentage points.

44.　　a. If a broker is a co-owner of a property and the other owners authorize the broker to represent the property for sale, the broker's agency is coupled with an interest.

45.　　a. A stigmatized property is a property having a condition that certain persons may find materially negative in a way that does not relate to the property's actual physical condition.

46.　　c. Until Olivia receives an acceptance of her counteroffer from Bob, she is free to accept another offer regardless of whether it is superior to Bob's offer.

47.　　c. The parol evidence rule is a rule of evidence that prohibits the introduction of extrinsic evidence of preliminary negotiations, oral or written, and of contemporaneous oral evidence, to alter the terms of a written agreement that appears to be whole. In a court action for specific performance, the amount of consideration is important. Specific performance is an equitable remedy commonly sought by one party to a real estate contract seeking a court order requiring the other party to perform what was specifically stated in the contract (such as transferring the deed to the property), as an alternative to awarding damages. As a general rule, to obtain an equitable remedy (as opposed to a legal remedy of monetary damages), the fairness or adequacy of consideration will weigh heavily in the court's deliberations.

48.   b. Concealment refers to the act of preventing disclosure of something.

49.   a. Loan amount = $275,000 × .8 = $220,000.
Down payment = purchase price - loan amount = $280,000 - $220,000 = $60,000.

50.   c. See diagram below.

A theoretical township showing numbered sections (large bold type) and adjacent township sections (smaller regular type).							
36	31	32	33	34	35	36	31
1	6	5	4	3	2	1	6
12	7	8	9	10	11	12	7
13	18	17	16	15	14	13	18
24	19	20	21	22	23	24	19
25	30	29	28	27	26	25	30
36	31	32	33	34	35	36	31
1	6	5	4	3	2	1	6

51.   a. Variance refers to an exception that may be granted in cases where damage to the value of a property from the strict enforcement of zoning ordinances would far outweigh any benefit to be derived from enforcement.

52.   b. The principle of contribution (also referred to as the principle of diminishing marginal returns) states that improvements made to a property will contribute to its value or that, conversely, the lack of a needed improvement will detract from the value of the property.

53.   c. An ostensible agent's agency is created when a principal intentionally, or by want of ordinary care, causes a third person to believe another to be his agent who is not actually employed by the principal.

54.   b. An open listing agreement may be made by a seller to any number of brokers, though only one commission would be paid, going to the agent who first procurers an offer acceptable to the seller. The seller also reserves the right to sell the property to a buyer procured by the seller, without paying a commission to any broker. Furthermore, the sale of the property automatically terminates all outstanding open listing agreements for the property, without the need for notification on the part of the seller to the brokers to whom the seller gave an open listing. For these reasons, few agents are willing to spend time on open listings.

55.   d. George and Emily have no contract because a counteroffer is a rejection of the prior offer, and they have not agreed on a price.

56.   c. In a strict foreclosure, the lender merely gives the debtor proper notice and prepares the proper papers; a court sets a period of time for the debtor to redeem the property by paying all past-due payments; and if the debtor fails to so redeem the property, title passes to the lender and the debtor loses all rights and interests (including equity) in the property.

57.   d. The Civil Rights Act of 1866 prohibits *all* racial discrimination in the lease or sale of real and personal property. The fact that John's property is exempt from the FFHA does not mean that his property is exempt from all other applicable antidiscrimination laws.

58.   d. ($468,000 - $100,000) × .012 = $4,416.

59.   b. A mechanics lien is a specific lien; a judgment lien is a general lien. Both mechanics liens and judgment liens are involuntary liens.

60.   d. A section of a township contains 640 acres.
Therefore, ¼ × ¼ × ¼ × 640 acres = 10 acres.

61.   c. The Comprehensive Environmental Response, Compensation, and Liability Act (also referred to as the Superfund Law) is intended to clean up sites contaminated with pollutants and toxic wastes.

62.   b. The income approach estimates the value of an income-producing property as being an investment (like stocks or bonds) worth the present value of the future income of the property through a three-step process: (1) determine the net annual income, (2) determine an appropriate capitalization rate, and (3) divide the net income by the capitalization rate to obtain the estimate of value; i.e., value = net income ÷ capitalization rate.

63.   c. One of the disadvantages of an FHA-insured loan is upfront mortgage insurance premiums (upfront MIP) and annual MIP premiums.

64.   c. If Greg were a dual agent, the listing agent or Susan's attorney in fact, he would owe fiduciary duties to Susan, which would involve holding Susan's financial condition confidential.

65.   c. Megan's law is an informal name for various federal and state laws that provide for the registration of sex offenders and for the making available to the public information regarding the location of these offenders.

66.   b. The EPA pamphlet Protect Your Family From Lead In Your Home must be given to tenants as well as to buyers.

67.   b. Larry's assuming Emily's mortgage results in Emily's receiving an $85,000 benefit, so $85,000 should be credited to Larry and debited to Emily.

68.   b. Placing a number on the Do-Not-Call Registry prohibits commercial calls from persons with whom the receivers of the calls have no established business relationship.

69.   c. Finding where 4% and a 15-year term intersect in the table, we obtain the number $7.397 which is the dollar amount per month per $1,000 of the initial loan.
$7.397/$1,000 = $1,275/loan amount. Therefore,
loan amount = ($1,275 ÷ $7.397) × $1,000 = $172,367.

70.   b. Real estate taxes, special assessments, and subordination agreements present exceptions to the general lien priority of first to record, first in right.

71.   b. Under the Residential Lead-Based Paint Hazard Reduction Act, a seller is not required by to pay for a lead-based paint inspection.

72.   c. The process of ascertaining value by comparing and evaluating values obtained from different valuation approaches is called reconciliation.

73.   c. Persons who served in the National Guard or Selected Services are also eligible, usually with six years service.

74.   d. Typically, real estate law does not require that a licensee who is acting *solely* as a principal in a real estate transaction must reveal his or her status as a licensee.

75.   c. Known external conditions that, because of their severity, may rise to the level of material facts (such as neighbors who throw loud parties, neighbors with dogs that bark throughout the night, gang activity nearby, etc.) should be disclosed.

76.   a. A lease transfers an estate in the real property leased. A lease also constitutes an executory bilateral contract between landlord and tenant that governs such matters as the landlord's maintenance of the property and the tenant's duty to make lease payments.

77.   c. The IRS requires escrow agents to report every sale of real estate on Form 1099-S, giving the seller's name, Social Security number, and the gross sale proceeds. A market value appraisal of the property is not required.

78.   d. Even though a broker may not be personally at fault, because the employees and associated licensees are agents of the broker, the broker can be held responsible for the negligent conduct of employees or agents who act within the scope of their employment or agency.

79.   b. Kathy's broker's gross is 3% of the sales price of $845,000, which is $.03 \times \$845,000 = \$25,350$. The broker's net is 55% of $25,350 = $13,942.50.

80.   a. An easement in gross is an easement that benefits a legal person rather than other land.

81.   a. Because Bob clearly violated a condition in the deed restriction, Arnold may bring an action to enforce the condition through forfeiture of title.

82.   b. A CMA takes into consideration many potential adjustments in comparable properties, including square footage.

83.   d. A blanket mortgage is a mortgage used to finance two or more parcels of real estate.

84.   c. In any dual agency, conflicts of loyalty and confidentiality can arise, such as when, for example, the buyer wants to know whether the seller is willing to take a lower price, or conversely, when the seller wants to know whether the buyer is willing to pay a higher price. In such cases, a dual agent must not disclose price concessions from either party without the consent of the other party.

85.   c. A holder of a mortgage or deed of trust with a power-of-sale clause may, if so desired, use judicial foreclosure; however, many states have a one-action rule, under which a choice of either judicial or non-judicial foreclosure must be made.

86.   a. Nonconforming use refers to an exception for areas that are zoned for the first time or that are rezoned and where established property uses that previously were permitted do not conform to the new zoning requirements. As a general rule, such existing properties are "grandfathered in," allowing them to continue the old use but not to extend the old use to additional properties or to continue the old use after rebuilding or abandonment.

87.   b. Stating only the APR in an advertisement does not trigger the requirement for additional financial term disclosures.

88.   d. A voidable contract is a contract that is enforceable at the option of one party but not at the option of the other, as when the consent of one party (the party who may elect to have the contract enforced) is obtained by fraud (not forgery, which would render the contract void), coercion, misrepresentation, or undue influence.

89.   c. In an option contract, the *optionor* grants to the *optionee* the right to purchase property for a specific sum at any time during the option term without creating an obligation by the optionee to do so.

90.   b. The after-acquired title warranty in a grant deed means that all interests in the property acquired by the grantor subsequent to the conveyance of the deed automatically pass to the grantee.

91.   c. $300,500 = $500 × 601.
601 × $.75 = $450.75.

92.   a. The largest real estate trade association in the United States is the National Association of Realtors® (N.A.R.), which was established in 1908.

93.   b. Under a deed of trust, the lender (beneficiary) holds the promissory note; the trustee holds legal title with power to sell upon default by the borrower.

94.   d. The monthly gross income multiplier is calculated by dividing the sales price of the property by the monthly gross income (not just rental income).

95.   b. Escheat is a process whereby property passes to the state (or in some cases the county) if a person owning the property dies intestate without heirs. If no heirs of a decedent can readily be found, publication is made to locate heirs, but if none comes forward to claim the property within a statutorily mandated time, the court will order an escheat of the property to the state.

96.   c. The life estate continues for the duration of John's life, regardless of the duration of the life tenant's life.

97.   b. The number of days the buyer must reimburse Bob for is 31-15 = 16. The daily rate of the homeowner's fee for October was $465 ÷ 31 = $15. Therefore the buyer must reimburse Bob in an amount of $15 × 16 = $240.

98.   c. Some states permit a broker to act *not* as an agent who represents one or more parties to a real estate transaction, but to act as a mere middleman who brings the parties together and lets the parties do all of the negotiating among themselves. Such a nonagent broker (also referred to as a *transactional broker, facilitator, intermediary, coordinator,* or *contract broker*) does not owe fiduciary duties to either party and is therefore not held to the same legal standards of conduct as is an agent. However, the states that permit this kind of nonagent status impose an obligation on the nonagent to act fairly, honestly, and competently to find qualified buyers or suitable properties.

99.   c. A subordination clause states that the mortgage or deed of trust will have lower priority than a mortgage or deed of trust recorded later.

100.   c. Market allocation occurs when competitors agree to divide up geographic areas or types of products or services they offer to customers. It is no defense that Emily and Olivia may have honestly thought that their agreement was in their clients' best interest.

GLOSSARY

1031 exchange — under Internal Revenue Code section 1031, a tax-deferred exchange of "like kind" properties.

1099-S Reporting — a report to be submitted on IRS Form 1099-S by escrow agents to report the sale of real estate, giving the seller's name, Social Security number, and the gross sale proceeds.

abendum clause — a clause in a deed, usually following the granting clause and beginning with the words "to have and to hold," that describes the type of estate being transferred.

acknowledgment — a written declaration signed by a person before a duly authorized officer, usually a notary public, acknowledging that the signing is voluntary.

acknowledgment of satisfaction — a written declaration signed by a person before a duly authorized officer, usually a notary public, acknowledging that a lien has been paid off in full and that the signing is voluntary.

abandonment — failure to occupy or use property that may result in the extinguishment of a right or interest in the property.

abatement — a legal action to remove a nuisance.

abstract of judgment — a summary of the essential provisions of a court monetary judgment that can be recorded in the county recorder's office of the county or counties in which the judgment debtor owns property to create a judgment lien against such properties.

abstract of title — a chronological summary of all grants, liens, wills, judicial proceedings, and other records that affect the property's title.

abstractor — the person who prepares an abstract of title.

acceleration clause — a clause in either a promissory note, a security instrument, or both that states that upon default the lender has the option of declaring the entire balance of outstanding principal and interest due and payable immediately.

acceptance — consent (by an offeree) to an offer made (by an offeror) to enter into and be bound by a contract.

accession — the acquisition of additional property by the natural processes of accretion, reliction, or avulsion, or by the human processes of the addition of fixtures or improvements made in error.

accretion — a natural process by which the owner of riparian or littoral property acquires additional land by the gradual accumulation of soil through the action of water.

accrued depreciation — depreciation that has happened prior to the date of valuation.

acknowledgment — a written declaration signed by a person before a duly authorized officer, usually a notary public, acknowledging that the signing is voluntary.

acknowledgment of satisfaction — a written declaration signed by a person before a duly authorized officer, usually a notary public, acknowledging that a lien has been paid off in full and that the signing is voluntary.

active investor — an investor who actively contributes to the management of the business invested in.

actual agency — an agency in which the agent is employed by the principal, either by express agreement, ratification, or implication.

ad valorem — a Latin phrase meaning "according to value." The term is usually used regarding property taxation.

adjustable-rate mortgage (ARM) — a mortgage under which interest rates applicable to the loan vary over the term of the loan.

adjusted cost basis — the dollar amount assigned to a property after additions of improvements and deductions for depreciation and losses are made to the property's acquisition cost.

adjustment period — the time intervals in an adjustable-rate mortgage during which interest rates are not adjusted.

administrator — a person appointed by a probate court to conduct the affairs and distribute the assets of a decedent's estate when there was no executor named in the will or there was no will.

advance fee — a fee charged in advance of services rendered.

adverse possession — the process by which unauthorized possession and use of another's property can ripen into ownership of that other's property without compensation.

after-acquired interests — all interests in a property acquired subsequent to a transfer of the property.

affirmative covenant — a contractual promise to do certain acts, such as to maintain a party wall, the remedy for breach thereof being either monetary damages or injunctive relief, not forfeiture.

age-life method — *see*, straight-line method.

agency — the representation of a principal by an agent.

agent — a person who represents another.

alienation clause — a due-on-sale clause

alluvium — addition to land acquired by the gradual accumulation of soil through the action of water.

ambulatory instrument — a document that can be changed or revoked, such as a will.

amended public report — a report that a subdivider must apply for if, after the issuance of a final public report, new conditions arise that affect the value of the subdivision parcels.

Americans with Disabilities Act — a federal act that prohibits discrimination against persons with disabilities, where "disability" is defined as "a physical or mental impairment that substantially limits a major life activity."

amortization — in general, the process of decreasing or recovering an amount over a period of time; as applied to real estate loans, the process of reducing the loan principal over the life of the loan.

anchor bolt — a bolt inserted into concrete that secures structural members to the foundation.

annual percentage rate (APR) — expresses the effective annual rate of the cost of borrowing, which includes all finance charges, such as interest, prepaid finance charges, prepaid interest, and service fees.

appraisal — an estimate of the value of property resulting from an analysis and evaluation made by an appraiser of facts and data regarding the property.

appreciation — an increase in value due to any cause.

appropriation, right of — the legal right to take possession of and use for beneficial purposes water from streams or other bodies of water.

appurtenance — an object, right or interest that is incidental to the land and goes with or pertains to the land.

asbestos — a naturally occurring mineral composite that once was used extensively as insulation in residential and commercial buildings, in brake pads, and in fire-retardant products, such as furniture. As asbestos ages, it breaks down to small fibers that, if inhaled in sufficient quantity over sufficient time, can cause a variety of ailments, including a type of cancer known as mesothelioma.

assignment — the transfer of the rights and obligations of one party (the assignor) to a contract to another party (the assignee); a transfer of a tenant's entire interest in the tenant's leased premises.

associate broker — a person with a real estate brokers license who is employed as a salesperson by another broker.

assumption — an adoption of an obligation that primarily rests upon another person, such as when a purchaser agrees to be primarily liable on a loan taken out by the seller.

attachment lien — a prejudgment lien on property, obtained to ensure the availability of funds to pay a judgment if the plaintiff prevails.

attorney in fact — a holder of a power of attorney.

automatic homestead —a homestead exemption that applies automatically to a homeowner's principal residence and that provides limited protection for the homeowner's equity in that residence against a judgment lien foreclosure.

average price per square foot — the average price per square foot for a given set of properties is arrived at by adding the per-square-foot cost of each property in the set by the number of properties in the set.

avulsion — a process that occurs when a river or stream suddenly carries away a part of a bank and deposits it downstream, either on the same or opposite bank.

back-end ratio — the ratio of total monthly expenses, including housing expenses and long-term monthly debt payments, to monthly gross income.

balloon payment — a payment, usually the final payment, of an installment loan that is significantly greater than prior payments — "significantly greater" generally being considered as being more than twice the lowest installment payment paid over the loan term.

bankruptcy — a legal process conducted in a United States Bankruptcy court, in which a person declares his or her inability to pay debts.

beam — a horizontal member of a building attached to framing, rafters, etc., that transversely supports a load.

bearing wall — a wall that supports structures (such as the roof or upper floors) above it. In condominiums, non-bearing walls are owned by the individual condominium owners, whereas bearing walls usually are property owned in common.

beneficiary — (1) the lender under a deed of trust, (2) one entitled to receive property under a will, (3) one for whom a trust is created.

bequeath — to transfer personal property by a will.

bequest — a gift of personal property by will.

bilateral contract — a contract in which a promise given by one party is exchanged for a promise given by the other party.

bill of sale — a written document given by a seller to a purchaser of personal property.

blanket mortgage — a mortgage used to finance two or more parcels of real estate.

blight — as used in real estate, the decline of a property or neighborhood as a result of adverse land use, destructive economic forces, failure to maintain the quality of older structures, failure to maintain foreclosed homes, etc.

blind ad — an advertisement that does not disclose the identity of the agent submitting the advertisement for publication.

blockbusting — the illegal practice of representing that prices will decline, or crime increase, or other negative effects will occur because of the entrance of minorities into particular areas.

board foot — a unit of measure of the volume of lumber, equivalent to the volume of lumber of 1 square foot and 1 inch thick; 144 cubic inches.

bona fide — in good faith; authentic; sincere; without intent to deceive.

book depreciation — a mathematical calculation used by tax authorities and accountants to determine a depreciation deduction from gross income.

book sale — a "sale" for accounting purposes regarding tax-delinquent property; this "sale" does not entail an actual transfer property.

boot — cash or other not like-kind property received in an exchange.

bridge loan — a short-term loan (often referred to as a swing loan) that is used by a borrower until permanent financing becomes available.

broker — a person who, for a compensation or an expectation of compensation, represents another in the transfer of an interest in real property.

brownfields — as defined by the EPA, "real property, the expansion, redevelopment, or reuse of which may be complicated by the presence or potential presence of a hazardous substance, polluted, or contaminant."

BTU (British Thermal Unit) — A measure of heating (or cooling) capacity equivalent to the amount of heat required to raise the temperature of 1 pound of water 1° Fahrenheit (from 39°F to 40°F).

buffer zone — in zoning, a strip of land to separate, or to ease the transition from, one use to another, such as a park separating a residential zone from a commercial zone, or a commercial or industrial zone separating residential zones from busy streets or highways.

bulk sale — a sale, not in the ordinary course of the seller's business, of more than half of the value of the seller's inventory as of the date of the bulk sale agreement.

bundle of rights — rights the law attributes to ownership of property.

business opportunity — involves the sale or lease of the assets of an existing business enterprise or opportunity, including the goodwill of the business or opportunity, enabling the purchaser or lessee to begin a business.

buyer's agent — a real estate broker appointed by a buyer to find property for the buyer.

capital asset — permanent, non-inventory assets held for personal or investment purposes, such as householders' homes, household furnishings, stocks, bonds, land, buildings, and machinery.

capital gain — the amount by which the net sale proceeds from the sale of a capital asset exceeds the adjusted cost value of the asset.

capitalization approach — *see*, income approach

capitalization rate — the annual net income of a property divided by the initial investment in, or value of, the property; the rate that an appraiser estimates is the yield rate expected by investors from comparable properties in current market conditions.

capture, law of — the legal right of a landowner to all of the gas, oil, and steam produced from wells drilled directly underneath on his or her property, even if the gas, oil, or steam migrates from below a neighbor's property.

carryover —under an adjustable-rate loan, an increase in the interest rate not imposed because of an interest-rate cap that is carried over to later rate adjustments.

caulking — a putty-like material used to seal cracks and joints to make tight against leakage of air or water, as in making windows watertight.

CC&Rs — an abbreviation of "covenants, conditions, and restrictions" — often used to refer to restrictions recorded by a developer on an entire subdivision.

certificate of occupancy — a written document issued by a local governmental agency, stating that a structure intended for occupancy has been completed, inspected, and found to be habitable.

chain of title — a complete chronological history of all of the documents affecting title to the property.

chattel real — personal property that contains some interest in real property, the most common example being a lease.

Civil Rights Act of 1866 — a federal law enacted during Reconstruction that stated that people of any race may enjoy the right to enforce contracts, to sue, be parties, and give evidence, to inherit, purchase, lease, sell, hold, and convey real and personal property, and to full and equal benefit of all laws.

Civil Rights Act of 1968 — a federal law (often referred to as the Fair Housing Act) that prohibited discrimination in housing based on race, creed, or national origin. An amendment to this Act in 1974 added prohibition against discrimination based on gender, and an amendment in 1988 added prohibition against discrimination based on a person's disabilities or familial status.

client — an agent's principal

closing — in reference to an escrow, a process leading up to, and concluding with, a buyer's receiving the deed to the property and the seller's receiving the purchase money.

cloud on title — any document, claim, lien, or other encumbrance that may impair the title to real property or cast doubt on the validity of the title.

coastal zone — a region where significant interaction of land and sea processes occurs.

Coastal Zone Management Act (CZMA) — a federal act intended to protect coastal zones, including the fish and wildlife that inhabit those zones, of the Atlantic, Pacific, and Arctic oceans, the Gulf of Mexico, Long Island Sound, and the Great Lakes from harmful effects due to residential, commercial, and industrial development.

collar beam — a beam connecting pairs of opposite rafters well above the attic floor.

column — a circular or rectangular vertical structural member that supports the weight of the structure above it.

commercial acre — the buildable part of an acre that remains after subtracting land needed for streets, sidewalks, and curbs.

commingling — regarding trust fund accounts, the act of improperly segregating the funds belonging to the agent from the funds received and held on behalf of another; the mixing of separate and community property.

commission — an agent's compensation for performance of his or her duties as an agent; in real estate, it is usually a percent of the selling price of the property or, in the case of leases, of rentals.

common interest development (CID) — a subdivision in which purchasers own or lease a separate lot, unit, or interest, and have an undivided interest or membership in a portion of the common area of the subdivision.

community apartment project — a development in which an undivided interest in the land is coupled with the right of exclusive occupancy of an apartment located thereon.

community property — property owned jointly by a married couple or by registered domestic partners, as distinguished from separate property. As a general rule, property acquired by a spouse or registered domestic partner through his/her skills or personal efforts is community property.

community property with right of survivorship — property that is community property and that has a right of survivorship. Upon the death of a spouse or registered domestic partner, community property with right of survivorship passes to the surviving spouse or domestic partner without probate.

comparable property — a property similar to the subject property being appraised that recently sold at arm's length, where neither the buyer nor the seller was acting under significant financial pressure.

comparative market analysis (CMA) — a comparison analysis made by real estate brokers using recent sales, and current listings, of similar nearby homes to determine the list price for a subject property.

competitive market analysis (CMA) — *see*, comparative market analysis.

compound interest — the type of interest that is generated when accumulated interest is reinvested to generate interest earnings from previous interest earnings.

concealment — the act of preventing disclosure of something.

condemnation proceeding — a judicial or administrative proceeding to exercise power of eminent domain.

condition subsequent — a condition written into the deed of a fee estate that, if violated, may "defeat" the estate and lead to its loss and reversion to the grantor.

conditional use — a zoning exception for special uses such as churches, schools, and hospitals that wish to locate to areas zoned exclusively for residential use.

condominium — a residential unit owned in severalty, the boundaries of which are usually walls, floors, and ceilings, and an undivided interest in portions of the real property, such as halls, elevators, and recreational facilities.

conduit — a (usually) metal pipe in which electrical wiring is installed.

conflict of interest — a situation in which an individual or organization is involved in several *potentially* competing interests, creating a risk that one interest *might* unduly influence another interest.

conforming loan — a loan in conformance with FHFA guidelines.

consideration — anything of value given or promised, such as money, property, services, or a forbearance, to induce another to enter into a contract.

conspiracy — in antitrust law, occurs when two or more persons agree to act and the agreed-upon action has the effect of restraining trade.

construction mortgage — a security instrument used to secure a short-term loan to finance improvements to a property.

constructive eviction — a breach by the landlord of the covenant of habitability or quiet enjoyment.

constructive notice — (1) notice provided by public records; (2) notice of information provided by law to a person who, by exercising reasonable diligence, could have discovered the information.

contingency — an event that may, but is not certain to, happen, the occurrence upon which the happening of another event is dependent.

contract — a contract is an agreement to do or to forbear from doing a certain thing.

conventional loan — a mortgage loan that is not FHA insured or VA guaranteed.

conversion — the unauthorized misappropriation and use of another's funds or other property.

cooperating broker — a broker who attempts to find a buyer for a property listed by another broker.

co-ownership — joint ownership

cost approach — an appraisal approach that obtains the market value of the subject property by adding the value of the land (unimproved) of the subject property to the depreciated value of the cost (if currently purchased new) of the improvements on subject property.

cost recovery — the recoupment of the purchase price of a property through book depreciation; the tax concept of depreciation.

cost-to-cure method — a method of calculating depreciation by estimating the cost of curing the curable depreciation and adding it to the value of the incurable depreciation.

counteroffer — a new offer by an offeree that acts as a rejection of an offer by an offeror.

coupled with an interest — an aspect of an agency that refers to the agent's having a financial interest in the subject of the agency, which has the legal effect of making the appointment of the agent irrevocable.

covenant — a contractual promise to do or not do certain acts, such as on a property, the remedy for breach thereof being either monetary damages or injunctive relief, not forfeiture.

crawlspace — the space between the ground and the first floor that permits access beneath the building.

credit bid — a bid at a foreclosure sale made by the beneficiary up to the amount owed to the beneficiary.

credits — in reference to an escrow account, items payable to a party. This definition of a debit does not conform to its use in double-entry bookkeeping or accounting.

cubic-foot method — a method of estimating the replacement or reproduction cost of a structure that is similar to the square-foot method except that it uses the volume of recently constructed similar buildings. This method often is used for warehouses and other industrial buildings

curable depreciation — depreciation that results from physical deterioration or functional obsolescence that can be repaired or replaced at a cost that is less than or equal to the value added to the property.

debits — in reference to an escrow account, items payable by a party. This definition of a debit does not conform to its use in double-entry bookkeeping or accounting.

deed — a document that when signed by the grantor and legally delivered to the grantee conveys title to real property.

deed in lieu of foreclosure — a method of avoiding foreclosure by conveying to a lender title to a property lieu of the lender's foreclosing on the property.

defeasance clause — a provision in a loan that states that when the loan debt has been fully paid, the lender must release the property from the lien so that legal title free from the lien will be owned by the borrower.

defendant — the one against whom a lawsuit is brought.

deferred maintenance — any type of depreciation that has not been corrected by diligent maintenance.

deficiency judgment — a judgment given to a lender in an amount equal to the balance of the loan minus the net proceeds the lender receives after a judicial foreclosure.

deliberate misrepresentation — *see*, intentional misrepresentation

designated agent — an agent authorized by a real estate broker to represent a specific principal to the exclusion of all other agents in the brokerage. This designated agent owes fiduciary responsibilities to the specified principal, but other agents in the brokerage may represent other parties to the same transaction that the specified principal is a party to without creating a dual agency situation. Where this practice of designated agency is allowed, disclosure of the designated agency relationship is required.

demand — the level of desire for a product.

Depository Institutions Deregulation and Monetary Control Act (DIDMC) — a federal law that exempts from state usury laws interest paid on residential mortgage loans.

deposit receipt — a written document indicating that a good-faith deposit has been received as part of an offer to purchase real property; also called a purchase and sale agreement.

depreciation — the loss in value due to any cause.

depreciation deduction — an annual tax allowance for the depreciation of property.

devise — (1) (noun) a gift of real property by will; (2) (verb) to transfer real property by a will.

devisee — a recipient of real property through a will.

discounted rate — a rate (also called a teaser rate) on an adjustable-rate mortgage that is less than the fully indexed rate.

discount points — a form of prepaid interest on a mortgage, or a fee paid to a lender to cover cost the making of a loan. The fee for one discount point is equal to 1% of the loan amount.

disintegration — the phase when a property's usefulness is in decline and constant upkeep is necessary.

divided agency — an agency in which the agent represents both the seller and the buyer without obtaining the consent of both.

documentary transfer tax — a tax imposed by counties and cities on the transfer of real property within their jurisdictions.

dominant tenement — land that is benefited by an easement appurtenant.

Glossary

dormer — a projecting structure built out from a sloping roof that is used to provide windows and additional headroom for the upper floor.

down payment — the amount of money that a lender requires a purchaser to pay toward the purchase price.

drywall — prefabricated sheets or panels nailed to studs to form an interior wall or partition.

dual agent — a real estate broker who represents both the seller and the buyer in a real estate transaction.

due diligence — the exercise of an honest and reasonable degree of care in performing one's duties or obligations. A real estate agent's due diligence involves investigating the property to ensure that the property is as represented by the seller and to disclose accurate and complete information regarding the property.

due-on-sale clause — a clause in the promissory note, the security instrument, or both that states that the lender has the right to accelerate the loan if the secured property is sold or some other interest in the property is transferred.

duress — unlawful force or confinement used to compel a person to enter into a contract against his or her will.

earnest money deposit — a deposit that accompanies an offer by a buyer and is generally held in the broker's trust account.

easement — a non-possessory right to use a portion of another property owner's land for a specific purpose, as for a right-of-way, without paying rent or being considered a trespasser.

easement appurtenant — an easement that benefits, and is appurtenant to, another's land.

easement by necessity —arises as a creation of a court of law in certain cases were justice so demands, as in the case where a buyer of a parcel of land discovers that the land he or she just purchased has no access except over the land of someone other than from the person from whom the parcel was purchased.

easement in gross — an easement that benefits a legal person rather than other land.

eaves — the overhang of a roof that projects over an exterior wall of a house.

economic life — the period of time that the property is useful or profitable to the average owner or investor.

economic obsolescence — *see*, external obsolescence.

EER and SEER — Air-conditioners have an efficiency rating that states the ratio of the cooling capacity (how many BTUs per hour) to the power drawn (in watts). For room air conditioners the ratio is the EER (energy efficiency ratio); for central air conditioners the rating is the SEER (seasonal energy efficiency ratio). The higher the EER or SEER, the greater the efficiency of the air-conditioning unit. Significant savings in electricity costs can be obtained by installing more efficient air-conditioning units.

effective age — the age of an improvement that is indicated by the condition of the improvement, as distinct from its chronological age.

effective demand — demand coupled with purchasing power sufficient to acquire the property from a willing seller in a free market.

effective gross income — income from a property after an allowance for vacancies and uncollectible rents is deducted from gross income.

ejectment — a legal action to recover possession of real property from a person who is not legally entitled to possess it, such as to remove an encroachment or to evict a defaulting buyer or tenant.

emancipated minor — a minor who, because of marriage, military service, or court order, is allowed to contract for the sale or purchase of real property.

emblements — growing crops, such as grapes, avocados, and apples, that are produced seasonally through a tenant farmer's labor and industry.

eminent domain — right of the state to take, through due process proceedings (often referred to as condemnation proceedings), private property for public use upon payment of just compensation.

employee — a person who works for another who directs and controls the services rendered by the person.

employer — a person who directs and controls the services rendered by an employee.

encroachment — a thing affixed under, on, or above the land of another without permission.

encumber — To place a lien or other encumbrance on property.

encumbrance — A right or interest held by someone other than the owner the property that affects or limits the ownership of the property, such as liens, easements, licenses, and encroachments.

Endangered Species Act — a federal law that is intended to provide a means whereby the ecosystems upon which endangered species and threatened species depend may be conserved, and to provide a program for the conservation of such endangered species and threatened species.

Environmental Impact Statement (EIS) — a written document that federal agencies must prepare for any development project that a federal agency could prohibit or regulate, and any development project for which any portion is federally financed. An EIS can include comments on the expected impact of a proposed development on such things as air quality, noise, population density, energy consumption, water use, wildlife, public health and safety, and vegetation.

Equal Credit Opportunity Act (ECOA) — a federal law that prohibits a lender from discriminating against any applicant for credit on the basis of race, color, religion, national origin, sex, marital status, or age (unless a minor), or on the grounds that some of the applicant's income derives from a public assistance program.

equal dignities rule — a principle of agency law that requires the same formality to create the agency as is required for the act(s) the agent is hired to perform.

equilibrium — the period of stability when the property changes very little.

equitable title — the right to possess and enjoy a property while the property is being paid for.

escalator clause — a provision in a lease that provides for periodic increases in rent in an amount based on some objective criteria not in control of either the tenant or the landlord, such as the Consumer Price Index.

escheat — a process whereby property passes to the state if the owner of the property dies intestate without heirs, or if the property becomes abandoned.

escrow — a neutral depository in which something of value is held by an impartial third party (called the escrow agent) until all conditions specified in the escrow instructions have been fully performed.

escrow agent — an impartial agent who holds possession of written instruments and deposits until all of the conditions of escrow have been fully performed.

escrow holder — an escrow agent

escrow instructions — the written instructions signed by all of the principals to the escrow (buyers, sellers, and lenders) that specify all of the conditions that must be met before the escrow agent may release whatever was deposited into escrow to the rightful parties.

estate — the degree, quantity, nature, duration, or extent of interest one has in real property.

estate at sufferance — a leasehold that arises when a lessee who legally obtained possession of a property remains on the property after the termination of the lease without the owner's consent. Such a holdover tenant can be evicted like a trespasser, but if the owner accepts rent, the estate automatically becomes a periodic tenancy.

estate at will — an estate (or tenancy) in which a person occupies a property with the permission of the owner; however, the tenancy has no specified duration, and, in most states, may be terminated at any time by either the tenant or the owner of the property upon giving proper notice.

estate for years — a leasehold that continues for a definite fixed period of time, measured in days, months, or years.

estate from period to period — a leasehold that continues from period to period, whether by days, months, or years, until terminated by proper notice.

estate of inheritance — a freehold estate.

estoppel — a legal principle that bars one from alleging or denying a fact because of one's own previous actions or words to the contrary. Ostensible agency can be created by estoppel when a principal and an unauthorized agent act in a manner toward a third-party that leads the third party to rely on the actions of the unauthorized agent, believing that the actions are authorized by the principal.

exclusive agency listing — a listing agreement that gives a broker the right to sell property and receive compensation (usually a commission) if the property is sold by anyone other than the owner of the property during the term of the listing.

exclusive authorization and right to sell listing — a listing agreement that gives a broker the exclusive right to sell property and receive compensation (usually a commission) if the property is sold by anyone, including the owner of the property, during the term of the listing.

executed contract— a contract that has been fully performed; may also refer to a contract that has been signed by all of the parties to the contract.

executor — a person named in a will to carry out the directions contained in the will.

executory contract — a contract that has not yet been fully performed by one or both parties.

express contract — a contract stated in words, written or oral.

external obsolescence — depreciation that results from things such as (1) changes in zoning laws or other government restrictions, (2) proximity to undesirable influences such as traffic, airport flight patterns, or power lines, and (3) general neighborhood deterioration, as might result from increased crime.

Fair Housing Act — *see*, Civil Rights Act of 1968

false promise — a promise made without any intention of performing it.

Fannie Mae — a U.S. government conservatorship originally created as the Federal National Mortgage Association in 1938 to purchase mortgages from primary lenders.

federally designated targeted area — federally designated locations where homeownership is encouraged and incentivized.

fee simple absolute estate — the greatest estate that the law permits in land. The owner of a fee simple absolute estate owns all present and future interests in the property.

fee simple defeasible estate — a fee estate that is qualified by some condition that, if violated, may "defeat" the estate and lead to its loss and reversion to the grantor.

FHA — the Federal Housing Administration is a federal agency that was created by the National Housing Act of 1934 in order to make housing more affordable by increasing home construction, reducing unemployment, and making home mortgages more available and affordable.

FHFA — the Federal Housing Finance Agency is a U.S. government agency created by the Housing and Economic Recovery Act of 2008 to oversee the activities of Fannie Mae and Freddie Mac in order to strengthen the secondary mortgage market.

FICO score — a credit score created by the Fair Isaac Corporation that ranges from 300 to 850 and is used by lenders to help evaluate the creditworthiness of a potential borrower.

fiduciary relationship — a relationship in which one owes a duty of utmost care, integrity, honesty, and loyalty to another.

final map —a final map that a planning commission must approve after consideration of a tentative map before regulated subdivided property may be sold.

final public report — a report that the Real Estate Commissioner issues after determining that a subdivision offering meets certain consumer protection standards.

finder — a person who merely introduces a buyer to a seller, but does nothing else to facilitate a transaction between the buyer and seller, such as rendering assistance in negotiating terms.

fire stop — a block or board placed horizontally between studs to form a tight closure of a concealed space, thereby decreasing drafts and retarding the spread of fire and smoke.

first mortgage — a security instrument that holds first-priority claim against certain property identified in the instrument.

fixed lease — a gross lease

fixture — an object, originally personal property, that is attached to the land in such a manner as to be considered real property.

flashing — sheet metal or other material used in roof and wall construction to prevent water from entering.

flat fee listing — a listing in which the broker's compensation is a set amount rather than a percentage of the sale price.

floodplain — an area of low, flat, periodically flooded land near streams or rivers.

flue — a channel in a chimney through which flame and smoke passes upward to the outer air.

footing — concrete poured on solid ground that provides support for the foundation, chimney, or support columns. Footing should be placed below the frost line to prevent movement.

forbearance — the act of refraining from taking some action.

foreclosure — a legal process by which a lender, in an attempt to recover the balance of a loan from a borrower who has defaulted on the loan, forces the sale of the collateral that secured the loan.

foreclosure prevention alternative — a first lien loan modification or another available loss mitigation option.

Foreign Investment in Real Property Tax Act (FIRPTA) — a federal act that, with certain exceptions, requires the buyer in a real estate transaction to determine whether the seller is a non-resident alien; and if so, the buyer has the responsibility of withholding 10% of the amount realized from the sale and sending that 10% of the IRS.

Form Report — *see*, Summary Report.

four unities — refers to the common law rule that a joint tenancy requires unity of possession, time, interest, and title.

Freddie Mac — a U.S. government conservatorship originally created as the Federal Home Loan Mortgage Corporation in 1968 to purchase mortgages from primary lenders.

freehold estate — an estate in land whereby the holder of the estate owns rights in the property for an indefinite duration.

front-end ratio — the ratio of monthly housing expenses to monthly gross income.

fully amortized loan — a loan whereby the installment payments are sufficient to pay off the entire loan by the end of the loan term.

fully indexed rate — on an adjustable-rate mortgage, the index plus the margin.

functional obsolescence — depreciation that results (1) from deficiencies arising from poor architectural design, out-dated style or equipment, and changes in utility demand, such as for larger houses with more garage space, or (2) from over-improvements, where the cost of the improvements was more than the addition to market value.

gable roof — a roof with two sloping sides but not sloping ends.

gambrel roof — a roof sloped on two sides, each side having a steep lower slope and a flatter upper slope.

Garn-St. Germain Act — a federal law that made enforceability of due-on-sale provisions a federal issue.

general agent — an agent who is authorized by a principal to act for more than a particular act or transaction. General agents are usually an integral part of an ongoing business enterprise.

general lien — a lien that attaches to all of a person's nonexempt property.

general partnership — a partnership in which each partner has the equal right to manage the partnership and has personal liability for all of the partnership debts.

general plan — a comprehensive, long-term plan for the physical development of a city or county that is implemented by zoning, building codes, and other laws or actions of the local governments.

gift deed — a deed used to convey title when no tangible consideration (other than "affection") is given. The gift deed is valid unless it was used to defraud creditors, in which case such creditors may bring an action to void the deed.

Ginnie Mae — the Government National Mortgage Association is a wholly owned U.S. government corporation within HUD to guarantee pools of eligible loans that primary lenders issue as Ginnie Mae mortgage-backed securities.

good-faith improver — a person who, because of a mistake of law or fact, makes an improvement to land in good faith and under erroneous belief that he or she is the owner of the land.

goodwill — an intangible asset derived from the expectation of continued public patronage.

graduated lease — a lease that is similar to a gross lease except that it provides for periodic increases in rent, often based on the Consumer Price Index.

grantee — one who acquires an interest in real property from another.

grantor — one who transfers an interest in real property to another.

gross income — total income from a property before any expenses are deducted.

gross income multiplier (GIM) — a number equal to the estimated value of a property divided by the gross income of the property.

gross lease — a lease under which the tenant pays a fixed rental amount, and the landlord pays all of the operating expenses for the premises.

gross rent multiplier (GRM) — a number equal to the estimated value of a property divided by the gross rental income of the property.

ground lease — a lease under which a tenant leases land and agrees to construct a building or to make other significant improvements on the land.

group action — in antitrust law, two or more persons agreeing to act in a certain way.

group boycott — in antitrust law, the action of two or more brokers agreeing not to deal with another broker or brokers.

heir — a person entitled to obtain property through intestate succession.

hip roof — a sloping roof that rises from all four sides of the house.

holographic will — a will written, dated, and signed by a testator in his or her own handwriting.

home equity line of credit (HELOC) — a revolving line of credit provided by a home equity mortgage.

home equity mortgage — a security instrument used to provide the borrower with a revolving line of credit based on the amount of equity in the borrower's home.

homeowner's exemption — and exemption of $7,000 from the assessed value of a homeowner's residence.

Homeowner's Protection Act (HPA) — a federal law that requires lenders to disclose to borrowers when the borrowers' mortgages no longer require PMI.

homestead declaration —a recorded document that claims a particular dwelling (such as a house, condominium, boat, or mobile home) as the owner's principal place of residence and that provides limited protection for the claimant's equity in the dwelling.

homestead exemption — the amount of a homeowner's equity that may be protected from unsecured creditors.

horizontal property act — a law that provides for the creation of condominiums and establishes regulations regarding the condominiums and the condominium owners.

HUD-1 Uniform Settlement Statement — an escrow settlement form mandated by RESPA for use in all escrows pertaining to the purchase of owner-occupied residences of 1-4 dwelling units that use funds from institutional lenders regulated by the federal government.

implication — the act of creating an agency relationship by an unauthorized agent who acts as if he or she is the agent of a principal, and this principal reasonably believes that the unauthorized agent is acting as his or her actual agent.

implied contract— a contract not expressed in words, but, through action or inaction, understood by the parties.

implied easement — an easement arising by implication, as when a purchaser of mineral rights automatically acquires an implied right to enter the property to extract the minerals.

impound account — *see*, reserve account

inclusionary zoning — a zoning law that requires builders to set aside a specific portion of new construction for people of low to moderate incomes.

income approach — an appraisal approach that estimates the value of an income-producing property as being worth the present value of the future income of the property through a three-step process: (1) determine the net annual income, (2) determine an appropriate capitalization rate, and (3) divide the net income by the capitalization rate to obtain the estimate of value.

incurable depreciation — depreciation that results from (1) physical deterioration or functional obsolescence that cannot be repaired at a cost that is less than or equal to the value added to the property and (2) economic obsolescence (which is beyond the control of the property owner).

independent contractor — a person who performs work for someone, but does so independently in a private trade, business, or profession, with little or no supervision from the person for whom the work is performed.

index — under an adjustable-rate mortgage, the benchmark rate of interest that is adjusted periodically according to the going rate of T-bills, LIBOR, or the like.

innocent landowner defense — a defense to liability for cleanup of toxic waste under CERCLA (the Superfund Law) by one who acquires contaminated property after the contamination occurred and who acquired the property by inheritance or bequest or who, prior to purchasing the property, performed "all appropriate inquiries" to determine that the property had not been contaminated.

installment note — a promissory note in which periodic payments are made, usually consisting of interest due and some repayment of principal.

installment sale — a sale in which the seller receives at least one payment in a later tax period and may report part of the gain from the sale for the year in which a payment is received.

integration — the growth and development stage of property.

intentional misrepresentation — the suggestion, as a fact, to a party that which is not true committed by another party who does not believe it to be true and who makes the suggestion with the intent to deceive the first party, who was deceived to his or her detriment, such as by being induced to enter into a contract.

interest — the compensation fixed by the parties for the use of money.

interest-rate cap —under an adjustable-rate mortgage, the maximum that the interest rate can increase from one adjustment period to the next or over the life of the entire loan.

interpleader — an action that allows for a neutral third party (such as a real estate agent) to avoid liability to two or more claimants (such as a seller and buyer) to the same money or property (such as an earnest money deposit) by forcing the claimants to litigate among themselves, letting the court determine who deserves what while not enmeshing the neutral third party in the litigation.

Interstate Land Sales Full Disclosure Act — a federal consumer protection act that requires that certain land developers register with the Consumer Financial Protection Bureau if they offer across state lines parcels in subdivisions containing 100 or more lots. Subdivisions where each lot in the subdivision contains at least 20 acres are exempt from this registration requirement. A developer must provide each prospective buyer with a Property Report that contains pertinent information about the subdivision and that discloses to the prospective buyer that he or she has a minimum of 7 days in which to rescind the purchase agreement.

intestate — not having made, or not having disposed of by, a will.

intestate succession — transfer of the property of one who dies intestate.

inverse condemnation — a judicial or administrative action brought by a landowner to force the condemnation of the landowner's land where nearby condemned land or land used for public purposes (such as for noisy airports) severely reduces the value of the landowner's land.

involuntary lien — a lien created by operation of law, not by the voluntary acts of the debtor.

jamb — the vertical sides of a door or window that contact the door or sash.

joint ownership — ownership of property by two or more persons.

joint tenancy —a form of joint ownership which has unity of possession, time, interest, and title.

joist — one of a series of parallel heavy horizontal timbers used to support floor or ceiling loads.

Jones v. Mayer — a landmark 1968 United States Supreme Court case that held that the Civil Rights Act of 1866 was constitutional and that the Act prohibited all racial discrimination, whether private or public, in the sale or rental of property.

judicial foreclosure — a foreclosure carried out not by way of a power-of-sale clause in a security instrument, but under the supervision of a court.

judgment — a court's final determination of the rights and duties of the parties in an action before it.

jumbo loan — a mortgage loan the amount of which exceeds conforming loan limits set by the FHFA on an annual basis.

junior mortgage — a mortgage that, relative to another mortgage, has a lower lien-priority position.

land contract — a real property sales contract.

land installment contract — a real property sales contract.

lateral support — the support that soil receives from the land adjacent to it.

lease extension — a continuation of tenancy under the original lease.

lease-option — a lease (also referred to as a lease with an option to purchase) that provides the tenant with the right, but not the obligation, to purchase the leased property at a specified price within a specified period of time.

lease-purchase — an agreement (also referred to as a lease with an obligation to purchase) that provides for the purchase of property preceded by a lease under which a portion of each lease payment is applied to the purchase price.

lease renewal — a continuation of tenancy under a new lease.

leasehold estate — a less-than-freehold estate.

legatee — one who acquires personal property under a will.

lessee — a person (the tenant) who leases property from another.

lessor — a person (the landlord) who leases property to another.

less-than-freehold estate — an estate in which the holder has the exclusive right to possession of land for a length of time. The holder of a less-than-freehold estate is usually referred to as a lessee or tenant.

level payment note — a promissory note under which all periodic installment payments are equal.

leverage — a method of multiplying gains (or losses) on investments by using borrowed money to acquire the investments.

license to use —a personal right to use property on a nonexclusive basis. A license to use is not considered an estate.

lien —an encumbrance against real property that is used to secure a debt and that can, in most cases, be foreclosed.

lien priority — the order in which lien holders are paid if property is sold to satisfy a debt.

lien stripping — a method sometimes used in Chapter 13 bankruptcies to eliminate junior liens on the debtor's home.

lien theory — a legal theory of mortgage, holding that the mortgagor retains both legal and equitable title of the property, including exclusive possession and use of the property. The mortgagee simply possesses a lien against the property (usually a lien of higher priority than certain other liens, such as judgment liens). Upon default, the mortgagee must go through a formal (judicial) foreclosure proceeding to obtain legal title and possession.

life estate — a freehold estate the duration of which is measured by the life of a natural person — either by the life of the person holding the estate, or by the life or lives of one or more other persons.

limited liability partnership — a partnership in which there is at least one general partner and one or more limited partners. The limited partners have no liability beyond their investment in and pledges to the partnership.

lintel — a horizontal support made of wood, stone, concrete, or steal that lies across the top of a window or door and supports the load above.

liquidated damages — a sum of money that the parties agree, usually at the formation of a contract, will serve as the exact amount of damages that will be paid upon a breach of the contract.

lis pendens — (Latin for "action pending") a notice of pendency of action.

listing agreement — a written contract between a real estate broker and a property owner (the principal) stipulating that in exchange for the real estate broker's procuring a buyer for the principal's property, the principal will compensate the broker, usually with a percentage of the selling price.

loan flipping — the practice of frequently refinancing loans that result in little more than the generation of additional loan fees.

loan modification — a restructuring or modification of a mortgage or deed of trust on terms more favorable to the buyer's ability (or desire) to continue making loan payments.

loan servicing — the administration of a loan from the time the loan proceeds are dispersed to the time the loan is paid off in full.

loan-to-value ratio (LTV) — the amount of a first mortgage divided by the lesser of (1) the appraised value of the property or (2) the purchase price of the property.

long-term capital gain — the capital gain on the sale of a capital asset that was held for a relatively long period of time, usually more than one year.

lot, block, and tract land system — (see " recorded map or plat system ")

maker — the person who makes a promissory note.

margin — a number of percentage points, usually fixed over the life of the loan, that is added to the index of an adjustable-rate mortgage to arrive at the fully indexed rate.

market allocation — in antitrust law, the process of competitors agreeing to divide up geographic areas or types of products or services they offer to customers.

market price — the price actually paid for a particular property.

market value — as defined for appraisal purposes by HUD/FHA is: "The most probable price which a property should bring in a competitive and open market under all conditions requisite to a fair sale, the buyer and seller, each acting prudently, knowledgeably and assuming the price is not affected by undue stimulus."

material fact — a fact that is likely to affect the decision of a party as to whether to enter into a transaction on the specified terms.

mechanics lien — a specific lien claimed by someone who furnished labor or materials for a work of improvement on real property and who has not been fully paid.

median price per square foot — the median price per square foot of a set of properties is the price per square foot of the property whose price per square foot is such that half of the properties in the set have an equal or lower price per square foot and half have an equal or higher price per square foot.

Megan's Law — an informal name for various federal and state laws that provide for the registration of sex offenders and for the making available to the public information regarding the location of these offenders.

menace — a threat to commit duress or to commit injury to person or property.

meridians — (see and compare "base lines")

metes and bounds land description — a method of describing a parcel of land that uses physical features of the locale, along with directions and distances, to define the boundaries of the parcel.

moldings — patterned strips, usually of wood, used to provide ornamental finish to cornices, bases, windows, and door jambs.

mortgage banker — a primary lender that uses its own money in creating a mortgage loan.

mortgage broker — an individual or company that finds borrowers and matches them with lenders for a fee.

mortgagee — a lender or creditor to whom a mortgagor gives a mortgage to secure a loan or performance of an obligation.

mortgage loan originator (MLO) — a person who takes, or offers to take, a residential mortgage loan application or offers or negotiates terms of a residential mortgage application for compensation or gain or in expectation of compensation or gain.

mortgagor — the borrower who gives a mortgage on his or her property to secure a loan or performance of an obligation.

mudsill — for houses built on a concrete slab, the wood sills that are bolted to all sides of the slab, providing a means of attaching portions of the framing for the house to the foundation.

multiple listing service — an organization (MLS) of real estate brokers who share their listings with other members of the organization.

mutual consent — refers to the situation in which all parties to a contract freely agree to the terms of the contract; sometimes referred to as a "meeting of the minds."

National "Do Not Call" Registry — a registry established by the Federal Trade Commission to protect consumers from unwanted commercial telephone solicitations.

National Association of Real Estate Brokers — a real estate trade association whose members are called Realtists®.

National Association of Realtors® — the largest real estate trade association in the United States, founded in 1908, whose members are called Realtors®.

National Environmental Policy Act (NEPA) — a federal law intended to protect, and to promote the enhancement of, the environment.

negative amortization — a loan repayment scheme in which the outstanding principal balance of the loan increases because the installment payments do not cover the full interest due.

negative amortized loan (NegAm loan) — a loan by which the installment payments do not cover all of the interest due — the unpaid part of the interest due being tacked onto the principal, thereby causing the principal to grow as each month goes by.

negative covenant — a contractual promise not to do certain acts, such as build a fence on a property, the remedy for breach thereof being either monetary damages or injunctive relief, not forfeiture.

negative fraud — the act of not disclosing a material fact which induces someone to enter into a contractual relationship and that causes that person damage or loss.

negligent misrepresentation — an assertion not warranted by the information of the party making the assertion that an important fact was true, which was not true, relied on by another party to that party's detriment.

net income — income from a property remaining after expenses are deducted from gross income.

net lease — a lease under which the tenant pays a fixed rental amount plus some of the landlord's operating expenses.

net listing — a listing agreement providing the broker with all proceeds received from the sale over a specified amount. Net listings are not legal in many states.

NMLS — the Nationwide Mortgage Licensing System and Registry is a mortgage licensing system developed and maintained by the Conference of State Bank Supervisors and the American Association of Residential Mortgage Regulators for the state licensing and registration of state-licensed loan originators.

nonconforming loan — a loan not in conformance with FHFA guidelines.

nonconforming use — a zoning exception for areas that are zoned for the first time or that are rezoned and where established property uses that previously were permitted to not conform to the new zoning requirements. As a general rule, such existing properties are "grandfathered in," allowing them to continue the old use but not to extend the old use to additional properties or to continue the old use after rebuilding or abandonment.

non-judicial foreclosure — a foreclosure process culminating in a privately conducted, publicly held trustee's sale. The right to pursue a non-judicial foreclosure is contained in the power-of-sale clause of a mortgage or deed of trust, which, upon borrower default and the beneficiary's request, empowers the trustee to sell the secured property at a public auction.

notice of cessation — a written form that notifies that all work of improvement on a piece of real property has ceased, and that limits the time in which mechanics liens may be filed against the property.

notice of completion — a written form that notifies that a work of improvement on real property has been completed, and that limits the time in which mechanics liens may be filed against the property.

notice of default (NOD) — a document prepared by a trustee at the direction of a lender to begin a non-judicial foreclosure proceeding.

notice of pendency of action — a notice that provides constructive notice to potential purchasers or encumbrancers of a piece of real property of the pendency of a lawsuit in which an interest in that piece of real property is claimed.

notice of sale — a document prepared by a trustee at the direction of a lender that gives notice of the time and place of sale of an identified foreclosed property.

novation — a substitution of a new obligation or contract for an old one, or the substitution of one party to a contract by another, relieving the original party of liability under the contract.

nuisance — anything that is indecent or offensive to the senses, or an obstruction to the free use of property, so as to interfere with the comfortable enjoyment of life or property.

nuncupative will — an oral will.

offer — a proposal by one person (the offeror) to enter into a contract with another (the offeree).

offeree — one to whom an offer to enter into a contract is made.

offeror — one who makes an offer to enter into a contract.

open listing — a listing agreement that gives a broker the nonexclusive right to sell property and receive compensation (usually a commission) if, but only if, the broker is the first to procure a buyer for the property.

opinion of title — a written rendering of an opinion on the condition of ownership of title in a real estate transaction prepared by an attorney after examination of an abstract of title.

option contract — a contract that gives the purchaser of the option the right to buy or lease a certain property at a set price any time during the option term.

ordinary interest — interest calculated by the 30/360 day count convention.

origination fee — the fee a lender charges to cover expenses of processing a loan, such as purchasing credit reports, inspection reports and appraisals, and paying office expenses and salaries of personnel who interview borrowers and analyze the reports and appraisals.

ostensible agency — an agency in which the principal intentionally, or by want of ordinary care, causes a third person to believe another to be his agent who was not actually employed by him.

parol evidence rule — a rule of evidence that prohibits the introduction of extrinsic evidence of preliminary negotiations, oral or written, and of contemporaneous oral evidence, to alter the terms of a written agreement that appears to be whole.

partially amortized loan — an installment loan under which monthly payments pay all of the interest due but not enough of the principal to fully pay off the loan at the end of the loan term. In such a case, a balloon payment would be due at the end of the loan term.

partial release clause — a clause in a blanket mortgage that allows a developer to sell off individual parcels and pay back, according to a release schedule, only a proportionate amount of the blanket loan.

partition —a court-ordered or voluntary division of real property held in joint ownership into parcels owned in severalty.

passive income — in general, income from either rental activity or from a business in which the taxpayer does not materially participate.

passive investor — an investor who does not actively contribute to the management of the business invested in.

patent, land — an instrument used to convey government land.

payee — the person to whom a promissory note is made out.

payment cap —under an adjustable-rate mortgage, the maximum amount that installment payments may increase from one adjustment period to the next or over the life of the loan.

percentage lease — a lease, often used in shopping centers, under which the tenant typically pays a base rent amount plus a percentage of the gross receipts of the tenant's business.

period of redemption — a period of time after a sheriff's sale in a judicial foreclosure proceeding during which the borrower may redeem his or her property by paying off the entire debt plus costs.

periodic tenancy — an estate from period to period.

physical deterioration — depreciation that results from wear and tear of use and from natural causes.

physical life — the period of time that the property lasts with normal maintenance.

pitch — the degree of inclination or slope of a roof.

plaintiff — the one who brings a lawsuit.

plaster — a mixture of lime or gypsum, sand, water, and fiber that is applied to walls and ceilings and that hardens into a smooth coating.

point of beginning — the fixed starting point in the metes and bounds method of land description.

point — in finance, a point is equal to 1% of the loan amount. The term is used by lenders to measure discount charges and other costs such as origination fees and private mortgage insurance premiums.

police power — the power of a government to impose restrictions on private rights, including property rights, for the sake of public welfare, health, order, and security, for which no compensation need be made.

portfolio loans — loans that primary lenders retain in their own investment portfolios rather than sell into the secondary market.

post-dated check — a check dated with a date after the date the check is written and signed.

potentially responsible party — as defined by the EPA, anyone who ever owned or operated a contaminated property, as well as anyone who produced the waste, transported the waste to the property, or disposed of the waste on the property.

power of attorney — a special written instrument that gives authority to an agent to conduct certain business on behalf of the principal. The agent acting under such a grant is sometimes called an attorney in fact.

power-of-sale clause — a clause contained in most trust deeds that permits the trustee to foreclose on, and sell, the secured property without going to court.

preapproval —an evaluation of a potential borrower's ability to qualify for a loan that involves a credit check and verification of income and debt of the potential borrower.

predatory lending — the imposition of unfair, deceptive, abusive, or fraudulent loan terms on borrowers.

prepayment penalty — a fee charged to a borrower for paying off the loan faster than scheduled payments call for.

prequalification — an initial unverified evaluation of a potential borrower's ability to qualify for a mortgage loan.

prescription — a method of acquiring an interest in property by use and enjoyment for five years.

prescriptive easement — an easement acquired by prescription.

price fixing — an agreement between competitors to set prices or price ranges.

price per square foot — the price per square foot of a specific property is determined by dividing the price (either selling or listing) by the property's square footage. Appraisers determine the square footage of a property by using the *outside* measurement of the property.

primary financing — first mortgage property financing.

primary lender — lenders who originate mortgage loans.

primary mortgage market — the market where mortgage loans are originated.

principal — the one whom an agent represents.

principle of anticipation — principle that value is derived from a calculation of anticipated future benefits to be derived from the property, not from past benefits, though past benefits may inform as to what might be expected in the future.

principle of balance — principle that the maximum value of property, its highest and best use, is created and maintained when land use by interacting elements of production are in equilibrium or balance.

principle of change — principle that property values are in a constant state of flux due to economic, environmental, political, social, and physical forces in the area.

principle of competition — principle that increased competition results in increased supply in relation to demand, and thereby to lower profit margins.

principle of conformity — principle that the maximum value of land is achieved when there is a reasonable degree of social, economic, and architectural conformity in the area.

principle of contribution — principle that improvements made to a property will contribute to its value or that, conversely, the lack of a needed improvement will detract from the value of the property.

principle of four-stage life cycle — principle that property goes through a process of growth, stability, decline, and revitalization.

principle of plottage — states that assembling two or more parcels of land into one parcel results in the larger parcel having a greater value than the sum of the values of the smaller parcels.

principle of progression — principle that the value of a residence of less value tends to be enhanced by proximity to residences of higher value.

principle of regression — principle that the value of a residence of higher value tends to be degraded by the proximity to residences of lower value.

principle of substitution — principle that the value of a property will tend toward the cost of an equally desirable substitute property.

principle of supply and demand — principle that the value of property in a competitive market is influenced by the relative levels of supply and demand: the greater level of demand in relation to the level of supply, the greater the value.

principle of the highest and best use — principle that the best use of a property in terms of value is the use most likely to produce the greatest net return (in terms of money or other valued items).

private mortgage insurance (PMI) — mortgage insurance that lenders often require for loans with an LTV more than 80%.

privity of contract — a legal doctrine that states that a legally enforceable relationship exists between the persons who are parties to a contract.

privity of estate — a legal doctrine that states that a legally enforceable relationship exists between the parties who hold interests in the same real property.

probate — a legal procedure whereby a superior court in the county where the real property is located or where the deceased resided oversees the distribution of the decedent's property.

Glossary

procuring cause — a common law legal concept developed by the courts to determine the proportioning of commissions among agents involved in a real estate transaction In general, an agent who is a procuring cause of a sale originated a chain of events that resulted in the sale and is thereby entitled to at least some part of the total commission generated by the sale.

profit á prendre — the right to enter another's land for such purposes as to drill for oil, mine for coal, or cut and remove timber.

promissory note — a contract whereby one person unconditionally promises to pay another a certain sum of money, either at a fixed or determinable future date or on demand of the payee.

property disclosure statement — a statement filled out by the seller of residential property consisting of 1 to 4 dwelling units, disclosing to potential purchasers defects in the property that are known to the seller, or that should be known to the seller upon reasonable inspection.

proration — an adjustment of expenses that either have been paid or are in arrears in proportion to actual time of ownership as of the closing of escrow or other agreed-upon date.

protected class — a group of people protected from discrimination by federal or state law.

protection clause — *see*, safety clause.

public dedication — a gift of an interest in land to a public body for public use, such as for a street, a park, or an easement to access a beach.

public grant — public land conveyed, usually for a small fee, to individuals or to organizations, such as to railroads or universities.

puffing — the act of expressing a positive opinion about something to induce someone to become a party to a contract.

purchase money loan — a deed of trust or mortgage on a dwelling for not more than four families given to a lender to secure repayment of a loan which was in fact used to pay all or part of the purchase price of that dwelling, occupied entirely or in part by the purchaser.

pyramid roof a hip roof that has no ridge.

quantity survey method — the most detailed method of estimating the replacement or reproduction cost of a structure, in which an estimate is made of the cost of all of the raw materials needed to replace the building. Such material-cost information is available in construction cost handbooks

quiet title action — *see*, suit to quiet title

quitclaim deed — a deed that contains no warranties of any kind, no after-acquired title provisions, and provides the grantee with the least protection of any deed; it merely provides that any interest (if there is any) that the grantor has in the property is transferred to the grantee.

rafter — one of a series of parallel sloping timbers that extend from the ridgeboard to the exterior walls, providing support for the roof.

ratification —the act of creating an agency relationship by a principal who accepts or retains the benefit of an act made by an unauthorized agent.

194

real estate investment trust (REIT) — a company that invests in and, in most cases operates, income-producing real estate and that meets numerous criteria, such as the necessity of being jointly owned by at least 100 persons.

real estate owned (REO) — property acquired by a lender through a foreclosure sale.

real estate professional — a real estate investor who (1) materially participates for at least 750 hours during the tax year in the real estate business and (2) spends more than 50% of his or her personal services performed in all businesses during the tax year in the real estate business that he or she materially participates in.

Real Estate Settlement Procedures Act (RESPA) — a federal law designed to prevent lenders, real estate agents, developers, title insurance companies, and other agents (such as appraisers and inspectors) who service the real estate settlement process from providing kickbacks or referral fees to each other, and from facilitating bait-and-switch tactics.

real property sales contract — an agreement in which one party agrees to convey title to real property to another party upon the satisfaction of specified conditions set forth in the contract and that does not require conveyance of title within one year from the date of formation of the contract.

Realtist® — a member of the National Association of Real Estate Brokers.

Realtor® — a member of the National Association of Realtors®.

reconciliation — the process of ascertaining value by comparing and evaluating values obtained from comparables or from different valuation approaches; the process of comparing what is in a trust fund account with what should be in the account.

reconveyance deed — a deed executed by the trustee of a deed of trust after the promissory note is paid off in full by the borrower and the lender instructs the trustee to so execute the reconveyance deed, which reconveys legal title to the borrower

recorded map or plat system — a method of land description that states a property's lot, block, and tract number, referring to a map recorded in the county where the property is located.

rectangular survey system — a method of land description based on a grid system of north-south lines ("ranges") and east-west lines ("tier" or "township" lines) that divides the land into townships and sections.

red flag — a condition that should alert a reasonably attentive person of a potential problem that warrants further investigation. Examples include stains on ceilings or walls, the smell of mold, and warped floors or walls.

redlining — the illegal practice of refusing to make loans for real property in particular areas.

Regulation Z — the set of regulations that implement the Truth-in-Lending Act (TILA).

reinforced concrete — concrete poured around steel bars or metal netting to increase its ability to withstand tensile, shear, and compression stresses.

rejection — the act of an offeree that terminates an offer. An offer may be rejected (1) by submitting a new offer, (2) by submitting what purports to be an acceptance but is not because it contains a variance of a material term of the original offer, or (3) by express terms of rejection.

rejuvenation — the phase when a property is rebuilt, remodeled, or otherwise revitalized to a new highest and best use.

reliction — a natural process by which the owner of riparian or littoral property acquires additional land that has been covered by water but has become permanently uncovered by the gradual recession of water.

remainder — the residue of a freehold estate where, at the end of the estate, the future interest arises in a third person.

remainder depreciation — depreciation that will occur after the date of valuation.

remainderman — a person who inherits or is entitled to inherit property held as a life estate when the person whose life determines the duration of the life estate passes away.

replacement cost — the cost of replacing improvements with those having equivalent utility, but constructed with modern materials, designs, and workmanship.

reproduction cost — the cost of replacing improvements with exact replicas at current prices.

request for a reconveyance — an instrument that a lender sends to a trustee requesting that the trustee execute and record a deed of reconveyance that is then sent to the borrower.

rescission — the cancellation of a contract and the restoration of each party to the same position held before the contract was entered into.

reserve account — in reference to loan servicing, the escrow account from which the loan servicer typically pays, on behalf of the borrower, property taxes, hazard insurance, and any other charges (such as mortgage insurance) with respect to the loan.

residual value — an estimate of the reasonable fair market value of a property at the end of its useful life.

respondeat superior — in agency law, the doctrine that a principal is liable for the acts of an agent if those acts were performed within the scope of the agent's authority. (See, vicarious liability.)

retaliatory eviction — an eviction action brought to retaliate against a tenant for making a habitability complaint or for asserting other of the tenant's legal rights.

return on investment (ROI) — an investor's cash flow (net income minus financing charges) divided by the investor's actual cash investment (as distinct from the purchase price).

reverse mortgage — a security instrument for a loan for homeowners over the age of 62 who have a large amount of equity in their homes, usually designed to provide such homeowners with monthly payments, often over the lifetime of the last surviving homeowner who either moves out of the house or dies.

reversion — the residue of a freehold estate where at the end of the estate, the future interest reverts to the grantor.

revocation — the withdrawal of an offer by the person who made the offer.

rezoning amendment — an amendment to a zoning ordinance that property owners may request if they feel that their area has been improperly zoned.

ridgeboard — a horizontal board placed on edge at the apex of a roof to which the upper ends of the rafters are attached.

right of first refusal — the right to be given the first chance to purchase a property at the same price, terms, and conditions as is offered to third parties if and when the property is put up for sale.

right of survivorship — the right to succeed to the interest of a joint tenant or, if community property with right of survivorship, to succeed to the interest of a spouse or registered domestic partner. Right of survivorship is the most important characteristic of joint tenancy.

riparian rights — the rights of a landowner to use water from a stream or lake adjacent to his or her property, provided such use is reasonable and does not injure other riparian owners.

robocall — a pre-recorded, auto-dialed telephone call.

R-value — a measure of the resistance of insulation to heat transfer. The FTC requires sellers of new homes to disclose the R-value of each home's insulation. The higher the R-value, the greater is the effectiveness of the insulation.

SAFE Act — the Safe and Fair Enforcement for Mortgage Licensing Act of 2008 was designed to improve consumer protection and reduce mortgage fraud by setting minimum standards for the licensing and registration of mortgage loan originators.

safety clause — a provision in a listing agreement, providing that the broker will earn the full commission if the property is sold within a specified number of days after the termination of the listing to a buyer with whom the broker has dealt in certain specified ways regarding the property.

sales comparison approach — an appraisal approach that compares recent sales of similar properties in the area to evaluate the market value of the subject property.

salesperson — a natural person who is employed by a licensed real estate broker to perform acts that require having a real estate license.

salvage value — residual value.

sandwich lease — a leasehold interest that lies between a primary lease and a sublease.

sash — frames that contain one or more windowpanes.

scarcity — a lack of abundance.

scrap value — residual value.

second mortgage — a security instrument that holds second-priority claim against certain property identified in the instrument.

secondary financing — second mortgage and junior mortgage property financing

secondary mortgage market — the market where mortgages are sold by primary mortgage lenders to investors.

secret profit — any compensation or beneficial gain realized by an agent not disclosed to the principal. Real estate agents must always disclose any interest that they or their relatives have in a transaction and obtain their principals' consent.

section — one square mile, containing 640 acres.

security instrument — the written instrument by which a debtor pledges property as collateral to secure a loan.

SEER — (see EER)

self-help eviction — a landlord's denial of possession of leased premises to a tenant without complying with the legal process of eviction.

seller carry back loan — a loan or credit given by a seller of real property to the purchaser of that property.

seller's agent — a real estate broker appointed by the seller to represent the seller.

selling agent — the real estate agent who sells or finds and obtains a buyer for the property in a real estate transaction.

senior mortgage — a mortgage that, relative to another mortgage, has a higher lien-priority position.

separate property — property that is owned in severalty by a spouse or registered domestic partner. Separate property includes property acquired before marriage or the registering of domestic partnership, and property acquired as a gift or by inheritance during marriage or registered domestic partnership.

servient tenement — land that is burdened by an easement.

setback — a designation of a governing body as to how far a structure must be situated from something else, such as a curb or a neighboring property.

settlement — *see*, closing

severalty — ownership of property by one person.

severance — the act of detaching an item of real property that changes the item to personal property, such as the cutting down of a natural tree. Also, the act of terminating a relationship, such as the act of partitioning by court order for the transfer of an interest that changes a joint tenancy into a tenancy in common.

severance damages — damages paid to an owner of land partially taken by eminent domain where the value of the remaining portion of the owner's land is severely reduced by the severance of the condemned a portion of owner's land.

sheriff's deed — a deed given at the foreclosure of a property, subsequent to a judgment for foreclosure of a money judgment against the owner or of a mortgage against the property. A sheriff's deed contains no warranties and transfers only the former owner's interest in the property.

sheriff's sale — a sale of property following a judicial foreclosure.

Sherman Act — the federal law passed in 1890 that prohibits agreements, verbal or written, that have the effect of restraining free trade.

short sale — a pre-foreclosure sale made by the borrower (usually with the help of a real estate agent) with lender approval of real estate for less than the balance due on the mortgage loan.

short-term capital gain — the capital gain on the sale of a capital asset that was held for a relatively short period of time, usually one year or less.

sill — the board or metal forming the lower side of the frame for a window or door; the lowest part of the frame of a house, resting on the foundation and providing the base for the studs.

simple interest — the type of interest that is generated only on the principal invested.

single agent — an agent who represents only one party in a given transaction.

single point of contact — an individual or team of personnel employed by a mortgage loan servicer, each of whom has the ability and authority to assist a borrower in assessing whether the borrower may be able to take advantage of a foreclosure prevention alternative offered by, or through, the mortgage servicer.

situs — the legal location of something; also refers to the preference for a particular location to live, work, or invest in

special agent — an agent for a particular act or transaction.

special assessment — a tax levied against properties in a particular area that are benefited by improvements such as for streets, water, and sewers.

specific lien — a lien that attaches only to specific property.

specific performance — a court order that requires a person to perform according to the terms of a contract.

spot zoning —refers to the zoning of isolated properties for use different from the uses specified by existing zoning laws. To spot zone a particular property may, in some cases, be a violation of the requirement that police power apply similarly to all property similarly situated, which in turn arises from the constitutional guarantee of equal protection under the law.

square-foot method — the most widely used method of estimating reproduction or replacement cost of a building, involving the collection cost data on recently constructed similar buildings and dividing the total cost by the square footage to obtain cost per square foot

standard subdivision — is a subdivision with no common areas of ownership or use among the owners of the subdivision parcels.

standby loan commitment — a commitment by a lender to make a take-out loan after construction on a property is completed

statute of frauds — a law that requires certain types of contracts, including most real estate contracts, to be in writing and signed by the party to be bound in order for the contract to be enforceable.

statute of limitations — a law that requires particular types of lawsuits to be brought within a specified time after the occurrence of the event giving rise to the lawsuit.

steering — the illegal practice of directing people of protected classes away from, or toward, housing in particular areas.

stigmatized property — a property having a condition that certain persons may find materially negative in a way that does not relate to the property's actual physical condition.

stock cooperative — a corporation formed or availed of primarily for the purpose of holding title to improved real property either in fee simple or for a term of years.

straight note — a promissory note under which periodic payments consist of interest only.

straight-line depreciation — the expensing of a property by equal amounts over the useful life of the property, determined by subtracting from the cost of the property the estimated residual value of the property and dividing that amount by the useful life of the property measured in years.

straight-line method — a method of calculating annual depreciation of an improvement by dividing the cost of the improvement by the estimated useful life of a typical such improvement.

strict foreclosure — a foreclosure process permitted in a few states, whereby no public sale of the property is made — full title simply passes to the lender.

subagent — an agent of an agent.

subjacent support — the support that soil receives from land beneath it.

subject to — acquiring real property that is burdened by a mortgage without becoming personally liable for the mortgage debt.

subjective value — (also referred to as *value in use*) is value placed on the amenities of a property by a specific person.

sublease — a transfer of a tenant's right to a portion of the leased premises or to the entire premises for less than the entire remaining lease term.

subordination clause — a provision in a mortgage or deed of trust that states that the mortgage or deed of trust will have lower priority than a mortgage or deed of trust recorded later.

subrogation — the substitution of one party for another in regard to pursuing a legal right, interest, or obligation. Subrogation is a legal right used by insurance companies to acquire the right from a policyholder to sue in the place of the policyholder for damages the insurance company paid to the policyholder for some act committed by a third party.

suit to quiet title — a court proceeding intended to establish the true ownership of a property, thereby eliminating any cloud on title.

take-out loan — a loan that provides long-term financing for a property on which a construction loan had been made.

tax assessor — the county or city official who is responsible for appraising property.

tax auditor — the county or city official who maintains the county tax rolls.

tax collector — the county or city official who is responsible for collecting taxes.

tax deed — the deed given to the successful buyer at a tax sale. A tax deed conveys title free and clear from private liens, but not from certain tax liens or special assessment liens, or from easements and recorded restrictions.

Taxpayer Relief Act of 1997 — a tax relief act that contained several tax reduction provisions, including a large exemption for profits on the sale of a personal residence.

tenancy at sufferance — see, estate at sufferance.

tenancy at will — see, estate at will.

tenancy by the entirety — recognized in some states, a special form of joint tenancy between a married couple, in which, as in a joint tenancy, there is the right of survivorship, but in which, unlike in a joint tenancy, neither spouse may convey his or her interest in the property during the lifetime of the other spouse without the consent of the other spouse.

tenancy for years — see, estate for years.

tenancy from period to period — see, estate from period to period.

tenancy in common — a form of joint ownership that is presumed to exist if the persons who own the property are neither married nor registered domestic partners and they own undivided interests in property. Tenants in common may hold unequal interests; however, if the deed does not specify fractional interests among the tenants, the interests will be presumed to be equal.

tenancy in partnership — a form of joint ownership in which the partners combine their assets and efforts in a business venture.

term loan — see, straight loan.

testament — a will.

testator — one who dies leaving a will.

time-share estate — an estate in real property coupled with the right of occupancy for certain periods of time.

time-share use — a right to occupancy during certain periods of time, not coupled to an estate in real property.

title plant — a duplicate of county title records maintained at title insurance companies for use in title searches.

title search — an examination of all relevant public documents to determine whether there exist any potential defects (such as judicial liens, lis pendens, or other encumbrances, including tax liens and special assessments) against the title.

title theory — a legal theory of mortgage, holding that a mortgage transfers legal title to the mortgagee (the lender) while the mortgagor (the borrower) retains equitable title to the property, which permits the mortgagor exclusive possession and use of the property. Upon default, the mortgagee is entitled to immediate possession and use (such as to collect rents) of the property.

townhouse — a form of condominium in which the individual units are connected by a common wall and, in general, (unlike in a high-rise condominium complex) a deed to the land beneath the townhouse is granted to the townhouse owner.

township — six square miles, containing 36 sections.

trade fixtures — objects that a tenant attaches to real property for use in the tenant's trade or business. Trade fixtures differ from other fixtures in that, even though they are attached with some permanence to real property, they may be removed at the end of the tenancy of the business.

transactional broker — a nonagent middleman who brings the parties to a real estate transaction together and lets the parties do all of the negotiating among themselves. States that permit this kind of nonagent-facilitator status impose an obligation on the transactional broker to act fairly, honestly, and competently to find qualified buyers or suitable properties, but the transactional broker does not owe fiduciary legal obligations to any of the parties.

transferability — the ability to transfer some interest in property to another.

triggering term — any of a number of specific finance terms stated in an advertisement for a loan that triggers Regulation Z disclosure requirements in the advertisement.

triple net lease — a lease under which the tenant pays a fixed rent plus the landlord's property taxes, hazard insurance, and all maintenance costs.

trust account — an account set up by a broker at a bank or other recognized depository in the state where the broker is doing business, into which the broker deposits all funds entrusted to the broker by principles or others.

trust deed — a three-party security device, the three parties being the borrower (trustor), the lender (beneficiary), and a third-party (trustee) to whom "bare legal title" is conveyed.

trust fund overage — a situation in which a trust fund account balance is greater than it should be.

trust fund shortage — a situation in which a trust fund account balance is less than it should be.

trustee — a person who holds something of value in trust for the benefit of another; under a deed of trust, a neutral third-party who holds naked legal title for security.

trustor — a borrower who executes a deed of trust.

Truth-in-Lending Act (TILA) — a federal consumer protection law that was enacted in 1968 with the intention of helping borrowers understand the costs of borrowing money by requiring disclosures about loan terms and costs (in particular, the APR) and to standardize the way in which certain costs related to the loan are calculated and disclosed.

tying arrangement — occurs in antitrust law when the seller conditions the sale of one product or service on the purchase of another product or service.

underwriter — one who analyzes the risk of, and recommends whether to approve, a proposed mortgage loan.

undivided interest — an ownership interest in property in which an owner has the right of possession of the entire property and may not exclude the other owners from any portion by claiming that a specific portion of the property is his or hers alone.

undivided interest subdivision — a subdivision in which owners own a partial or fractional interest in an entire parcel of land. The land in an undivided interest subdivision is not divided; its ownership is divided.

unenforceable contract — a contract that a court would not enforce.

Uniform Commercial Code (UCC) — a set of laws that established unified and comprehensive regulations for security transactions of personal property and that superseded existing laws in that field.

unilateral contract — a contract in which one party gives a promise that is to be accepted not by another promise but by performance.

uninformed misrepresentation — *see*, negligent misrepresentation.

unit-in-place method — a method of estimating the replacement or reproduction cost of a structure by calculating the unit cost of components of the structure.

unity of interest — in reference to joint ownership, refers to each of the owners having equal interests in the property.

unity of possession — in reference to joint ownership, refers to each of the owners having an equal, undivided right to possession of the entire property.

unity of time — in reference to joint ownership, refers to each of the owners having acquired his/her interest in the property at the same time.

unity of title — in reference to joint ownership, refers to each of the owners having received ownership in the property from the same deed.

universal agent — an agent given power of attorney to act on behalf of a principal for an unlimited range of legal matters.

unlawful detainer — a legal action to regain possession of real property.

useful life — the estimated period during which a property generates revenue (if the property is an income property) or usefulness (if the property, such as a private residence, has value other than income value).

U.S. government survey system — see rectangular survey system

usury — the charging of interest in excess of that allowed by law.

utility — the usefulness of property; its ability to satisfy a potential buyer's need or desire, such as to provide shelter or income.

VA — the Department of Veterans Affairs is a federal agency designed to benefit veterans and members of their families.

valid contract — a contract that is binding and enforceable in a court of law.

value — the present worth to typical users or investors of all rights to future benefits, arising out of property ownership.

variance — an exception that may be granted in cases where damage to the value of a property from the strict enforcement of zoning ordinances would far outweigh any benefit to be derived from enforcement.

vendee — the purchaser in a real property sales agreement

vendor — the seller in a real property sales agreement.

vicarious liability — liability imposed on a person not because of that person's own acts but because of the acts of another. (See, respondeat superior.)

void contract — a purported contract that has no legal effect.

voidable contract — a contract that, at the request of one party only, may be declared unenforceable, but is valid until it is so declared.

voluntary lien — a lien obtained through the voluntary action of the one against whose property the lien attaches.

warranty deed — a deed in which the grantor warrants that the title being conveyed is good and free from defects or encumbrances, and that the grantor will defend the title against all suits.

warranty of habitability — mandated by both statutes and by common law, an implied warranty in any residential lease that the premises are suitable for human habitation.

wetlands — as defined by the EPA, "areas that are soaked or flooded by surface or groundwater frequently enough or for sufficient duration to support plants, birds, animals, and aquatic life. Wetlands generally include swamps, marshes, bugs, estuaries, and other inland and coastal areas, and are federally protected."

will — a document that stipulates how one's property should be distributed after death; also called a testament.

writ — a court order commanding the person to whom it is directed to perform an act specified therein.

writ of attachment — a writ ordering the seizure of property belonging to a defendant to ensure the availability of the property to satisfy a judgment if the plaintiff wins.

writ of execution — a writ directing a public official (usually the sheriff) to seize and sell property of a debtor to satisfy a debt.

writ of possession — a court order that authorizes the sheriff or other eviction authority to remove a tenant and the tenant's possessions from leased premises.

zoning — laws of a city or county that specify the type of land-use that is acceptable in certain areas.

INDEX

Index

Made in the USA
Lexington, KY
16 September 2016